WORLD HERITAGE SITES

ANCIENT *C*IVILIZATIONS

vmb
PUBLISHERS

Texts by
Marco Cattaneo
Jasmina Trifoni

Graphic design
Patrizia Balocco Lovisetti

Graphic layout
Maria Cucchi

2 Processions of tributaries in relief crowd the registers on the east steps of the Apadana (generic Persian term for palace, in this case it refers to the audience hall built by the King of Kings, Darius, in the sixth century BC). Here we see the delegation from Bactria, a region of Central Asia, bringing a camel as tribute.

7 The painted reliefs in the main corridor of Ptahhotep's mastaba at Saqqarah are the best preserved from the Old Kingdom. Ptahhotep was the priest of the goddess of truth, Ma'at, and vizier to Unas, the last king of the fifth Dynasty (2375-2345 BC). This period preceded the end of Egypt's first glorious period by two centuries.

Published in the USA by
VMB Publishers®
An imprint of White Star, Italy

© 2004 White Star S.r.l.
Via Candido Sassone, 22/24
13100 Vercelli, Italy
www.whitestar.it

TRANSLATION
Timothy Stroud

ISBN 88-540-0228-3

REPRINTS:
1 2 3 4 5 6 08 07 06 05 04

Printed in Korea
Color separation by
Grafotitoli, Milan

Contents

PREFACE
PAGE 8

INTRODUCTION
PAGE 10

Ancient Civilizations

Preface

ITALIAN NATIONAL COMMISSION

After the volumes Treasures of Art, dedicated to the World Heritage sites of cultural and architectural importance, and Nature Sanctuaries, devoted to the natural sites, Edizioni White Star offers the third in the series entitled Ancient Civilizations, which illustrates the UNESCO sites important for their historical and archaeological significance.

With the same high quality writing and superb photographs seen in the previous two volumes, Ancient Civilizations tells the history of Man and his cultures from humanity's beginnings to the most recent manifestations of civilizations that have produced an outstanding artistic and cultural heritage.

From magical places inhabited at the outset of Man's evolution, such as the famous caves at Lascaux and Altamira, which, with innumerable other sites, constitute the early nucleus from which European civilization developed, to Buddhist and Pre-Columbian sculptures, the temples of Angkor and Boroburdur, and that splendid example of a cradle and crossroads of culture, the fortified city of Hatra in Iraq, this volume provides a fascinating journey in search of the ancient places that have contributed to the evolution of modern Man.

The *Paris Convention in 1972 for the Protection of the World Heritage*, now ratified by 176 countries and still the most important international agreement in this field, protects and safeguards the heritage left to us by great civilizations and cultures, so that we might in turn leave it to future generations. The List drawn up by the Convention has become our 'physical memory' and the sites inscribed have been made the responsibility of governments, associations and private individuals.

Faced by an increasingly globalized world and the standardizing of cultures that may follow from this, UNESCO intervenes to protect and safeguard the equal dignity of all cultures and their vocation to enhance and enrich one another.

I should also like to mention that, in addition to the 1972 Convention, UNESCO has recently adopted an *International Convention for the Safeguarding of the Immaterial Cultural Heritage* and is undertaking the study for the development of prescriptions for the protection of cultural diversity.

This new and last volume that Edizioni White Star has devoted to the great cultural debates to encourage the knowledge of, and therefore respect for, different civilizations is therefore very topical. Like the previous titles, it will stimulate the interest of an increasingly wide public, who, it must be recalled, besides being the main recipients will also be the principal guarantor of the world's cultural, natural, material and immaterial heritage.

Ambassador Francesco Caruso,
Italy's Permanent Representative
to UNESCO

8 The eighth-century Stele H was created as one of a pair erected in the Great Plaza at Copán. At that time the Maya kingdoms were prosperous but fragmented. However, within two hundred years they all disappeared for reasons unknown: a devastating people's revolt, an epidemic, over-exploitation of the soil, famine …

Introduction

11 The face of an apsara
(a creature that cheered the
divine palaces of the Khmer
rulers) emerges from the
elaborate decorations at
Angkor Wat in Cambodia.
Here, Hinduism and Buddhism
overlapped in the twelfth and
thirteenth centuries, coexisting
for a long time.

12-13 This fresco was found
in the triclinium of the House
of the Gold Bracelet in
Pompeii. With exuberant
naturalism it illustrates a
garden with bird pools,
paintings, and oscilla (masks,
though sometimes also shields)
that "fluctuate" in the
composition and reproduce
domestic ornaments.

In Paris on November 23, 1972, the UNESCO General Conference drew up the institutive convention of the World Heritage List, which became active on December 17, 1975. The ambitious aim of the United Nations Educational, Scientific, and Cultural Organization was to identify, study, and safeguard monuments, complexes, and sites – whether natural or manmade – that have "outstanding universal value" from a historical, artistic, scientific, naturalistic, archaeological, or anthropological standpoint.

Thirty years later, the World Heritage List is an extraordinary inventory of places and works embracing the twin histories of man and the earth, providing a tool for understanding nature, culture and, above all, the profound link that unites them. In short, the list is a summary of the planet's historical development. The aim of this book is to present a cross-section of the priceless legacy under the aegis of UNESCO.

In order to deal with such a vast collection of sites, the subject matter has been divided into three volumes, dedicated respectively to treasures of art and architecture, natural sites, and ancient civilizations. The distinction between cultural and natural properties was explicitly defined in the convention, but the demarcation line between architectural sites and sites of archaeological interest was more difficult to define. A purely temporal criterion would probably have misrepresented historical understanding. Therefore, it has been considered opportune to include in this volume all the sites characterized by significant cultural development – though the requirement of continuous habitation may be lacking due either to the decline of the civilizations that constructed them or to abandonment – and the places where evidence has been found that contributes to understanding the evolution of the human species.

To merit inscription in the World Heritage List as a cultural property, the monument, complex, or site must meet at least one of the following criteria:

represent a masterpiece of human creative genius;

demonstrate an important interchange of human values, over a span of time or within a cultural area of the world, involving developments in architecture or technology, monumental arts, town planning, or landscape design;

bear a unique or at least exceptional testimony to a cultural tradition or to a civilization which is living or has disappeared;

be an outstanding example of a type of building, or an architectural or technological ensemble, or a landscape which illustrates (a) significant stage(s) in human history;

be an outstanding example of a traditional human settlement or land-use which is representative of a culture (or cultures), especially if it has become vulnerable or is under the effects of irreversible change;

be directly or tangibly associated with events or living traditions, with ideas or beliefs, or with artistic or literary works of outstanding universal significance.

Using these criteria as a starting point, UNESCO's World Heritage Sites number 188 properties of archaeological interest in 66 countries. One hundred have been selected for description in this volume in an attempt to offer as complete a picture as possible of the ancient civilizations of man without, however, neglecting those places that have been of importance from an evolutionary viewpoint, nor those in which the first examples of figurative art were produced.

Nonetheless, an objective assessment of the legacy passed down the centuries by certain particularly influential cultures has inevitably led to emphasis being placed on the remains of the civilization of Ancient Egypt, the empires of the ancient Romans and Greeks, and – across the Atlantic – the world of the great pre-Columbian cultures.

List of the Sites

Europe

Placing rigid limits on the continent's geographic borders, Europe is home to 56 of the 188 archaeological sites on the World Heritage List, almost one third of the total. For reasons of historical consistency, many centers in the Mediterranean area – from Morocco to Tunisia and from the Middle East to Turkey – should be included, being for the most part the result of the expansion of the Roman empire to the south and east.

The art of the ancient Greeks and Romans dominates that of Europe as a whole, featuring outstanding, timeless monuments such as the Acropolis in Athens and the historic center of Rome; other examples include Delphi, Olympia, and Delos, Agrigento and Pompeii, Segovia, Merida, Arles, and Orange, Split, where Diocletian built his imperial palace, and the immense fortification that Hadrian constructed in England to separate the Romans from the barbarians. With their wealth of decoration, the profusion of columns, sculptures, and reliefs, and the many temples, sumptuous villas, and refined mosaics, ancient Greek and Roman art has influenced the Old Continent more than that of any other civilization, dominating its history for at least a millennium, both before and during the Christian era.

Yet a quick scan of the list of sites protected by UNESCO soon produces places built by peoples that dared to challenge the hegemony first of Athens, then of Rome: the Thracian necropolises at Kazanlak and Sveshtari, the Dacian forts in Romania, the ancient civilizations that developed in almost total isolation on the Mediterranean islands of Malta and Cyprus, and the unique defensive structures known as *nuraghi* built by the Sardinian peoples as early as the Bronze Age.

By taking a few steps back in time, the picture of Europe's archaeological heritage becomes far more varied than might be expected. The rock paintings in Tanum in Sweden and Alta in Norway shed light on the Scandinavian peoples of the Bronze Age whereas rocks covered with runic inscriptions at Jelling in Denmark illustrate the customs of Nordic pagan cultures. The mines at Spiennes in Belgium represent the first known mineral extraction of the Neolithic period, and the Boyne Valley and Stonehenge mark the triumph of the age of megalithic constructions.

Going further back in time to man's primordial origins, Europe is still not lacking in wonders. The fossil beds of Atapuerca, where remains of hominids from one million years ago have been found, recently lost its title as the earliest inhabited site on the continent but remains one of the cornerstones of the World Heritage List in the reconstruction of the history of human migration. Moreover, the wealth of European rock art describing the life of the first modern *Homo sapiens* has no equal on Earth. These include the rock carvings in Valcamonica in Italy and the Côa Valley in Portugal, but above all, the ancient painted masterpieces in the caves of Altamira in Spain and Lascaux in France, which compete with each other for the title of the "Prehistoric Sistine Chapel."

The Rock Incisions at Tanum

SWEDEN

BOHUSLÄN
REGISTRATION: 1994
CRITERIA: C (I) (III) (IV)

With 12,000 inhabitants mostly living in tiny fishing villages along the coast of the North Sea, Tanum is the largest municipality in the province of Bohuslän in southern Sweden. It lies in an unspoiled natural setting enriched by an exceptionally fertile marine environment providing sustenance to almost all the inhabitants. Smooth rocks and open grassy areas stretching down to the sea dominate the coastline. Inland areas feature a quiet agricultural region with a series of narrow valleys. Where these valleys come together meadows have been formed that were first inhabited by man over 4,000 years ago.

At least 350 groups of wall paintings have been found in the area featuring a total of over 1,500 subjects. They date from between 1800 and 500 BC and are spread across an area of roughly 19 square miles. At Tanum, in particular, archaeologists have found a vast collection of these prehistoric paintings, which can be grouped into 13 types of motifs including zoomorphic figures, anthropomorphic figures, trees, handprints and footprints, ancient ships, and even images resembling sleds. They were all painted using the same technique: sharp tools were used to cut an outline and the cracks were then

filled with red pigment.

Among the most important compositions at Tanum are a plow pulled by a pair of oxen guided by an anthropomorphic figure, a human figure confronting a snake, two armed figures fighting, and a boat with nine stylized men who seem to be gesticulating. An entire rock is covered with different motifs: scenes of life at sea and plowing are shown beside handprints and anthropomorphic figures. Another rock bears close-up images of two boats loaded with stylized human figures, while, in the background, there is an agricultural scene. These are indicative of the complexity of a society that had already reached a significant level of figurative representation. Overall, the images provide a cross-section of life in the Bronze Age in Northern Europe.

Painted close to the shore, today the rock paintings at Tanum are roughly 80–100 feet above sea level, and it is the sea, which has lain at the center of the local economy for thousands of years, that presents one of the greatest threats to the art of the Bronze Age. The brackish water combined with the harsh weather and, above all, with the fumes from motor vehicles, is rapidly endangering the paintings, which threaten to disappear completely within a short while. Swedish and Norwegian specialists have been testing different techniques in an attempt to protect the incisions from further deterioration, and in particular, to prevent the formation of deposits of sulfur and acid rain, which dissolve the most fragile minerals, and to prevent algae, mosses, and lichens from attaching to the rocks.

In the meantime, research in the area continues. Recently different teams of Scandinavian archaeologists have discovered entire villages in Bohuslän

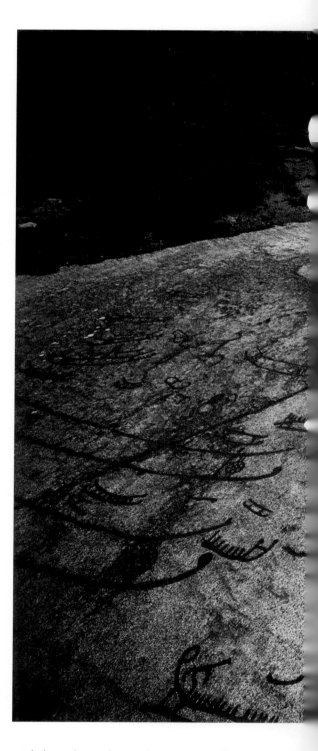

with hearths and paved areas, as well as the remains of houses and pottery fragments. To contribute to an understanding of the history of the site, a state-of-the-art museum was opened in 1998 at Vitlycke, in the heart of the UNESCO World Heritage site, which is actively involved in the research studies conducted on the sites and where a Bronze Age village has been reconstructed to throw some light on the daily life of our ancestors.

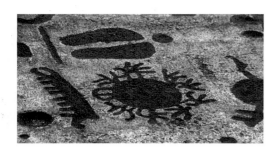

16 The Fossum rock wall, seen here in a general view, has an extraordinary variety of subjects: anthropomorphic figures, animals, trees, and even boats with their crews.

16-17 The figure of a warrior 7'2" tall stands out on the broad flat surface of the rock at Vitlycke. He is surrounded by 120 other rock paintings, some of which seem to represent sleds.

17 top This figure is interpreted as a symbol of the sun and is one of the 350 groups of rock paintings in the Tanum area. The main groups are at Vitlycke (where there is a museum), Fossum, Litsleby, and Aspeberget.

17 right A warrior about to let fly an arrow on the wall at Fossum. Painted between 1800 and 500 BC, the rock pictures at Tanum provide a unique cross-section of life in the Bronze Age in northern Europe.

17 bottom Known as the "Calendar Man" (on the left of the picture), this anthropomorphic figure is one of the most fascinating and mysterious at Tanum.

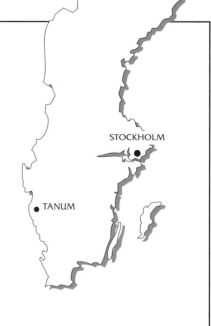

STOCKHOLM

TANUM

The Megalithic Monuments of the Boyne Valley

IRELAND

COUNTY MEATH
REGISTRATION: 1993
CRITERIA: C (I) (III) (IV)

Lying thirty or so miles north of Dublin, the green hill of Newgrange – literally meaning "new farm" – owes its modern name to the fact that, in 1142, it became part of the agricultural property of the Abbey of Mellifont. However, the place, which was identified as the burial site of the legendary kings of Tara and, even earlier, as the *Tuatha de Danann*, the abode of supernatural beings led by the goddess Danu, had long been the subject of fabulous tales.

In 1699, during the construction of a road, a mysterious underground cavity was discovered. At that time, perhaps for fear of disturbing ancient and fearsome gods, it was preferred to not investigate the origin of the cavity any further. As a result of superstition, it was thereafter only entered sporadically, until 1962 when archaeologists decided to examine it properly. What they found was a passage tomb dating back to approximately 3200 BC.

Today Newgrange is the most important and best conserved site in what in Gaelic is called *Brú na Bóinne*, an area of just five square miles lying along the Boyne River that is the location of 30 monumental megalithic structures from the Neolithic period. It represents the highest concentration of prehistoric constructions in Europe. Similar in size and appearance to the megalithic monuments of Knowth and Dowth (the other two archaeological complexes in the region under the protection of UNESCO), Newgrange is a mound of about 85 yards in diameter that encloses a burial chamber in the shape of a cross. It is accessed along a 21-yard-long corridor lined with 22 pillars on the west wall and 21 on the east wall. The corridor was built to take advantage of a curious astronomic phenomenon governed by its size, shape, and slope. From December 19 to 23, for a duration of 17 minutes, the first rays of the rising sun quickly filter down the narrow passage to suddenly light up the chamber.

On the outside, the perimeter of the mound – built from earth, stones, and schist and covered with grass – is marked by 97 very regularly shaped stones called

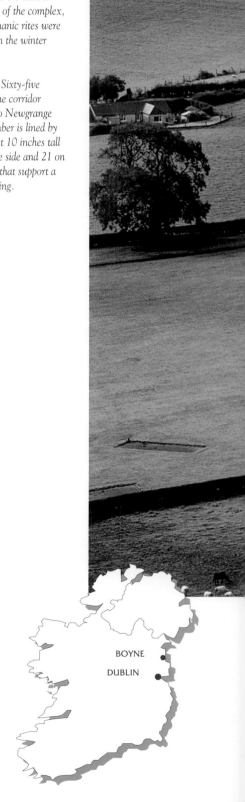

18 top A stone offerings' plate at the center of the burial chamber at Newgrange. It is thought that this was the sancta sanctorum of the complex, where shamanic rites were practiced on the winter solstice.

18 bottom Sixty-five feet long, the corridor that leads to Newgrange burial chamber is lined by stones 7 feet 10 inches tall – 22 on one side and 21 on the other – that support a stone covering.

BOYNE

DUBLIN

"kerbstones" by archaeologists. Some of these, like the one by the entrance, are decorated with lovely engravings of spirals, diamond shapes, zigzags, squares, and concentric circles. Thanks to a reconstruction project using materials found on site, the southwest wall of the mound shines with white quartzite slabs.

Although excavations inside the burial chamber at Newgrange have led to the discovery of two tombs containing the remains of at least three bodies, seven marble tablets, four pendants, bone beads, and a blade of flint, archaeologists agree that this and the other megalithic

to enter Newgrange Tomb and witness the sun illuminating the stones in the chamber. For this reason, since 2000 the site managers have organized a sort of lottery so that of the more than 20,000 aspiring "sun priests," 50 are chosen. These are divided into five groups of ten each, one group for each of the five days. You can bet that they all pray for a cloudless dawn.

monuments in *Brú na Bóinne* were not merely funerary in nature but also ceremonial and social. The mounds containing passage tombs at Knowth and Dowth also bear clear references to the movement of the sun, and at the first site there is a stele considered to be the earliest sundial in the world. They also

contain stones decorated with mysterious incisions that were probably connected with ancient shamanic rites.

Places of enigmatic appeal, the monuments in the Boyne Valley are visited by 200,000 people every year, and, for the five days around the winter solstice, there is a mile-long waiting list

18-19 The tumulus at Newgrange in the green countryside of County Meath. The site dates back to around 3200 BC and it is thought that it took 300 men 20 years to build.

19 top A stone engraved with spiral motifs on the Knowth Tumulus. Boulders incised with circles, triangles and zigzags have been found in all the megalithic sites in the valley. These signs have been interpreted as representations of the Sun, Moon, and Man.

Hadrian's Wall

UNITED KINGDOM

COUNTIES OF CUMBRIA, NORTHUMBRIA, AND TYNE AND WEAR
REGISTRATION: 1987
CRITERIA: C (II) (III) (IV)

It is not often that a literary masterpiece becomes a bestseller, yet this is what happened to Marguerite Yourcenar's *Memoirs of Hadrian*. The French author, an expert and lover of the Classical world, wrote the book in the form of a long letter from the Roman emperor, close to death, to Marcus Aurelius. In it, he recounts his life, insists on the importance of serving his country right up to the last moment, and warns Marcus of his realization that the empire must inevitably decline. More than any contemporary biography of Hadrian, Marguerite Yourcenar's book succeeded in communicating the emperor's complex psychological state of mind and revealing his "pacifist"

philosophy. Having inherited from Trajan, in AD 117, an immense territory that the Romans proudly referred to as "the known world," Hadrian, unlike his predecessors, was never impassioned by conquest. Even the most important of his military works – the wall that he had built at the northern tip of the empire – is a monument lacking any particularly bellicose significance.

Hadrian planned its construction in AD 122 during a trip to Britain. His intention was that the wall should physically separate the Romans from the barbarians, provide an observation point, and be used to control any trading that took place between the two sides. It took six years to build the colossal fortification from coast to coast. It measures 20 feet high, ten wide, and stretches 80 Roman miles (72 modern miles) from what is now Bowness on the Irish Sea to the mouth of the river Tyne near Wallsend, on the North Sea. A gateway marked every mile of the wall, which were topped by small forts each able to accommodate a garrison of 32 soldiers. At a distance of a third of a mile between each gate were two lookout towers guarded by shifts of four sentinels. Their role was principally to create a chain of messengers that permitted a rapid exchange of information from one coast to the other. Later, to provide even greater

protection to the wall, a V-shaped dike was dug ten feet deep and 33 feet wide, and 16 forts were built to hold up to 10,000 men.

Around these forts, the best conserved of which is Chester, traces remain of extensive civilian settlements, attesting to the intense commercial activity between the two sides of the wall. Recently, excavation has unearthed many handmade objects of different provenance and about 400 wooden tablets on which detailed descriptions were engraved regarding the daily life of the soldiers. These are the oldest written documents found in Great Britain.

The wall was an *ante litteram* multicultural experiment. To build it, Hadrian sent three legions of soldiers from all over the empire, with the aim of keeping his men busy and motivated even during times of peace. He encouraged religious freedom and successfully strengthened the soldiers' sense of being Romans despite any national (according to modern standards) divisions. It is ironic that, once the Roman Empire began to disintegrate, the wall took on a completely different significance, and even today, some of the British consider the ancient construction to mark the boundary between the two historical rivals – England and Scotland.

20 top left The ruins of the baths at Chester Fort. The traces of an extensive civilian settlement around the stronghold are evidence of busy commercial activity between the two sides of the wall.

20 bottom left The wall near Berwick-on-Tweed in Northumbria. At 80 Roman miles long (72 modern miles), in several places the wall marks the current border between England and Scotland.

20 top right A granary in Carrawburgh Fort, which once held a garrison of 500 men. Along the length of the wall, 16 forts were built to provide barracks for a total of 10,000 soldiers.

21 An aerial view of Housestead Fort, one of the best preserved along Hadrian's Wall. A hospital and the commander's lodgings have been discovered inside the defensive walls.

NEWCASTLE

LONDON

Stonehenge and Avebury

UNITED KINGDOM

COUNTY OF WILTSHIRE, WESSEX, ENGLAND
REGISTRATION: 1986
CRITERIA: C (I) (II) (III)

22 An aerial view of Stonehenge, the most famous and mysterious megalithic site in the world, built between 3100 and 1600 BC. Myths and folklore aside, today not even the scientific community is able to provide unequivocal explanations of its purpose and use.

AVEBURY

STONEHENGE

LONDON

Who built Stonehenge? Over the centuries, dozens of legends have flourished and all kinds of serious and not-so-serious hypotheses have been put forward. Was it the Celts, the Saxons, the ancient Egyptians, the Romans, or the people of Atlantis? Then again, perhaps people from outer space? Or – as is claimed by some – were the stones placed "strategically" by a group of fanatical British in search of new forms of spirituality in 1968 at the height of Beatlemania?

The answer is no, at least to the last idea. The first written reference to Stonehenge dates back to 1135. In his *History of the Kings of Britain*, Geoffrey of Monmouth claimed that the stones were brought from Africa to Ireland by a tribe of giants, and then made to fly from there across the sea by Merlin the magician, where they were then mounted on Salisbury Plain in homage to King Arthur. However, the Druids, the priests of the Celtic people, have always claimed their forebears were responsible for the construction. Until 1985, the ancient order of the Druids used to visit the monument, dressed in white tunics and carrying harps and trumpets, to celebrate initiation rites on the summer solstice.

Not even the scientific community is in a position to give unequivocal answers regarding the world's most famous megalithic site. In the most recent study, published in 2003 by the gynecologist Anthony Perks in the *Journal of the Royal Society of Medicine*, it was suggested that the ring formed by the stone blocks represented the female sexual organ through which the Earth Mother– the main divinity during the Neolithic era – gave birth to the plants and animals. However, this was met by a chorus of protests and was refuted in writing by David Miles, the archaeologist who has been director of the site for years.

Whoever was responsible for Stonehenge (the name is derived from an ancient Anglo-Saxon word meaning "hanging rocks"), the monument was constructed in three phases between 3100 and 1600 BC. In the earliest phase, a circular earthwork was raised measuring roughly 100 yards in diameter; it was bounded by a dike and, a short distance away, by a ring of 56 holes that were once filled by an equal number of wooden poles. These holes are known as Aubrey Holes after the person who first described them in 1666. In the second phase, around 2550 BC, the first stones appeared. Called "bluestones," they are the smallest stones on the site, despite the fact that they each weigh about five tons. They were transported – first probably by sea, then up the river Avon, and finally across land – the 236 miles to Salisbury Plain from quarries in Pembroke in southwest Wales. During the third phase, which started around 2100 BC, Stonehenge was given the structure seen today, composed of megaliths each weighing about 30 tons. They were brought from the hills of Marlborough, about 19 miles away. These blocks from the Eocene epoch are called *sarsen*, a word meaning "foreigner" in the ancient language of Wessex.

The outermost element in the Stonehenge site is an avenue about 650 yards long lined on either side by dikes that run parallel at a distance of 25 yards from one another. The avenue leads to the Heel Stone, another sarsen that, during the summer solstice, projects its shadow to the exact center of the site. Further along, the avenue leads to the circular earthwork. At its entrance is the Slaughter Stone, whose name was given by the red marks in the rock from iron "melted" by the rain over the millennia. From here, the central part of the site formed by concentric megalithic structures can be seen. The external ring is composed of 30 sarsens of which 17 are still in place; they stand 13 feet high and are connected to one another by a series of architraves held in place by mortise-and-tenon joints. Ten feet away from this circle, there is another ring, this time of 60 bluestones (many of which have fallen or are broken), standing nearly seven feet high. At the center of the two circles stands a massive horseshoe-shaped structure (today incomplete) consisting of five trilithons, the tallest of which stands 23 feet tall, each formed by two standing stones supporting a horizontal one. Finally, a modest horseshoe of bluestones rings the so-called Altar Stone at the center, though this does not have the drainage system typical of

23 top This view shows the circle of sarsen stones, the enormous blocks that were transported to Stonehenge 3,000 years ago from the hills of Marlborough 19 miles away.

23 bottom A detail of the five massive triliths (two uprights and an architrave) that stand in a horseshoe shape inside the ring of Stonehenge. The tallest measures 25 feet 6 inches in height.

24 *The county of Wiltshire has many stone circles, menhirs and, above all, burial mounds. Those in the picture stand in wheat fields close to Avebury.*

24 The county of Wiltshire has many stone circles, menhirs and, above all, burial mounds. Those in the picture stand in wheat fields close to Avebury.

24-25 Covering almost 29 acres, the stone circle at Avebury is the largest in the world. At one time the earthwork stood 56 feet high from the bottom of the dike to the highest point of the wall.

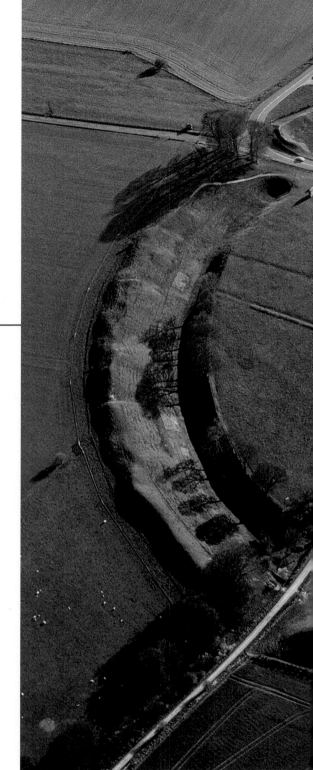

altars in sacrificial temples built elsewhere during the same period.

The fame and dramatic nature of Stonehenge obscures the fact that Wiltshire boasts many Neolithic sites, such as Silbury Hill (the largest prehistoric burial mound in Europe), West Kennet Long Barrow (the largest chamber grave in England), and Avebury. This last site is the largest stone circle in the world, covering an area of roughly 28 acres. At one time it was formed by an earthwork exactly one mile in diameter, which enclosed a circle of 98 stones (27 of which are still in place). Like the large ones at Stonehenge, they also came from the Marlborough Downs. Avebury has several megaliths of huge size, including the Swindon Stone weighing 66 tons, and the Devil's Chair, which was named after a popular belief that it was possible to make the devil appear there if you ran around the stone 100 times counterclockwise.

Although scholars agree that Stonehenge and Avebury were places of worship, there are innumerable speculations overlaid on this certainty relating, for example, to the remarkable astronomical coincidences of its layout. It is not clear if the site could have been an *ante litteram* observatory for the study of the heavens, as many claim, nor whether it was simply a calendar to mark the events of the seasons, such as sowing and harvesting the grain. Some go further, claiming that it was used to forecast eclipses, although it was utterly improbable that the ancient people of Stonehenge had such advanced knowledge.

Unless – and here another theory enters the picture – Stonehenge was designed by an individual from a more advanced culture who arrived at Salisbury Plain to teach the locals the knowledge required to erect the megaliths. Moreover, this person would have had to return regularly over the period of 1,500 years during which the monument was built. Nevertheless, this is a theory that is only good for those who believe in extraterrestrials and flying saucers.

25 bottom left Some of the stones at Avebury. The most interesting are the Swindon Stone (the largest, with a weight of 60 tons) and the Devil's Chair.

25 bottom right Today only 27 of the original 98 stones remain. Over the centuries, the others were destroyed by building fires around them to heat them, then throwing cold water over them. The broken fragments were then used to build the village of Avebury.

The Roman Monuments of Trier

GERMANY

RHEINLAND-PFALZ
REGISTRATION: 1986
CRITERIA: C (I) (III) (IV) (VI)

26 top The best preserved section of the imperial baths in ancient Treveris, the largest baths' complex outside of Rome. This section comprises a hall with three apses bounded by towers.

26 bottom The ruins of the elliptical arena of the amphitheater are now surrounded by countryside. Built at the end of the first century AD, in the Middle Ages the amphitheater was used to provide building materials.

26-27 Nigra Gate is the most important of the Roman remains in Trier. Its façade is 39 yards long, made more interesting by the 144 arched windows.

The façade of the seventeenth-century Rotes Haus in Trier's market square bears the inscription, *"Ante Romam Treveris stetit annis mille trecentis – Perstet, et aeterna pace fruatur, amen"* (Trier existed one thousand three hundred years before Rome – May it last and enjoy eternal peace, amen). Though a bit exaggerated, it does contain a grain of truth, given that evidence has been found of settlements in the area dating back to the third millennium BC. Trier is therefore the oldest city in Germany.

The legionaries of Julius Caesar arrived in 50 BC to subjugate the Celts, and in 16 BC, during the reign of Octavian Augustus, they founded the Roman colony *Augusta Treverorum*. The place was of almost no importance until the end of the third century, when Maximian (who ruled the Western empire while Diocletian governed the Eastern one) made it the seat of his court, as did his successors Constantus Clorus and Constantine. At around the same time, Treveris (as it was called then) became a center of Christianity; the religion had made its appearance here at the end of the first century after being imported by Syriac merchants. In 314, the city became the first bishopric north of the Alps.

Trier still features many important relics from the Roman era (partly incorporated in constructions from later eras), which, along with the Church of Our Lady of Trier and St. Peter's Cathedral, have been nominated UNESCO World Heritage sites. The most imposing Roman monument is the Nigra Gate, which dates back to the end of the second century. It was built when Treveris, which was until then an open city, was given a defensive wall 23 feet high, though today it no longer exists. Despite being built in pale sandstone, this gate (one of the seven largest in the Roman world) owes its name to the black patina that over the centuries has covered its rough blocks of stone held together with iron. It measures 98 feet high, 72 feet deep, and has a façade 118 feet wide with two entrances 23 feet high. The massiveness of the structure is softened by the 144 arched windows that open out of the gate's two levels. The Syriac monk Simeon once lived on top of the gate, in honor of whom a church was built in 1041, but this was almost entirely destroyed by the troops of Napoleon.

To the east of the city, a Roman bridge crosses the Moselle River. It was built in AD 45 during the reign of Claudius to support a wooden structure for carriages, but only a very few of its original granite blocks remain. An amphitheater was built a little past the bridge but today there is little to see of the original structure as its

27 bottom left Austere and cyclopic, the Aula Palatina was built using the spaces, and part of the walls, of what was once the throne room in the imperial palace built in 312 by Constantine.

27 bottom right An aerial view of Trier and the Moselle River. Many of the city monuments are medieval or seventeenth-century, and all are dominated by the Gothic bell tower of the Liebfrauenkirche.

materials were used for other buildings during the Middle Ages. However, the ellipse that measured 82 by 54 yards can still be seen, which marked the cavea around which 22,000 spectators could sit. The two monumental entrances to the amphitheater were surmounted by vaults with fine decorations. Other Roman monuments in Trier are the foundations of the baths of Saint Barbara (first century AD) and the imperial baths. Only smaller than the baths in Rome, they were begun in the third century and completed during the reign of Constantine.

What was once the gigantic Aula Palatina – the throne room in the imperial palace built for Constantine in 312 – was used as a "container" for the so-called Basilika, today a Protestant church, and only one wall of the original construction has survived. Construction of the Cathedral was begun in the eleventh century over the foundations of a Christian basilica, of which recent excavation work has revealed superb remains. All of Trier's historic center is the result of generations of architectural styles starting in antiquity and continuing through the Gothic era to the baroque, each new style adopting from previous ones. Moreover, these additions are interesting evidence of the city's continuous development, also known for having been the birthplace of Karl Marx.

27

BERLIN

TRIER

The Painted Grottoes in the Vallée de la Vézère

FRANCE

AQUITAINE, DORDOGNE
REGISTRATION: 1979
CRITERIA: C (I) (III)

The climb up the hill overlooking the village of Montignac on the left bank of the Vézère River in the Dordogne was supposed to be nothing more than a fun outing for Marcel Ravidat, Jacques Marsal, Georges Agnel, and Simon Coencas. Instead, it turned out to be one of the most famous archaeological discoveries of the twentieth century.

It was September 12, 1940 and the four boys, armed with only a dim flashlight and their natural sense of recklessness, decided to climb into the pit left by a fallen tree in the middle of the wood. Sliding down a heap of stones that had filled the entrance to a cave, they suddenly found themselves in a wide opening that today is known as the Great Hall of the Bulls. The rock paintings in the Great Hall of the Bulls are probably the most outstanding examples of Paleolithic art in the world. They cover about 200 square feet on both walls that curve over to form a vault in an

almost circular ravine, and consist of three groups of animals: horses, bulls, and deer.

Amazed at the incredible works of art that they had found, the boys told their teacher, and news of their discovery ended up in the school newspaper. From that moment on, archaeologists began to arrive in Lascaux, starting with Abbot André Glory, who was to spend more than a quarter of a century meticulously copying

all the incisions. It took this much time because the Lascaux Cave continues for over 110 yards into the depths of the mountain and includes at least seven more areas with significant paintings. On the left, the Painted Gallery is the natural continuation of the Great Hall of the Bulls, featuring zoomorphic figures that cover as much of the walls as in the cave's vault, consequently nicknamed the French

"Prehistoric Sistine Chapel." To the right, there is the Lateral Passage, followed by the Main Gallery, and then the Chamber of Felines, which is the most internal of the decorated areas. A side passage leads to the Chamber of Engravings and then the Shaft of the Dead Man, which, besides the wall paintings, was found to contain a vast range of handmade objects. They included 21 finely worked lamps made from rough stone, 14 bone spearheads, a painter's "palette," thanks to which it was possible to study the pigments used by Paleolithic artists, and eight mineral agglomerates from which the pigments were extracted.

Overall, there have been almost 1,500 incisions catalogued on the walls and vault of the grotto, which were painted around 17,000 years ago according to some, or 15,000 according to others. Whichever it was, they represent the apex of Paleolithic rock painting, widespread throughout the Dordogne region during the period of the Magdalenian culture between 18,000 and 11,000 years ago. In just the Vallée de la Vézère, 147 prehistoric sites and 25 painted caves have been found, which have made it possible to reconstruct features of the lifestyle of *Homo sapiens* during the phase immediately preceding the introduction of farming.

The marvels of Lascaux, however, have been inaccessible to the public for around 40 years now. Already by 1955, due to the excess of carbon dioxide in the air, the first traces of deterioration in the paintings were noticed, and some years later, the first worrying green stains produced by algae and mosses started to appear. In consequence, André Malraux, the French Minister of Culture, decided to close the grotto on April 20, 1963.

Once the causes of environmental contamination had been eliminated, the paintings at Lascaux returned to their original state, however they have remained closed forever to the public. In 1980, the authorities decided to create a

28 top A bull with huge horns on a wall at Lascaux.

28 bottom left The rock paintings in the apse of the Hall of the Bulls are considered some of the best examples of Paleolithic art in the world.

28-29 Galloping cattle and horses animate the interior of the Hall of the Bulls.

29 top and bottom To paint the almost 1,500 figures in the caves at Lascaux (bottom, the so-called "Chinese horse"), the people of the Paleolithic era used 12 pigments, ranging from pale yellow to black.

complete replica of the grotto, which they did with great accuracy and the use of materials that allowed the colors, incisions, and even the granular quality of the original rock to be perfectly reproduced. Lascaux II opened to the public in 1983.

In 2001, a new threat to the paintings in the original grotto was identified: colonies of bacteria and fungi were found on some of the rocks and cave floor, which had to be treated with fungicides and antibiotics. The problem has been solved but concern remains about the fragility of the biological environment of this extraordinary legacy from the dawn of civilization.

PARIS

VÉZÈRE

The Roman Theater and the Triumphal Arch of Orange

FRANCE

Vaucluse, Provence

Registration: 1981

Criteria: C (iii) (vi)

PARIS

ORANGE

Situated on the hill of Saint-Eutrope close to the Aigues River and dominating the vast plain stretching to the Rhone River, what is today the city of Orange was founded by a people of Celtic origin. Lying at the heart of the florid Roman province of *Gallia Narbonensis*, it was named Arausio after an indigenous water god. Its protected position made it a strategic site, and this role was expanded in 36 BC when veterans of the Second Gallic Legion, led by Octavian, seized it from the Gallic barbarians and founded *Colonia Iulia Firma Secundanorum Arausio*, in which the word *firma* means fortification.

After having become emperor and assumed the name Augustus, Octavian returned to the province on several occasions and encouraged construction there. In AD 10, he ordered the construction in Arausio of a triumphal arch to celebrate the foundation of the new Roman city and the establishment of the Pax Romana. Completed in AD 27, it stands at the northern edge of the city. Rectangular in plan, it measures 64 feet long and 28 feet wide, with a large arch at the center and a smaller one on either side. The two façades are adorned with grooved half-columns with Corinthian capitals, statues, and panels carved with scenes of land and sea battles. The inscriptions celebrating the emperor Tiberius were added at a later date.

During the same period and to meet the needs of the province's inhabitants (mostly soldiers and their families) who complained of a dearth of entertainment, the emperor ordered the construction of several theaters in Antipolis, Apta Julia, Aveno, Forum Julii, and, the most majestic, in Arausio. This last one was built not only for spectacles and performances but it was also designed for political purposes, being large enough to hold electoral and administrative assemblies and trials at which, in that period, the entire population participated. Adorned with statues, this theater could accommodate 9,000 spectators in three orders. It has a stage closed at the back by a large wall 125 feet high and 113 yards long that also formed the outside wall. As the provincial public was not at the same intellectual level as refined Rome, for many years the spectacles were popular in nature, featuring performances such as the *fabulae atellanae* farces, acrobats and mime artists, and the comedies of Plautus.

In the fourth century AD, as the decline of the Roman Empire set in and Christianity began to spread, the inhabitants' interest in spectacles waned. In 391, the bishop of Arausio denounced the theater as a pagan impiety and ordered its closure. With the arrival of the barbarians, the theater was turned into a weapon deposit, and warrens of wooden houses grew up against the massive façade over the centuries. The decrepit theater survived the war between the troops of Louis XIV and William III of Nassau (William the Orange), and the victorious Sun King, who had ordered the fort of the rebel prince to be razed to the ground, decided to save what he considered the "most beautiful wall in the kingdom."

In 1860, restoration of the theater began thanks to the instigation of the writer Prosper Mérimée, then director of

the *Monuments Historiques* of France. Today the theater in Orange is the setting for a summer festival, and its stage is trod by actors of international fame, like in the golden times of ancient Rome. Only once in that period of abandon lasting over 1,000 years did a great "actor" make an appearance there. One night, while traveling to Paris after fleeing exile on the island of Elba, Napoleon asked his coach-driver to stop in Orange. He entered the theater alone and, on that magnificent and spectral stage, savored the taste of what was to be his last, and ephemeral, triumph.

30-31 In a very good state of conservation, the theater can hold 9,000 spectators. The stage is closed at the back by a wall 112 yards long and 125 feet high that also acts as the external façade.

30 bottom A detail of the frieze on the upper attic of the triumphal arch. It shows a horseback battle between the Romans and Gauls, and represents the triumph of civilization over barbarism.

31 top The theater in Orange is the only one in the Roman world to have preserved its imperial statue intact. Octavian Augustus (at 11 feet 7inches tall) stands in a niche at the center of the proscenium.

31 bottom Built between 10 and 27 AD for emperor Augustus, the façades of the triumphal arch are decorated with a Corinthian order and fluted half-columns.

The Pont du Gard

FRANCE

PROVENCE
REGISTRATION: 1985
CRITERIA: C (I) (III) (IV)

In 1958, extreme flooding of the Gardon River caused enormous damage to the area of Nîmes in Provence. The modern railway bridge that crossed the river near Remoulins was literally swept away, but the Pont du Gard a little upstream, which had been standing for 2,000 years, stood impassively before the turbulent waters. Once the emergency had passed, everyone rejoiced for the wellbeing of the bridge built by the ancient Romans (this monumental construction receives more than two million visitors a year and is France's secondmost important provincial tourist attraction after Mont-Saint-Michel), though twentieth-

century engineers could not but feel they had been "beaten" by their ancient colleagues.

Historical documents attribute the design of the Pont du Gard as well as the entire aqueduct that carried water from the *Ucetia* spring (modern Uzès) to Nemausus (Nîmes) to no less than Marcus Agrippa, the son-in-law of Augustus. Known for his engineering skills, Agrippa visited Gaul in 19 BC and soon began work on the colossal hydraulic project.

Probably completed during the reign of Trajan (AD 98–117), the aqueduct follows a U shape 30 miles long, 22 of which run underground, with a total difference in height of just 56 feet. What is most striking is not the length of the aqueduct but its extraordinary precision: from the spring to the huge cistern (called the *castellum* by the Romans) situated in what was then the outskirts of Nîmes, the water ran down a constant slope of just 21.5 inches per mile. From the *castellum*, ten canals departed to supply the baths, public buildings, and houses of roughly 50,000 inhabitants with water. Thus, they were each allocated approximately 106 gallons per day, a quantity considered sufficient even by modern standards. It has also been calculated that the construction of the aqueduct cost 30 million sesterces, the equivalent of fifty years pay for 500 officers of the Roman legions.

The symbol of the magnificence of the entire construction is the Pont du Gard. Majestic, yet elegant and almost delicate, it is a little over 330 yards long and stands 157 feet high over the river in three orders of arches. The lowest order has six arches that vary in width from 52 to 70 feet and supports a road that was widened for carriages in the mid-eighteenth century. The second order has eleven arches, and the top one, over which the water canal passes, has 35 small arches. The bridge was made from stone dense with fossil

concretions quarried locally. Its yellowish hue blends perfectly with the surrounding landscape of green hills and vineyards. The blocks each weigh 6.6 tons and were assembled without mortar with surprising precision.

The continual habitation and constant development of this corner of Provence have been providential for the safeguarding of the bridge. The first

restoration project was carried out during the reign of Napoleon III, and the most recent, which have only just ended, cost 30 million euros, most of which financed the construction of a visitors' center. The reinforcement of the Roman monument entailed the replacement of 390 cubic yards of stone, roughly five percent of the entire structure.

32 This frontal view of the Pont du Gard reveals the harmony of the three orders of arches. The bridge is the second-largest tourist attraction in provincial France after Mont-Saint-Michel.

32-33 Majestic yet elegant and almost delicate, the Pont du Gard is about 325 yards long and rises 157 feet above the water. The yellowish stone harmonizes perfectly with the landscape.

33 bottom An aerial view of the Roman bridge, built as a section of the aqueduct that carried water 30 miles to Nemasus (Nîmes). It was designed by Marcus Agrippa, Augustus's son-in-law, around 19 BC and completed during the reign of Trajan.

The Roman Monuments of Arles

FRANCE

BOUCHES-DU-RHÔNE, PROVENCE
REGISTRATION: 1981
CRITERIA: C (II) (IV)

*S*pectators in the Arena at *Arles* by Vincent Van Gogh – today in the Hermitage Museum in St. Petersburg – is a magnificent painting. The warm colors and impetuous brushstrokes give a sense of anxious expectation and overwhelming passion, the same emotions, in fact, felt by the spectators at the *corrida*. In 1888, when it was painted, the amphitheater in Arles had only been restored about fifty years prior. After centuries of looting, it was turned into a fort and then a residential area for the poor, before being returned to its original vocation, a setting for cruel spectacles. Built between AD 90 and 100, it is elliptical (measuring 149 yards along its longest axis and 117 along its shortest), formed by two orders of 60 arches each, and can hold 24,000 people. The arena proper is separated from the cavea by a high wall that was built to protect spectators from the wild beasts used in the games. This superb construction is not the only one to survive from the city's Roman period. Colonized by veterans of Julius Caesar's Sixth Legion, Arles – or rather *Iulia Arelate Sextanorum* – was in 49 BC a small town on the left bank of the Rhone River inhabited by peoples of Celtic-Ligurian and Greek origin. Much closer to the sea then than it is now, the city soon established a flourishing economy and adopted an ambitious urban development plan. Covering 100 acres, it was enclosed within a defensive wall. The section of the road leading to Marseilles was used as a *decumanus*, whereas the *cardus* and other streets were traced out to create a grid. The construction of a theater for 10,000 spectators (today restored and back in use) and the forum date to 40–15 BC, during the reign of Octavian Augustus. The forum lay around the sanctuary of the Genius Augusti, which was surrounded by porticoes resting on crypto-porticoes.

Following a period of economic stasis from the second to mid-third century AD, Arles experienced a sort of renaissance thanks to the expansion of its textile industry and the skill of its chiselers, who were famous throughout the empire for their production of sarcophagi. In the fourth century, when he was elected emperor, Constantine decided to settle there and so awarded the city the appellative *Gallula Roma*. A monumental program of construction and expansion was undertaken to make Arles a worthy imperial residence; of what remains of the emperor's palace, today it is possible to see the baths and the crypto-porticoes beneath the Augustan sanctuary. Restored by Constantine, the crypto-porticoes consist of two galleries of arches 100 yards long. In one of these, the bases of two granite columns have been found bearing an inscription mentioning the monuments built by the emperor to beautify the city and the names of the people who oversaw the works.

34 top The thick round walls of the amphitheater at Arles are characterized by round arches alternating with rectangular cornices and towers. They surrounded the castrum built by Julius Caesar to garrison his legions during consolidation of the conquest of Gaul.

34 bottom Unlike the Colosseum in Rome, the underground rooms in the amphitheater have survived pretty much intact with their original covering. As with similar structures, the rooms were used to store the stage machines.

34-35 Arles' spectacular amphitheater is the most important Roman monument in Provence. Built between 90 and 100 AD, over the centuries it has been looted, turned into a fort, and even become a residential area.

PARIS

ARLES

35 bottom The elegant
theater was built during
the principate of Octavian.
Founded by the Celts,
Arles was colonized

by the Romans, who
endowed it with
monuments and
named it Iulia Arelate
Sextanorum.

The Cave at Altamira

SPAIN

Province of Santander, Region of Cantabria

Registration: 1985

Criteria: C (I) (III)

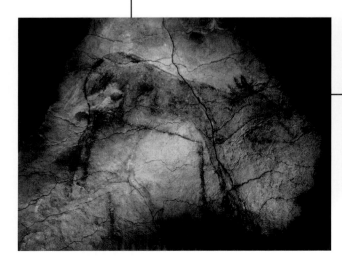

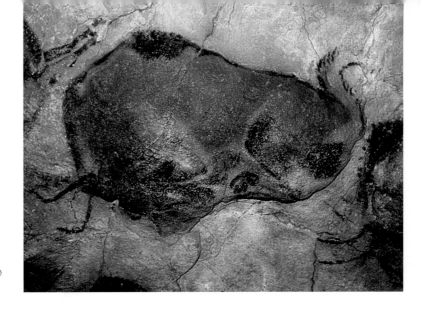

W as Paleolithic man capable of producing art? Certainly not said paleo-anthropologists at the end of the nineteenth century. At that time, those who had embraced the theory of evolution had taken up positions even more extreme than Darwin himself, and they were unable to imagine that prehistoric man – who they considered to be little more than a monkey – had a sense of aesthetics, or even technical capabilities.

So when in 1880 Marcelino Sanza de Sautuola, an amateur paleo-anthropologist published *Breves apuntes sobre algunos objetos prehistóricos de la provincia de Santander*, the scientific community considered the book a joke in bad taste. Sautuola had spent five years shut away in the cave at Altamira to catalog and describe the stone tools and rock paintings that he had found inside. The paintings in particular raised indignation and general hilarity, as they were considered too beautiful not to be fakes.

In fact, at the beginning of his studies, Sautuola had visited the caves several times without even noticing the paintings on the ceiling as he had simply not raised his eyes, and it was Maria, his twelve-year-old daughter, who drew his attention to them. Although it was clear to him that the prehistoric men who had left the bone and flint tools in the cave were the same ones that had painted the ceiling, he did not live long enough to win the recognition his intuition deserved.

It was only in the early twentieth century – following the discovery of other caves featuring rock drawings in Spain and France – that the scientific community agreed that the paintings at Altamira dated to the Upper Paleolithic. More recently, carbon-14 dating of the pigments has placed the paintings at between 18,500 and 10,000 years old, with some simple figures dating to the Aurignacian and Solutrean, and others (most of them) from the Magdalenian periods. The extraordinary skill – or perhaps it should be defined "art" – with which the paintings were executed has led to the cave being called the Spanish "Prehistoric Sistine Chapel."

Situated at the foot of Mount Vispieres, 512 feet above sea level, the Altamira cave comprises a series of chambers and galleries extending for 295 yards in the shape of an 'S'. On the ceiling and wall of the largest chamber, which measures 30 by 60 feet, there is a set of exceptional zoomorphic figures: a horse, a boar, several deer, and 15 large bison painted very realistically. Using yellow, brown, and reddish ocher, zinc oxide and pitch, the Magdalenian men painted the bison's coats with gradations of color. Moreover, the bodies of some of the bison were drawn to match the projections of the rock, thereby creating an amazing three-dimensional effect. Also of great interest are the paintings in the "polychrome corridor" where, with bison and other animals, there are also clearly defined anthropomorphic figures and handprints.

Though they have lasted for thousands of years in the darkness, the paintings are extremely delicate. Even the breath of the many visitors who have been to Altamira since the second half of the twentieth century is harmful to the pigments, so access to the cave is now restricted to scholars, and even then only a maximum of 150 per week. For the public, a new cave with an attached paleo-anthropological museum was opened nearby on July 17, 2001. The original paintings have been reproduced using "prehistoric" pigments and techniques in an artificial cave that recreates the shape of the original with a margin of error of less than one twenty-fifth of an inch! This very ambitious project cost 25.5 million euros. It could be argued that they lack the appeal of authenticity, or perhaps not, seeing that the structure already receives more than one million visitors a year.

36-37 Carbon dating of the pigments has dated the rock paintings at Altamira to between 18,500 and 10,000 years ago. The simpler figures are from the Aurignacian and Solutrean periods and others, more "artistic", from the Magdalenian.

36 bottom left A deer painted using yellow, red, and brown ochers and zinc oxide. What is so amazing is the precision with which primitive man has rendered the physical proportions of the animal.

36 bottom right The extraordinary ceiling of the "polychrome corridor" on which 15 bison and many other animals, including a horse, are painted. The series has earned Altamira the title of the "Sistine Chapel of Prehistory".

37 top The bison are the most skillfully painted. Their coats are rendered with an extraordinary variety of shading and color blends that give the representation a three-dimensional appearance.

Perched on a rocky spur similar in shape to the prow of a ship, and encircled by two rivers, the Río Eresma and Río Clamores, the old city of Segovia can boast having the most spectacular position of any city in Spain. The aqueduct, the only remnant of what was the important Roman military base of Segobriga, is like the rudder of this natural ship. Any traces of the ancient headquarters of those legionaries, built here in the second half of the first century BC over a previous Celtic settlement, has been lost in the turbulent history of this corner of Castile. After the Romans, the area was conquered by the

The Aqueduct of Segovia

SPAIN

Castilla y León
Registration: 1987
Criteria: C (i) (iii) (iv)

38-39 At 304 yards long, "el Puente", the most majestic section of the aqueduct, is formed by two orders of arches supported by 128 pillars. Probably built between AD 38 and 50, it is the best preserved aqueduct in the Roman world.

38 bottom Around 1500, the Catholic monarchs replaced the statue of a pagan god at the center of the structure with an effigy of the Virgin and Child.

39 A view of the old city of Segovia. In addition to the Roman aqueduct, Segovia has two more monuments registered by UNESCO on the World Heritage List: the Alcazár (eleventh century) and the Gothic cathedral (sixteenth century).

Visigoths and then the Moors, before becoming the setting for the political and amorous match between Ferdinand of Aragon and Isabella of Castile. Regardless of the wars and alternations of rulers, *El Puente*, as the inhabitants respectfully refer to the aqueduct, has always remained to dominate Segovia and perform, until the end of the nineteenth century, the important function for which it was built, becoming, of course, become the symbol of the city.

This masterpiece of hydraulic engineering, the best conserved in the Roman world, was built dry with 20,400 blocks of granite from the nearby Sierra de Guadarrama. It is ten and a half miles long and carries the waters of the Río Frio from a place called La Acebeda into the heart of the city, passing through a series of basins on its way. The raised section is 796 yards long, 304 of which are monumental and look down on the Plaza do Azoguejo. *El Puente* has two orders of round arches 93.5 feet high supported by 128 pillars, in turn crowned by an attic through which the water conduits pass. There is no written documentation of its construction but experts have noticed stylistic and technical similarities with the *Aqua Claudia*, one of the aqueducts that supplied ancient Rome with water, and thus are able to date it to between AD 38 and 50, or the end of the first century during the reign of Trajan. Given the size of the construction and the quantity of water it carried, it is estimated that Roman Segobriga had a population of about 50,000, the same as the modern city.

During the ninth century, some of the arches were damaged by the Moors but, due to its usefulness, in the sixteenth century the Catholic monarchs had it restored, including the substitution of the Roman statues of pagan gods at the center of the monumental section with an effigy of the Virgin of San Sebastián. Since that time, the massive structure has withstood both man and the elements miraculously well. Between 1992 and 1996, it was reinforced after a study found infiltrations of water that threatened the stability of the pillars. To avoid having to replace several of the blocks completely – as a result of which the aqueduct would have lost much of its charm – it was decided to replace just the inside of the blocks using the coring method.

In addition to the aqueduct, UNESCO has added two other monuments in Segovia to the World Heritage List: the Alcazár, built by the Moors, and the superb sixteenth-century Gothic cathedral. This apparently unrelated set of buildings represents the most important chapters in the city's history. Each is linked to the others by thin, though visible, threads: for example, ancient documents in the Vatican Libraries show that the Roman foundations on which the Alcazár was built are made of the same granite used in *El Puente*.

The Roman Monuments of Merida

SPAIN

PROVINCE OF BADAJOZ,
REGION OF ESTREMADURA
REGISTRATION: 1993
CRITERIA: C (III) (IV)

40 One of Merida's greatest treasures is the austere bridge over the Guardiana; this is the longest Roman bridge to have survived to the present day. Built towards the end of the first century AD, it has 81 arches and measures 866 yards long in its entirety.

40-41 The amphitheater in Merida was inaugurated in 8 BC on the occasion of the circus games. It could hold 14,000 spectators and was divided into three orders.

The Puente Lusitania was inaugurated in Merida in 1991. This slender structure across the Guadiana River is the pride of the residents, and not just because it was designed by Santiago Calatrava, one of the most famous contemporary architects. It is but the most recent manifestation of Merida's special relationship with bridges, which began when the first stone of a bridge was laid, thus marking the city's foundation.

41 bottom left 1,750 yards long, the San Lazaro (or Rabo de Buey, "bull's tail") Aqueduct crossed the Albarregas River to carry water from underground springs into the city.

In the year 25 BC, Publius Carisius, a legate of Emperor Augustus, reached the banks of the Guadiana. The surrounding area was fertile, numerous fresh-water springs flowed in the nearby hills, and there was an abundance of granite. These resources were enough to decide the foundation of the *Colonia Augusta Emerita*. It was populated by veterans of the Fifth Alaudae and Tenth Gemina legions, which had been victorious against the Cantabrian and Asturian peoples that represented the last pockets

of resistance to the expansion of the Roman Empire as far as the western edge of the known world.

The new colony built itself an aqueduct to bring water from the Proserpina Spring north of the city. It was 908 yards long, up to 80 feet high, and crossed the Albarregas River. Although today more than half of its arches have been destroyed, the grandeur of the structure is as evident as the elegance of the colors of the granite blocks and bricks with which it was built. The bridge over the Guadiana was built at the same time as the aqueduct. It has a span of 866 yards that is supported by 81 arches of an average height of 39 feet above the river level. Besides being the main means of reaching Roman Merida, from the sixteenth century on the bridge became a junction on the Via de la Plata, the road along which the Spanish transported the silver shipped from their American colonies to the state coffers in Madrid.

Soon the city flourished, and in 15 BC Marcus Agrippa (Augustus' son-in-law), arrived to preside over the celebrations held to mark the foundation of the Roman *provincia* of Lusitania, of which Merida was the capital. On this occasion, Agrippa inaugurated the theater that could hold 6,000 spectators and which had a cavea divided into three orders of seats for the different social classes. The amphitheater, which could seat 14,000 spectators and had been completed some years earlier, was used to stage gladiator fights, and together these buildings marked the start of a series of monumental constructions that were to

41 bottom right The Los Milagros Aqueduct is 908 yards long and 82 feet high. It was built in two stages between the end of the first century BC and the third century AD. It carried water to the city from the reservoir known as Lake Proserpina.

MADRID

MERIDA

make Merida the "*speculum et propugnaculum Imperii Romani.*"

Owing to the interest of the emperors of the Claudian dynasty, in the first century AD the city came to accommodate a garrison of 90,000 soldiers and witnessed a rapid growth of the economy in all of Roman Spain. The forum was paved with marble, and the Temple of Diana and a huge elliptical circus, able to seat 30,000, were built. The temple was the city's primary religious building and stood at the junction of the *cardus* and *decumanus*. Despite its name, it was dedicated to the imperial cult, which was determined by the discovery of a statue of the Genius Augustii and a sculptural group of Aeneas, Anchises, and Ascanius.

Merida reached its peak in the second century AD under Trajan and Hadrian, both natives of Spain. During this period, numerous patrician villas were built and decorated with mosaics – many examples of which are held today in the archaeological museum – or existing buildings were enlarged. The city's population also grew thanks to the arrival of troops from the North African provinces. These soldiers brought with them a new religion linked to the cult of Mars. Thus, from AD 155, Merida became one of the centers of Mithraism, as is demonstrated by the many bas-reliefs found in the city portraying the god fighting a bull. In fact, the Spanish passion for bull-fighting later originated in Merida.

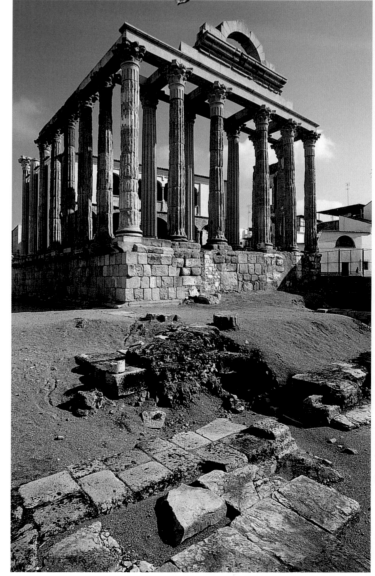

42 top left and right The large mosaic floor of harvest scenes (right, a detail) is the most interesting feature in the Roman House of the amphitheater. This is a notable example of a patrician residence from the late imperial age, and is arranged around a central patio embellished with a peristyle.

42 bottom Located in the center of modern Merida, the temple of Diana (built between the late-first and early-second centuries AD) is a superb peripteral, hexastyle building in granite whose base measures 45 by 24 yards.

42-43 Built in 15 BC by
Marcus Agrippa as a
tribute to the city designated
the capital of Lusitania,
Merida's Roman theater
could seat around 6,000
spectators.

43 bottom A panther hunt
in a fourth-century AD
mosaic panel in the
National Museum of
Roman Art. The museum
has an extraordinary
collection of mosaics,
sculptures, and frescoes
from Merida's Roman
villas, plus many objects
from the necropolis
discovered during
construction of the museum
itself.

Villa Adriana

ITALY

Tivoli, Province of Rome, Region of Lazio
Registration: 1999
Criteria: (i) (ii) (iii)

ROME
TIVOLI

44-45 Villa Adriana seen from the air. The perfect integration of the buildings with the landscape, and the apparently random placement of the various sections in the garden areas, make the villa an outstanding example of ancient architecture.

Having ascended to the imperial throne in AD 117, Hadrian, born in Spain like his predecessor Trajan, waited a year before arriving in Rome. The Roman aristocrats viewed Hadrian with distrust and never learned to appreciate him. For his part, Hadrian never loved the *Caput Mundi*, preferring – when duty called him back to Rome from his journeys to every corner of the enormous empire – to retire to Tivoli, to a magnificent villa he had designed himself.

The choice of the site was carefully made. A villa had already stood in that section of countryside dominated by woods of cluster pines since the first century BC. Its lands were delimited by two rivers that a little further downstream flowed into the Aniene, which was in those days navigable as far as the Tiber, and from there to Rome. The city, though, was also easily reached by road, down the Via Tiburtina. Built in two stages between AD 118 and 134, Villa Adriana covers an area of almost 300 acres. It is an exceptional compendium of architecture, sculpture, and mosaic art owing to the emperor's love of the Greek and Egyptian civilizations, and his enthusiasm for art, history, and philosophy. Prompted by these interests, he reproduced in miniature the principal monuments of his empire to create an "ideal city" of his own.

In fact, they were not simply copies, as Hadrian wanted them to be rebuilt in a "conceptual" manner. The Canopus, for example, resembles the canal built by the Egyptians to join the city of Canopus on the Nile Delta to Alexandria. Hadrian's version was 130 yards long and lined by a colonnade ending in the Serapeum, a building inspired by the Temple of Serapis that he used to host summer banquets. On the other hand, the Stoa Poikile is a direct copy of the original in Athens, though he included a garden and swimming pool at its center that he used for walks. The principal vestibule of the residence was named the Terrace of Tempe in honor of the famous valley in Thessaly. Though systematic excavation has not been carried out, it seems that in the underground tunnels a miniature version of Hades was built. The best-

conserved building in the villa is the Teatro Marittimo (Maritime Theater). It is a round construction with an Ionic portico and, inside, a canal circling an artificial island. Here, Hadrian built a small villa to which he would withdraw to read and study.

Piazza d'Oro (Gold Square) represents the hub of the complex and is lined by a series of reception buildings and a superb baths. Overall, what is exceptional about

46 The statue of Hermes from the Canopo. The decorative plan, overseen by the emperor himself, was designed to make the villa seem a "museum" of antiquity with reproductions of Greek works of art.

47 top left The Canopo is a set of buildings inspired by the Egyptian canal that joined Alexandria to the city of Canopo where the famous temple of Serapis stood. This is the northern end of the canal, framed by the curve of a colonnade with a mixtilinear architrave.

the Villa Adriana are its daring architectural innovations and its interminable sequences of straight lines and concave and convex curves that were to be taken up by the architecture of the baroque. Also surprising are the floors (though many have not survived), which were laid using the technique known as *opus sectile* with triangles, squares, and diamonds made from high-quality marbles, colored glass, and ivory to form geometric patterns. There are also mosaics created using *opus vermiculatum*, including the marvelous Dove Mosaic, now in the Capitoline Museums in Rome.

When Hadrian died, the villa was inhabited by his successor, Antoninus Pius, and other emperors to follow until Diocletian. Constantine, however, stripped it of many of its statues, taking them to his new capital, Constantinople, and becoming the first to plunder the villa's treasures in an operation that was to continue until the nineteenth century. It is estimated that at least 500 of the villa's statues are now in museums around the world, and its columns were taken to adorn the papal palaces. Villa Adriana has always been considered a "desirable object" by illustrious figures, many of whom wanted a piece of it for themselves. Others have limited themselves to leaving their mark on its ruins. A close observer will not miss an autograph left by a famous person who both loved and portrayed it: the great engraver Giovanni Battista Piranesi.

47 top right Along the west side of the Canopo, the columns are substituted by six caryatids, four of which are copies of those in the Erechtheum on the Acropolis in Athens. The outer figures are Greek mythological Sileni.

47 bottom Made using the refined opus vermiculatum technique, this mosaic of two theater masks was taken from Villa Adriana in the eighteenth century and is now displayed in the Capitoline Museums in Rome.

Ancient Rome

ITALY

PROVINCE OF LAZIO
REGISTRATION: 1980, 1990
CRITERIA: (I) (II) (III) (IV) (VI)

*P*anem et circenses, "bread and games": this was the basic formula of which Juvenal wrote in his AD 81 *Satire* that allowed the Roman rulers to maintain control of the masses. Distribution of food and working public baths on the one hand and gladiators, exotic animals, sports competitions, and theatrical performances on the other: these were the tools the emperors used to divert the discontent of the people.

Rome was the first true metropolis known to the world. With a million inhabitants, perhaps a million and a half, a complex city layout, and a natural setting that placed severe limitations on rational planning, the city already suffered problems of traffic and overcrowding as in modern-day metropolises, but with the added perils of poor hygiene, the ever-present risk of fire, and a lack of public order.

Consequently, it is hardly surprising that the emperors tried to distract the populace from their daily grind. When Juvenal wrote his caustic sentences, the most famous of the Roman monuments dedicated to games had only just been inaugurated. Commissioned by Vespasian and opened by Titus in AD 80, the Colosseum (or Flavian Amphitheater) stood 158 feet high, had four levels, was 205 yards across, and could seat 50,000 spectators. Three and a half million cubic feet of travertine and 330 tons of iron were required to build it. The first level was 34 feet six inches high and was decorated with Doric half-columns; the second was 38 feet ten inches high and was given Ionic columns; the third was 38 feet high and had Corinthian columns. The top level was made of brick and was given a system of poles that anchored the

velarium, a huge awning that sheltered the spectators from the sun.

Founded in 753 BC in the area of the Palatine Hill and surrounded by a number of villages, by the end of the eighth century BC Rome was one of the most important settlements in the Mediterranean. Under Tarquinius Priscus and Servius Tullius, the first public works were undertaken, with the construction of roads, squares, systems for drainage and water provision, and even the first street paving (625 BC), which can still be seen in the area of the Imperial Forums. From 509 BC on, the city was run by a system of republican government and, in the space of a few centuries, it became the capital of an empire. Victorious in the Punic wars in the third and second centuries BC, Rome became the uncontested ruler of the Mediterranean.

ROME

48 top Ritual in origin, the
munera gladiatoria
developed into cruel public
games in 105 BC. This
fourth-century AD mosaic
shows different types of
combatants with their real
or "professional" names.

48 bottom left and right
The Colosseum or, more
properly, the Flavian
Amphitheater, was built in
five years between AD 75
and 80 but only received its
fourth architectural order
some years later during the

reign of Domitian. The
emperor's and priests' rostra
were on opposite sides of
the structure's shorter axis.
The aerial view shows the
complexity of the animal
stalls and storerooms on the
level under ground.

49 The Roman Forum
stretching towards the
Colosseum: the most evident
characteristics are the well-
preserved temple of Antoninus
and Faustina and the basilica
of Maxentius (left), and the
three surviving columns from
the temple of Castor and Pollux.

The city monuments that have survived until the modern day, however, were all built to embellish the *Urbs* during the imperial age. The Forums were the heart of imperial Rome. Built to celebrate the greatness of the city and used to house administrative functions, they were constructed in an area that had been used for gladiatorial combats. There were five forums in all: Caesar's Forum, Augustus's Forum, the Forum of Peace, Nerva's Forum, and Trajan's Forum. Their construction marked the transition of Rome from a republic to an empire. Treading the same path as Julius Caesar, all the most important emperors wished to leave a mark of their own passing, resulting in a collective site that is one of the richest and most fascinating archaeological areas in the world.

Covering an area of 175 yards by 85, Caesar's Forum was a rectangular plaza lined by a dual colonnaded portico. At the far end stood the temple of Venus *Genetrix* (Venus the Begetter), which Caesar built to commemorate his victory in the battle of Pharsalus. Constructed to provide the Forum with greater importance, the temple was one of the most striking examples of political self-acclamation.

To make space for his own Forum, a little further north, Augustus had to buy up a large number of private houses in

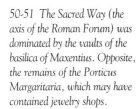

50 top left Created partly by the recycling of bas-reliefs from other monuments, Constantine's Arch celebrated the victory at the Milvian Bridge, following which the emperor legitimated Christian worship.

50 top right The gray columns of the Basilica Ulpia, partially integrated with bricks, frame Trajan's Column. The forum named after this emperor was the most magnificent in Rome.

50-51 The Sacred Way (the axis of the Roman Forum) was dominated by the vaults of the basilica of Maxentius. Opposite, the remains of the Porticus Margaritaria, which may have contained jewelry shops.

51 top Inspired by Trajan's Column, the column of Marcus Aurelius illustrates the military campaigns undertaken against the Sarmathians and Germans. The reliefs are a valuable source of information on the dress, life, and maneuvers of the imperial legions.

51 center The layout of Trajan's Forum, designed by Apollodorus of Damascus, is still visible in some parts. The white column in the semi-circular area stood in front of the market, where there were shops in buildings six stories high.

51 bottom The column of Marcus Aurelius is composed of 28 blocks of stone carved with 20 volutes in relief. The restoration in 1588 at the instigation of Pope Sixtus V led to the replacement of the statue of the emperor on the top with that of Saint Paul.

nearby Suburra. Inaugurated in 2 BC, the new forum was adorned with gigantic statues, including one of the emperor that was 56 feet tall and stood against a wall built to protect the Forum from fires. At the back of the plaza there was a gigantic temple dedicated to Mars Ultor (Mars the Avenger), the god of war, also in imitation of Caesar's Forum. Large grooved columns supported a triangular tympanum bearing images of Mars, Venus, Aeneas, and Romulus along its sides.

Both Vespasian's Forum, or the Forum of Peace, and Nerva's Forum were less spectacular. The former was a monumental square flanked by the *Templum Pacis* (Temple of Peace), built between AD 71 and 75, to celebrate the peace after the Civil Wars. Nerva's Forum – also known as the Transitorium as it lay in the narrow space between the forums of Augustus, Caesar, Vespasian, and the Republican Forum – had been begun by Domitian but was only inaugurated in AD 98 by Nerva, the succeeding emperor, who named it after himself.

The most majestic forum was built by Trajan to commemorate the Roman victory in Dacia in AD 105. To have it constructed he did not hesitate to remove a section of the Quirinale, where the Trajan Markets were built alongside the steep side of the hill. Trajan's Column was placed inside the forum and inaugurated on May 18, 113. It is made from massive blocks of marble that were hollowed out to create a tomb for the emperor in its base and a spiral staircase that leads to the top. A long spiral frieze on its exterior is carved with 2,500 figures illustrating the two Dacian campaigns.

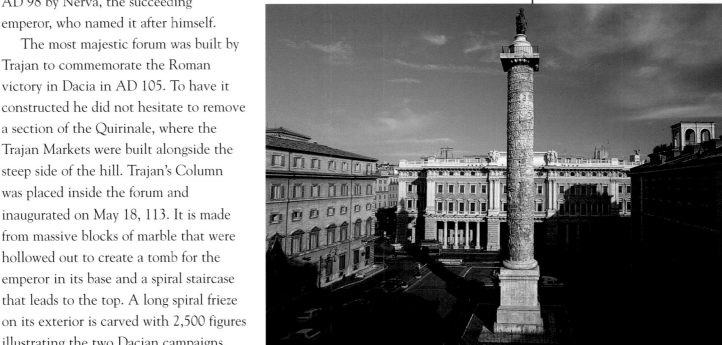

Columns were raised all over ancient Rome to celebrate military victories. In 176, Marcus Aurelius began to build a monument to commemorate his own victories against the Germans. It was completed in 192 and stood 100 Roman feet high (equal to about 96 modern feet), becoming a total of 138 feet tall if the statue of Saint Paul that Pope Sixtus V had placed on the top in 1589 is considered. Marcus Aurelius' column is composed of 28 drums of marble placed one atop the other and is decorated with a spiral bas-relief that winds around the column 21 times. Inside there is a spiral staircase with 203 steps that climbs up to the statue. Of the other monuments under the aegis of UNESCO, one of the most majestic and best conserved is the Pantheon. Built by Marcus Vipsanius Agrippa in 27 BC and rebuilt by Hadrian between AD 118 and 125, it is the result of the combination of a circular building, a hemispherical dome, and a colonnaded rectangular pronaos. A circular wall over 100 feet high supports the drum, and at the center of the dome there is an oculus 30 feet across that provides the interior with light. In 609, Pope Boniface IV transformed the building into a church, and today it is the site of the tombs of Raphael, Vittorio Emanuele II, Umberto I, and Margherita of Savoy. Nor should the funerary monuments be forgotten. Augustus's Mausoleum is truly impressive, begun in 28 BC after having defeated Antony and Cleopatra. With a diameter of roughly 285 feet and a height of 144, is has a cylindrical body lined with blocks of travertine at the center of which a doorway is preceded by a short flight of steps. On either side of the entrance, two pillars bear bronze tablets engraved with the *Res Gestae*, the emperor's autobiography. From the entry *dromos*, two round corridors were accessed that then encircled the burial chamber. At the center of the chamber there is a cylindrical nucleus lined with blocks of travertine around which the entire construction is focused. Equally remarkable is Hadrian's Tomb, construction of which was begun in AD 121. Today it has become Castel Sant'Angelo, located near the Vatican. Originally, it consisted of a square base on which the cylindrical body of the building we see today stood. This cylinder is 69 feet high and 210 in diameter. A second, smaller cylinder rose from the center in which Hadrian's ashes were placed. Higher up, where the angel bearing a sword now stands, there used to be a chariot drawn by four bronze horses that transported an effigy of the emperor towards the heavens. This has been just a brief summary of the monuments listed by UNESCO as justification for the ancient city's inclusion in the list of World Heritage sites.

52 top and 52-53 Augustus' Mausoleum, built in 28 BC, holds the ashes of the first emperor of Rome and of some of his relations and descendants. Despite the various uses the building was put to in the imperial era (fort, quarry, theater until 1936), it has still partially retained two of its three levels.

52 bottom Back in the imperial age, Hadrian's Tomb – now Castel Sant'Angelo – already performed the defensive functions that were to characterize its future. It even provided refuge for popes during times of tumult.

53 bottom left Coffers lighten the perfect hemisphere of the Pantheon's dome. The building is lit naturally through the 30-foot oculus that symbolizes the sun.

53 bottom right The Pantheon is one of the most daring and well-proportioned buildings in the world. It has survived in spite of the human and natural cataclysms that have always beset Rome. The concrete of which the dome is made is mixed with lighter and lighter material as it progresses towards the oculus.

52

54 top left Part of a two-tone mosaic, this figure of Eros riding a dolphin decorated the floor of a room in Caracalla's Baths, which at one time were the most magnificent in Rome.

54 top right Different wall paintings remain in the surviving rooms of Nero's Domus Aurea. Construction began in AD 64 but its delights were not long enjoyed by the emperor, who committed suicide in AD 68.

However, the incredible legacy left by the imperial age to the Eternal City would require many more pages. Just some of the buildings worth mentioning are Caracalla's Baths and the gigantic Circus Maximus, which could seat 350,000 spectators after Trajan had it rebuilt in the second century AD Not to be forgotten, there are recently discovered ancient sites like the Domus Aurea (Nero's magnificent residence) and the tombs along the Appian Way. The excavations carry on: Rome continues to yield more of the wonders of its ancient greatness.

54 center The indelible outline left by the Circus Maximus harks back to Rome's early centuries, to the kingdom of the Etruscan king, Tarquin. It was the setting for horse races from the fourth century BC to the sixth century AD, and it could hold 250,000 spectators.

54 bottom The Octagonal Room in the Domus Aurea was the focus of Nero's immense residence (it can only be visited today by booking). After the emperor's death, everything was done to take it to pieces and reuse the materials in other buildings, thereby dissipating his memory.

54-55 The human figure disappears among the magnificent rooms of the empire's most splendid baths. Built by Caracalla, the complex included hot- and cold-water pools, shops, libraries, massage rooms, beauty-treatment rooms, and gardens.

55 bottom Of the 323,000 square feet of wall paintings in the Domus Aurea, 1,200 have been restored. In part, the paintings have survived because the rooms were buried back in the Roman era beneath other monumental structures, and were thus filled with rubble.

Pompeii, Herculanum, and Oplontis

ITALY

Province of Naples, Region of Campania
Registration: 1997
Criteria: C (III) (IV) (V)

"A black and dreadful cloud bursting out in gusts of igneous serpentine vapor now and again yawned open to reveal long fantastic flames, resembling flashes of lightning but much larger... Soon afterwards the cloud... began to descend upon the earth, and cover the sea...." This short passage from one of the letters sent by Pliny the Younger to Tacitus described the catastrophic eruption of Vesuvius. When it occurred on August 24, AD 79, Pliny was still a boy; he was staying at the villa at Cape Misenum on the coast of Campania with his uncle, Pliny the Elder. Since early morning, the rumblings of minor earthquakes and the sinister smell of sulfur had persuaded the famous, elderly naturalist to take to the sea in an attempt to reach Pompeii and Herculanum where he would be able to observe and annotate the "terrible prodigy" from a closer viewpoint.

Together with many thousands of others, Pliny the Elder died in the eruption, but his nephew transcribed his notes, which today represent the most vivid account of the hecatomb that struck the magnificent cities on the Campanian coast. Vesuvius had begun to make its voice heard some days before and the inhabitants of Pompeii had hurriedly celebrated the *Vulcanalia*, the sacrificial rites to ingratiate themselves with the god of fire that lived in the bowels of the earth. Some decided to leave the city, but most were surprised by the deafening rain of pumice discharged from the mountain. And when, on the morning of August 25th, the volcano hurled a burning cloud of ash and small stones into the air at a speed of over 60 mph, there was no longer any means of escape. The two cities that had been the pride of the ancient Romans, places of relaxation and amusement for the patrician families, were buried beneath a blanket of ash 20 feet deep.

Founded by the Samnites in the sixth century BC over an earlier "mixed" settlement of Greek, Etruscan, and indigenous origins, Pompeii passed into Roman hands in 80 BC when the general Publius Cornelius Sulla established the *Colonia Cornelia Veneria Pompeianorum* there. The city, which stood on a plain overlooking the sea at the mouth of the Sarnus River and was surrounded by fertile fields, was soon embellished with public and private buildings, most importantly the temple dedicated to Venus. During the reigns of the emperors Augustus (27 BC–AD 14) and Tiberius (AD 14–37), it underwent a "frenzy of construction." Then, in AD 62, a violent earthquake struck the entire area around Vesuvius. This was so large that, 17 years later when the volcano erupted, Pompeii, Herculanum, and the villas all along the coast were still in a phase of reconstruction.

During the rule of the Bourbon monarchy, removal began of the thick layer of ash, thus revealing the cities exactly as they had appeared in AD 79 and providing the modern world with a fascinating snapshot of life in the Roman era. Temples, baths, houses, urban and rural villas, theaters, streets, aqueducts, shops of all kinds, and even brothels are now visible in their entire original splendor. In Herculanum, the town closest to the volcano, even wooden furniture and foods have been conserved.

56 bottom A tragic mask hangs over a naturalistic scene in the House of Venus Marina. Ironically, in AD 79, this beautiful domus, one of the least known in Pompeii, was being restored at the time of the eruption.

56-57 In this aerial view, the well-preserved cavea of the Great Theater is seen to be slightly oriented towards the northwest, perfectly in line with the cardus maximus and Vesuvius.

57 top left Painted during Nero's reign (the last years of Pompeii), this portrait of the baker Terentius Neus and his wife, now in the Archaeological Museum in Naples, was hung in the tablinum of the house named after the man.

57 top right "Sappho" is the conventional name given to this painting, though it probably was of an imaginary person. Writing was not a common pastime among Roman women.

57 center Apollo the archer, in the southeast corner of the blackened ruins of the temple dedicated to the god: an attempt may have been made to save the original of this statue (today in the National Museum in Naples), which was found outside the building.

57 bottom The fountains were often decorated with busts from which jets of water spurted. One of these, the face of a woman holding a cornucopia, gave the name to the Via dell'Abbondanza (in the photograph), one of the main streets in the city.

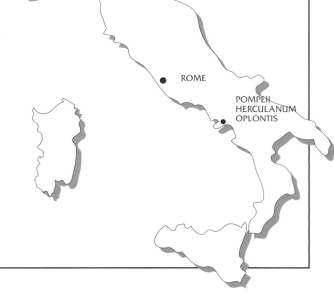

ROME

POMPEII
HERCULANUM
OPLONTIS

58 top Marble pools and a cupid in a peristyle in the House of the Vettii, which still has almost all its original furnishings.

58 bottom The oecus (the "room" cited by Pliny and Vitruvius) in the House of the Vettii is decorated with theatrical views and mythological illustrations, all of which were created with an extraordinary sense of volumes and perspective.

58-59 Alexander the Great (bareheaded on the left) prepares to hurl his spear beneath the disconcerted gaze of Darius. This famous mosaic is in the House of the Faun.

Excavation of Pompeii has extended over 109 of the 156 acres of the city and revealed a series of buildings of great historical and artistic value. There are temples (the most important being the Temple of Isis, built by Popidius Ampiatus, a freed slave who became the richest man in the city), the forum, baths, and a great number of superb private homes. The House of the Faun, named after the bronze statuette found standing in the middle of the *impluvium* (a basin that collected rainwater in the main courtyard), covers an area of 3,600 square yards. Built after the earthquake of AD 62 over a previous building, it is the most impressive of the houses in Pompeii. Its various frescoed rooms are arranged around two atria and two gardens with a peristyle. The superb sculptural and mosaic decorations, like the outstanding floor mosaic portraying the battle between the Persian king Darius and Alexander the Great, can now be seen in the archaeological museum in Naples. Typical of the houses of the nobility are the wall paintings in the style of "illusionistic realism," which are paintings of buildings and, sometimes, mythological figures meant to give rooms the impression of greater spaciousness.

59 bottom The Vettii were a rich family of freedmen who moved to Pompeii in the early years of the first century AD. The house named after them was restored after the serious earthquake of AD 62, the first serious warning of the imminent catastrophe. The new frescoes were executed in the Fourth Style, which was characterized by fantastic, almost ethereal motifs. This was the case with these cupids producing perfumes and, at the center, two characters grinding the ingredients.

60 top Traditional themes linked to the myths of Mars and Venus (left in the illustrated composition) make up the frescoes in the tablinum in the house of Marcus Lucretius Fronto. This name appears several times on walls recommending that he be elected to the construction magistracy.

60-61 The Villa of the Mysteries gets its name from the pictorial sequence that illustrates the various phases of an initiation rite into the Dionysiac "mysteries". The initiates of this practice, which was based on preferences different from that of the public religion, were bound to silence. Sileni, satyrs, maenads, and demons with whips populate a cycle that was already famous in antiquity.

Frequent in the gardens of houses of this kind are magnificent fountains, often adorned with sculptures.

These features are also found in the villas. In Pompeii, the most impressive is the Villa of the Mysteries, a luxurious residence that was also a *villa rustica* dedicated to agricultural production.

61 top A simple marble table today furnishes the atrium of the House of Fronto, with the impluvium visible in the foreground and the tablinum in the background. The house was cleared of ash in 1900 and immediately fitted with a roof to protect the paintings as they were gradually returned to the light of day.

62 top left A nymphaeum is visible in the background of the triclinium of the House of Neptune and Amphitrite, as well as a lovely polychrome mosaic (right) from which the house gets its name.

62 top right The Collegio degli Augustali is decorated with paintings in the Third Style. It was dedicated to the cult of the emperor and was administered by six men appointed for the period of one year. The divinization of Augustus was made official by Tiberius a few years before the eruption.

62-63 *This aerial view covers the entire excavation zone of Herculaneum. At top right there are the suburban baths, in the opposite corner the Collegio degli Augustali, and, in the center foreground, the city baths. Unlike Pompeii, Herculaneum was submerged beneath mud and volcanic detritus.*

63 top *A bust and a marble pool can be seen in the half-light of the suburban baths. The vestibule is illuminated by a light-well over the arcades.*

63 bottom *The House of the Deer, built between AD 55 and 70, is one of the largest in Herculaneum. The city buildings are very well preserved, particularly above ground. Together they formed a small town about one third the size of Pompeii, with roughly 5,000 inhabitants.*

The exceptionally fine Villa of the Papyruses, on the other hand, can be seen at Herculanum, where there is also a basilica, baths complex with annexed *palaestra*, and a theater that seated 3,000 spectators. Built on a series of terraces sloping down towards the sea, the Villa of the Papyruses boasted a 72-yard-long swimming pool, a 100-yard-long 40-yard-wide peristyle decorated with mosaics, 50 bronze statues, and 20 marble ones. Believed to have belonged to Appius Claudius Pulcrus, a man of culture and a friend of Cicero, this villa has been named after the important discovery inside its library of 1,758 papyruses bearing texts of the Epicurean philosopher Philodemus of Gadara.

Another two extraordinary residences are found at Oplontis, three miles from Pompeii where the modern town of Torre Annunziata stands. The first is a perfect example of a "villa of *otium*" (leisure) and is attributed to Poppea Sabina, the second wife of Emperor Nero. Enormous and magnificent with a very elegant baths area, it was built in the first century AD and enlarged during the reign of Claudius. The second villa, known as the "Villa of Lucius Crassius," was a residential complex with an attached farm that produced agricultural products and sold wine. At the moment of the eruption 54 men took refuge in the farm's storerooms, and of their bodies, like so many other people who died in Pompeii and Herculanum, archaeologists have been able to take casts by pouring liquid plaster into the hollows and cavities in the petrified ashes left by their disintegrated bodies. Today brought "back to life," even in the expressions on their faces and folds of their clothes, they are perhaps the most horrible and fascinating relics of that fateful day.

64 top Rose bushes, sycamores, chestnut and myrtle trees and laurel bushes adorned the gardens of the villa of Poppea, Nero's wife. When the huge complex was buried beneath the ashes of the volcano and suffered the same fate as Pompeii, its famous owner had already been dead for years.

64 center left The magnificent paintings that decorated the interior of the villa made frequent use of trompe l'oeil techniques imitating doors, columns, hangings, and architectural views that may have been inspired by theater scenery.

64 center right A restoration project interrupted for 2,000 years: that was the fate of Poppea's villa, buried during renovations and discovered by excavators as a sort of "open building site" beneath the ash. Modern restoration has been very careful: in addition to recreating the gardens using the same plants as existed originally, the Second (or "Architectural") Style paintings have been completed with white outlines on the new plaster, as can be seen in the triclinium.

64 bottom Mirror views on the opposite walls of the triclinium create a trompe l'oeil effect portraying the entrance gate to a luxurious villa. The expert painters interpreted Hellenistic decorations in Roman style, reflecting the transition and refinement of tastes that occurred between the austerity of the Republican era and the luxury of the imperial age.

65 Perhaps inspired by the furnishings in the gardens of the villa, the exuberant compositions in the triclinium were set like paintings in an overall decoration, similar to windows giving onto an immutable and perpetually dreamlike world.

Cilento and the Vallo di Diano with the Sites of Paestum and Velia

ITALY

PROVINCE OF SALERNO, CAMPANIA
REGISTRATION: 1998
CRITERIA: C (III) (IV)

Lauded by Virgil and other Roman poets, the roses of Paestum were for a long time more famous than its temples. In the drawings of Piranesi, they can be seen lush and blooming against the background of the ruins, and descriptions of them are found in Goethe's *Journey in Italy*. In 1802, the traveler Johann Gottfried Seume even set out on foot from distant Lipsia inspired by his desire to smell their intoxicating perfume.

The fertile plain on which Paestum stands is bounded on one side by the warm Tyrrhenian Sea, and, on the other, by the green hills of the Cilento, and boasts a climate and flora of extraordinary charm.

It was the landscape, abundant water, and proximity to the sea that, since remote times, brought the area of the Cilento and the flat strip of land referred to as the Vallo di Diano to play a fundamental role in the development of Mediterranean civilization. Inhabited since the Neolithic era, the zone had been colonized by Anatolic-Aegean populations before when, in the seventh century BC, people from Thessaly founded Poseidonia, the city that was renamed Paestum in 237 BC following the arrival of the Romans.

Linked to the myths of Odysseus and the sirens, Jason and the Argonauts, and the battle between the god Heracles and the Centaurs, Poseidonia grew to be rich and impressive, as attested to by the rose-colored limestone temples that have survived to this day in exceptional condition. The earliest building is the Basilica, a name that was attributed to it in the eighteenth century by archaeologists working for the Bourbons during the first excavation operations, though it was actually a temple dedicated

66 left The temple of Neptune (460 BC), the largest and best-preserved building in Paestum, was originally dedicated to Hera. It features six columns along the façade and fourteen on the longer sides. Its construction reflects great expertise, which can be noted in aspects such as its overall harmony.

66-67 The basilica, on the right side of the picture (the temple of Neptune is on the left), is the oldest monument in Paestum (circa 550 BC). Its name originated in the eighteenth century, when archaeologists mistakenly interpreted the temple, which was actually dedicated to Hera, as a civic building of the Roman era.

67 top The temple of Ceres, or the Athenaion, was built on the highest point in the city. Built around 500 BC, it is of great architectural interest as it merges two styles, the archaic Doric and the Ionic.

to Hera. Built in Doric style in the mid-sixth century BC, its tapered columns, whose shafts are fuller at the middle and whose capitals are decorated with leafy crowns, are miraculously still in intact. Aligned with the Basilica, the Temple of Neptune, or the *Poseidonion*, is the largest and best conserved of Paestum's buildings. Built between 460 and 450 BC

ROME

PAESTUM
VELIA

67 bottom The Romans arrived in Paestum in 273 BC and only partially modified the layout of the city. It was the Romans who built the amphitheater, shown here in an aerial photograph, as well as the temple dedicated to Jupiter, Juno and Minerva.

68 top The slab covering the Diver's Tomb is now displayed in the National Archaeological Museum of Paestum. Archaeologists agree that the delicate painting of the nude young man, in the act of diving, should be interpreted as a symbolic representation of the sudden transition between life and death.

68-69 and 69 bottom The lateral slabs from the Diver's Tomb depict a banquet. A comparison of this convivial scene with highly similar ones, found on Attic pottery, has made it possible to date the tomb to about 475-470 BC.

in Doric style, its majesty and style are reminiscent of the Temple of Zeus at Olympia. On the far side of the remains of the Amphitheater and civil buildings lies the *Athenaion*, renamed the Temple of Ceres, which dates back to 510 BC and owes its lighter and more elegant proportions than the other two temples to its blend of Doric and Ionic styles.

In the fourth century BC, the Greeks of Poseidonia came to coexist with the Lucanians and Etruscans, with the result that the different cultures slowly merged. The Lucanians were responsible for the construction of a massive quadrilateral defensive wall with smoothed corners. The Etruscans were responsible for the tombs in the vast necropolis that lay outside the city limits, discovery of which was made in 1968. Of these, the most interesting is the Tomb of the Diver, named after the famous painting on the ceiling slab of a young man about to dive from a springboard.

The city's contact with Rome in 273 BC led to the construction of the Italic Temple, which was dedicated to the triad of Jupiter, Juno, and Minerva.

Despite its name change, the city remained essentially autonomous for a long time, as did the nearby city of Elea, or Velia. Excavations of Velia are still in progress but much of the city was lost during the Middle Ages when the Normans used the stones of its temples to build a castle. Nevertheless, Velia preserves the memory of those glorious times when it was the birthplace of the philosophers Parmenides and Zeno, during that ancient period when the culture of Magna Grecia was the universal culture of the Mediterranean.

The Villa at Casale

ITALY

PIAZZA ARMERINA, PROVINCE OF ENNA, SICILY
REGISTRATION: 1997
CRITERIA: C (I) (II) (III)

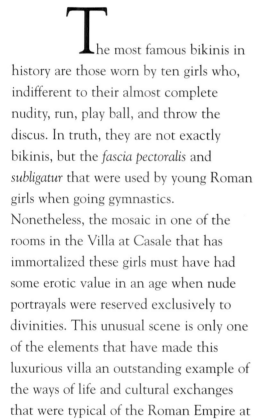

The most famous bikinis in history are those worn by ten girls who, indifferent to their almost complete nudity, run, play ball, and throw the discus. In truth, they are not exactly bikinis, but the *fascia pectoralis* and *subligatur* that were used by young Roman girls when going gymnastics. Nonetheless, the mosaic in one of the rooms in the Villa at Casale that has immortalized these girls must have had some erotic value in an age when nude portrayals were reserved exclusively to divinities. This unusual scene is only one of the elements that have made this luxurious villa an outstanding example of the ways of life and cultural exchanges that were typical of the Roman Empire at the peak of its power and the start of its decline.

The Villa at Casale was built in either the third or fourth centuries AD (an age marked by power struggles) in Sicily, the Roman province to which Justinian had conceded the title *Res suburbicaria*. This privilege signified that the island was directly dependent on Rome and, consequently, meant that large estates – the *latifunda* on which the economy of the island was to depend for many centuries to come – were handed out lavishly. It was near Piazza Armerina, at the center of one such *latifundum*, that the villa was built. It has survived in such good condition to the present day thanks to being covered by a mudslide during the age of the Normans, which protected

it from the elements until 1881 when the first excavation work was begun.

It is not known who the owner of the villa was. Its size – 4,200 square meters – and the profusion of decoration suggests that it was a dignitary of the senatorial class or perhaps even a member of the imperial family. The most accredited hypothesis is that the owner was Maximian, known as Herculius, a member of the Tetrarch that ruled the empire between AD 286 and 305.

Whoever it was, the building is a majestic complex of almost 50 rooms built on different levels of terraces. Entering the main gate, one passes

70 top left The villa (the photograph shows the peristyle) covers an area of 37,600 square feet. Its extension and sumptuous decoration indicate that its owner must have been a senatorial or imperial dignitary.

70 top right The octagonal frigidarium, surrounded by six apses and two pools, leads to the anointing room, used for massages.

70-71 and 71 top Some animals are being sent to Rome, where they will be used for cruel circus shows. This is the "final" part of the Great Hunt depicted in the floor mosaic in the corridor of the Great Hunt.

71 bottom left In this detail of the central part of the mosaic of the Great Hunt, soldiers on horseback defend themselves with large shields. They are the guards of Maximian, one of the tetrarchs who ruled the Empire between AD 286 and 305. He was probably the owner of the villa and is portrayed just beyond this section.

71 bottom right A hunter with a rhinoceros is portrayed in another detail of the mosaic of the Great Hunt. Hundreds of exotic animals are depicted, including panthers, lions, tigers, hippopotamuses, elephants, ostriches, antelopes, and dromedaries.

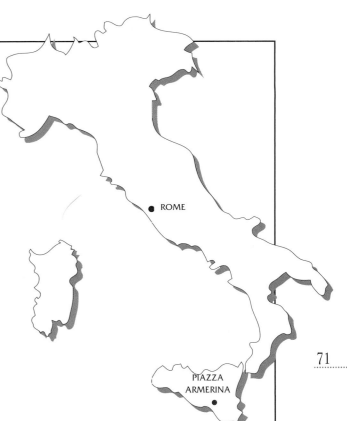

ROME

PIAZZA ARMERINA

through a polygonal courtyard to a *peristilium* around which were arranged the apartments of the owners, the guestrooms, and the Great Basilica in which official receptions were held. To the left of the entrance an area was reserved for banquets, and a sumptuous baths complex lies on the right.

More than the impressiveness of the buildings themselves, the floor mosaics make the villa truly unique. Laid by skilled African artists, they are remarkable for the realism and the detail seen in the compositions. Apart from the depiction of the female gymnasts, the most outstanding are the one in the Circus Room (the *palaestra* in the baths) portraying a chariot race in the Circus Maximus in Rome, another featuring the Labors of Hercules, and the Great Hunt found in the Ambulacrum. The floor of this 200-foot-long corridor illustrates an amazing scene of a large-game hunting expedition: panthers, lions, antelopes, ostriches, rhinoceroses, and hippopotamuses are captured and loaded on a boat that will take them to Rome, where they are destined for the arena of the Circus. Today it is these animals destined for the slaughter that fascinate and dismay visitors to the villa. To modern eyes, the girls in bikinis make an impact "only" because of their grace and beauty.

72-73 What makes the composition of the mosaic of the Great Hunt so extraordinary is the variety of the scenes, the realistic portrayal of the fights among beasts and between man and animal, the strong sense of action and movement, and the rich attention to detail.

72 bottom In the lower register of the famous mosaic known as the "mosaic of the ten girls in bikinis," the young girl wearing a mantle is about to crown an athlete, giving her the palm of victory. The young woman has completed exercises with a spoked wheel, turning it with a rod. Another girl standing next to the pair is awarded for her athletic prowess.

73 top left The vestibule is named for its stunning mosaic of Ulysses and Polyphemus. The scene depicts the ruse used by the hero from Ithaca to trick the monster, portrayed here with three eyes. Ulysses offered him a cup of wine that put him to sleep.

73 top right A detail of the maritime scene of the mosaic decoration on the floor of the frigidarium: depicted in a large pool (or perhaps a lake) surrounded by multicolor buildings are cupids, fishermen, Tritons, Nereids, and dolphins.

The Valley of the Temples in Agrigento

ITALY

AGRIGENTO, SICILY
REGISTRATION: 1997
CRITERIA: C (I) (II) (III) (IV)

Pindar described Agrigento as "the loveliest city of mortal men," where the inhabitants "lived as though they were to die the next day and built their houses as though they themselves were immortal." Observing the magnificent ruins, Guy de Maupassant wrote, "one gets the impression of being before the entire Olympus … of gods as fascinating, carnal,

and passionate as ourselves, who incarnated the sentiments of our hearts, the dreams of our minds, the instincts of our senses…."

History narrates that Agrigento was founded as the city of Akragas in 581 BC by a colony of Rhodians and Cretans. However, it is not exactly true that the men who built the city were Greeks. That colorful, perfumed corner of Sicily, bathed by the sun and caressed by soft breezes, must have seemed like paradise, and they behaved accordingly, induced by the beauty to build temples whose magnificence seems to challenge the gods, and whose arrogance looks down on the world of mere humans.

The temple dedicated to Zeus Olympus was built to celebrate victory over the Carthaginians at the battle of Himera (480–479 BC) and best represents Agrigentine pride, despite being reduced to a heap of splendid ruins. It had immense half-columns interspersed with 13-foot-high statues, called atlantes, that gave the impression of supporting the entire weight of the structure, just as Atlas was condemned by Zeus to hold up the world for having aided the Titans. The temple platform measures 371 feet four inches in length by 183 feet eight inches in width (essentially a double square) and could accommodate 42,000 people. Indeed, during the Carthaginian siege in 406 BC, the entire population of the city barricaded themselves inside the temple.

Seven Doric temples stood around the sanctuary, all built in tufa stone with golden tints, and originally lined with brightly colored stuccoes. They faced east so that the entrance and the effigies of the gods standing in front of them would be illuminated by the rising sun, the symbol of life. The best conserved of these other temples is the Temple of Concordia. It was built in the fifth century BC and avoided the fate suffered by the other religious buildings of the site – which were knocked down in the fourth century AD by Christians carrying out an edict by the Roman emperor Theodosius – and was transformed into a basilica dedicated to Saints Peter and Paul. Much later, in the middle of the eighteenth century, it was restored to its Classical forms. Its grooved columns are 22 feet tall and slightly inclined inwards so that, when seen from a distance, the building does not appear distorted due to perspective.

74 left All that remains of the temple of the Dioscuri, dedicated to Castor and Pollux, Zeus' twin sons, is the northwest corner. It seems to defy the laws of balance, and became popular because it was chosen as the symbol of the city.

74-75 Built in about 425 BC, the temple of Concord is one of the best-preserved monuments of the Hellenic world. Unlike other buildings in Agrigento, it escaped destruction because it was transformed into a church dedicated to Saints Peter and Paul.

Also splendid is the Temple of Hera Lacinia in which a statue of the goddess was prayed to by young brides and betrayed wives. The temple stood on the summit of a hill overlooking Akragas, and its six fallen columns on the short sides and 13 on the long ones were raised at the start of the twentieth century. The other monuments are even barer, like the elegant Temple of Heracles, the most ancient in the city, the Temple of the Dioscuri (dedicated to Castor and Pollux, the twin sons of Zeus), of which only four columns and a portion of the trabeation remain, and the temples sacred to the cults of Vulcan, the god of fire, and Asclepius, the god of medicine.

During the Christian era up until the eighteenth century, the Valley of the Temples was known as the Quarry of the Giants. Its stones were constantly carried off and even the Bourbons used them to build the wharf at Porto Empedocle, which is dedicated, ironically, to one of the most famous of Akragas's citizens, the philosopher and thaumaturge Empedocles. Nonetheless, the absent sections of the temples do not detract from the site's charm, and therefore seem to endorse the ancient Agrigentines' claim to immortality.

75

ROME

AGRIGENTO

The Historic Center of Split and the Palace of Diocletian
CROATIA

Central Dalmatia
Registration: 1979
Criteria: C (II) (III) (IV)

It was a series of fortuitous circumstances that led to the nomination as Roman emperor on November 20, 284 of a simple soldier of very humble origins. His name was Diokles and he had been born 41 years before at Salona, the capital of the Roman province of Dalmatia. In Rome nobody would have bet a *sesterce* on his reign lasting long, nor on his life, for in the half century before Diokles' appearance on the scene the Senate had elected no fewer than 20 emperors, who had been overthrown by at least as many usurpers. Instead, Gaius Aurelius Valerius Diocletianus – the Latin version of his name – proved all the predictions

wrong. In a shrewd move, he appointed his friend Maximian as co-regent and gave him the Western half of the empire to govern. For his own part, Diocletian ruled the Eastern half, moved to Nicomedia, and installed an absolute monarchy on the Persian model.

His reign was marked by a variety of successes and administrative and tax reforms, and it came to an end on May 1, 305 when the old man abdicated and

retired to his splendid new palace built on the site of the ancient Greek settlement of Aspalatos, close to Salona.

Built in top-quality limestone quarried on the nearby island of Brazza and embellished with granite columns and sphinxes transported from Egypt, Diocletian's palace is one of the most important monuments from the late imperial age. Rectangular in layout, it covers almost 35,000 square yards and has walls with 16 towers on the north, east, and west faces. The south side, which overlooks the sea, was not fortified but features a rather graceful series of arcades.

In its original form, the architectural layout reflected the building's dual nature: part villa and part military *castrum*. The *decumanus* ran east-west and divided the palace into a residential area for soldiers and servants and into a luxurious area for the emperor, where a monumental peristyle led to Diocletian's apartments, his mausoleum, three temples, and two sets of baths.

Upon Diocletian's death in 316, the palace remained an imperial possession until at least 480. The *Notitia Dignitarium*, written during that era, mentions that a textile factory was active there. During the same period, a cross was carved above a bas-relief of Victory, the first evidence of Christianity in the complex. The palace underwent a transformation in the seventh century as a result of the inhabitants of Salona taking refuge there from the invasion of the Slavs and Avars. Settlement in the

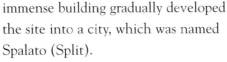

immense building gradually developed the site into a city, which was named Spalato (Split).

The new residents gave the city-palace an ecclesiastical organization, and it was the city's bishop, Giovanni da Ravenna, who transformed Diocletian's tomb into a Christian church (today it is the city cathedral) and the Temple of Jupiter into a baptistery. During the Middle Ages, Gothic buildings were built over the Roman remains – and even beneath them – and later Renaissance and Baroque palaces were added. By this time, Spalato had spread beyond the walls of the original palace site.

The view of the peristyle and the cathedral with an Egyptian sphinx in front is today the loveliest to be had of the historic center. It is an "architectural poem" that fascinated the Italian architect Andrea Palladio and later his English colleague Robert Adam, who in London in 1764 published a monograph on Diocletian's

palace. The beauty of ancient Spalato also persuaded Canaletto to paint a view of the peristyle and cathedral, though he left the sphinx out. However, this is not a great surprise, for he never actually visited the city.

The Thracian tomb of Kazanlak

BULGARIA

REGION OF KAZANLAK

REGISTRATION: 1979

CRITERIA: C (I) (III) (IV)

78 One of the most extraordinary pictorial works from the Hellenistic age, the circular frieze on the vault of the burial chamber represents, with – vivid colors and exquisite detail – the last meeting between a prince – probably Seute III, the Thracian ruler who it is believed was buried here – and his wife. A funeral procession departs in either direction from the central couple.

79 top The walls and ceiling of the dromos (the corridor in which those objects needed in the afterlife were placed) are decorated with three elegant bands of frescoes.

79 bottom Detail from the frescoes in the dromos: the lowest band, painted dark, is purely ornamental, while the upper band shows dramatic battle scenes on horseback.

The dignitary sits on a red- and white-striped cushion on the low metal chair, perhaps even made of silver, before a wooden table on which two loaves, fruit, and plates have been set. His wife sits on his left on a tall wooden seat decorated with silver and watches him sadly. The two hold hands as the ceremonial procession approaches from opposite directions. From the left, a woman in a dark *peplos* places a plate of fruit before her master. On the other side, two ladies-in-waiting with curly black hair, adorned with jewelry, bring gifts to the lady. Behind both of them, there are other servants and knights.

This is the scene painted on the large circular frieze on the vault of the burial chamber in the Thracian tomb of Kazanlak, one of the most extraordinary pictorial masterpieces from the Hellenistic period. Kazanlak lies in the middle of Bulgaria, between the Stara Planina and the mountains of Sredna Gora, in what has been known for centuries as the "Valley of the Roses." Here, in 1944, – not far from Seutopolis, the capital of the kingdom of the Odrisi founded by the king of Thrace, Seute III – a small tomb was discovered, whose frescoes provide a vivid picture of a civilization that reached its apogee between the fifth and third centuries BC.

Of the more than 500 burial mounds in the area of Kazanlak, the tomb (which may be that of Seute III himself, or of a high dignitary in his court) differs by being one of the few in "honeycomb" style. Built in brick – like few other tombs in Thrace – it is composed of three sections: an antechamber for the chariot, horses, and slaves that were sacrificed to accompany the lord to the world beyond the tomb; a *dromos*, or corridor, for objects that would be necessary in the afterlife; and the burial chamber where the body of the deceased was placed. The chamber is the largest of the three sections, with a circular plan eight feet seven inches in diameter and ten feet six inches high. The complex honeycomb structure was built using special curved bricks that are different in each row. The corridor is also made of brick, with walls that curve gradually inwards until they reach the center of the ceiling to form a vault.

Apart from the interesting and unusual architecture, the frescoes are the Kazanlak tomb's true masterpiece, partly because they are the only ones from the Hellenistic period that have been perfectly preserved. Above the aforementioned frieze located right in the middle of the dome of the burial chamber, three chariots are shown racing interspersed by Ionic columns. They most likely represent the chariot races held at the conclusion of funeral ceremonies.

There are other frescoes in the corridor. The walls are divided into three horizontal panels of almost the same height. The two lower ones are purely ornamental, but the third, which begins where the inclination of the walls is at its greatest, is divided into two friezes, one above the other. The first shows stylized acanthus leaves enclosed by elegant palm branches. The second shows battle scenes with two armies in formation at either end of the corridor whereas on the east wall, at the center of the corridor, two warriors challenge one another armed with daggers and shields. Opposite, on the west wall, one of the two warriors kneels to protect himself from the blows of the other. Although the elements of combat are undoubtedly linked to classical Greek art, the scene is natural, free of the stereotypes found in Hellenic bas-reliefs.

Recently two more tombs have been found in the region, at Muglizh and in the village of Krun. However, in neither of these, nor in those of Seutopolis (which today lies beneath the water of a reservoir), did the art of the fresco achieve the perfection of the tomb in Kazanlak.

SOFIA

KAZANLAK

Vergina
GREECE

PREFECTURE OF EMATHIA,
CENTRAL MACEDONIA
REGISTRATION: 1996
CRITERIA: C (I) (III)

*80 top and center left
The dazzling larnax that
held the ashes of Philip II,
father of Alexander the
Great, and his cuirass of
iron and gold are among
the most valuable finds
uncovered at Vergina.*

*80-81 Built towards the
middle of the fourth century
BC, the palace of Philip II
was set around a large
peristyle and included a
circular sanctuary (tholos),
banquet halls and a theater.*

"It is a marvelous place, situated right where the farthest slope of the mountains of Pieria meets the plain of Emathia, with woods of huge elms alternating with fields of corn and sesame…." The enthusiasm of the Frenchman Léon Heuzey is palpable in his description of the setting of his discovery. In 1861, a short distance from the village of Vergina, the archaeologist had identified the remains of Aigai, the first capital of the kingdom of Macedonia, built between the fourth and third centuries BC.

The palace with the annexed theater must have belonged to Philip II (382–336 BC). It is arranged around a large peristyle containing a circular temple (tholos), a luxurious banquet room, and various other rooms, one of which has a mosaic floor. There are also numerous references to the royal family in the Temple of Eukleia, which still features the bases of the votive statues put in place for Eurydice, the grandmother of Alexander the Great. In addition, the remains of Aigai also include fragments of a defensive wall, an acropolis, and, beyond the fortifications, a necropolis with about 300 burial mounds.

Excavation work has continued for more than a century and uncovered evidence of constant settlement since the early Bronze Age (third millennium BC). It has been proven that Aigai had already become a community of a certain size as of the early Iron Age (eleventh–eighth centuries BC) and had experienced two phases of remarkable development during the Archaic (seventh–sixth centuries BC) and the Classical (fifth-fourth century BC) ages. However, the sensational discovery of the royal Macedonian tombs occurred "only" in November 1977, thanks to the work of Greek archaeologist Manolis Andronikos. Beneath a mound of earth 42 feet high and measuring 120 yards across, probably created by king Antigonus Gonates to protect what remained of the tombs following looting by Pyrrhus in 274 BC, Andronikos identified an urn containing the remains of Alexander IV, son of Alexander the Great and Roxana. More remarkably, the remains of Philip II – assassinated during the wedding banquet of his daughter Cleopatra and the king of Epirus – and his sixth, or perhaps, seventh wife, also called Cleopatra, who threw herself onto the king's funeral pyre.

Andronikos had no doubts. The richness of the grave furnishings could only suggest that the partially carbonized remains of the skeletons belonged to these figures. Philip II's tomb, with painted walls and a marble door flanked by two Doric columns, contained two funeral beds decorated with ivory, glass, and gold reliefs of Dionysus and the Muses and a battle scene. Next to this was a gold chest weighing almost 20 pounds that contained the remains of the king wrapped in gold-embroidered cloth and a gold crown composed of 313 leaves and 68 acorns weighing one and a half pounds. The gold chest (larnax) is embossed with a 16-point star with two rosettes at the center; the innermost rosette still bears traces of blue enamel. A study published in 2000 in the authoritative magazine Science contradicts the theory that the remains belong to Philip II, claiming instead that they are those of Philip III Arrhidaeus, half-brother of Alexander the Great, who was poisoned by his own mother because he was mentally and physically handicapped. The proof offered is crushing and is based on analysis of both the bones and the grave furnishings. However, another dispute flared up recently in relation to the Macedonian star on the funeral chest. In 1992, the new independent state of Macedonia adopted it as its symbol to be featured on the national flag, thereby arousing the protests of the Greek government, which considered the star, not to mention the name "Macedonia," part of its inalienable cultural heritage. In 1995, Macedonia succeeded in negotiating the right to retain the name but at the price of the symbol on the flag. Now the star has eight points rather than 16 and resembles a radiant sun.

80 bottom right
Resembling an Ionic temple, Tomb A is one of the three Macedon burials in the tumulus at Bella. The graves in the necropolis of Vergina express both a sense of reverential awe in the face of death but also the magnificence of regal glory.

81 Pluto's abduction of Persephone is depicted in the fresco adorning the only cist tomb in the great tumulus of Vergina. In 1993, a building in reinforced concrete was constructed over the tumulus to protect the valuable paintings in the tombs from light and humidity.

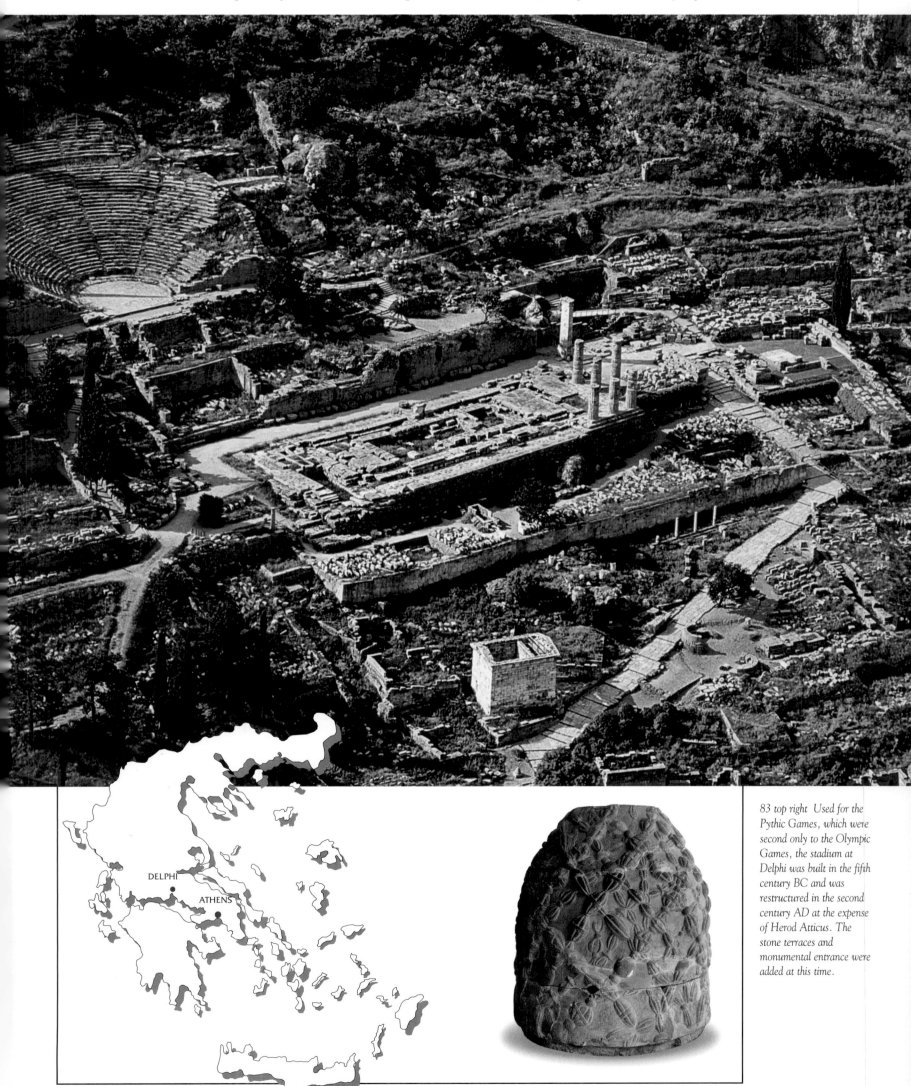

82-83 The presence of a place of worship in Delphi, visible here almost in its entirety, was documented as early as the Mycenaean era. However, the first sanctuary of the oracle was built at the beginning of the eighth century BC.

82 bottom The Omphalos or "navel," the stone that marked the center of the earth, was the sacral heart of Delphi. Though quite ancient, the stone at the local museum is not the original one, which was lost centuries ago.

83 left The work of Polymedes of Argos, who sculpted it between 610 and 580 BC, this kouros (over 6 and a half feet tall) in the archaic Doric style is one of a pair of statues portraying Kleobis and Biton, the two pious sons of one of Hera's priestesses. However, according to another interpretation they represent the Dioscuri. Found in the sanctuary of Apollo in 1893, the kouroi are now at the Museum of Delphi.

83 top right Used for the Pythic Games, which were second only to the Olympic Games, the stadium at Delphi was built in the fifth century BC and was restructured in the second century AD at the expense of Herod Atticus. The stone terraces and monumental entrance were added at this time.

Delphi

GREECE

PREFECTURE OF PHOKIS, STEREÁ ELLÁDA
REGISTRATION: 1987
CRITERIA: (I) (II) (III) (IV) (VI)

83 bottom right From the cavea of the theater at Delphi, which had 35 rows of seats, spectators could watch the paeans, stagings of Apollo's battle against Python, as well as ritual dances in the god's honor.

The legend of the origin of the most important religious site in ancient Greece begins with two eagles set free by Zeus in the antipodes of the world; the place where they met – later called Delphi – was where the king of the gods placed the Sacred Stone (the *omphalos*) that marked the center of the world. It was here that the goddess Gaea and her son, the serpent Python, dwelt until Apollo, enchanted by the beauty of the place, left Mount Olympus to take possession of it, defeating the serpent in order to do so. From that time on, Apollo lived in Delphi for nine months of the year, imposing on himself the other three months as a period of exile for having killed a rival. During his stay at Delphi, he spoke to humans through his oracle, the Pythia.

Passing from legend to history, the earliest evidence of a place of worship here dates back to the Mycenaean age, though the construction of a sanctuary to accommodate the oracle was not built until the eighth century BC. Authors from Greek and Roman literature such as Pliny, Plato, Aeschylus, Cicero, and Strabo all left behind abundant descriptions of the site and the prophecies that were announced there. Generals, colonizers and even simple citizens afflicted by problems of health and money, consulted the Pythia. The oracle's responses were also recorded in mythological stories, the most famous being that of Oedipus, who was told he would kill his father to marry his mother, and who tried, in vain and by all means possible, to evade his destiny.

The visible remains of the Temple of Apollo are those of a fourth-century-BC Doric building that was built over another, much older building. At the center of both was the *adyton* (prohibited area) where the Pythia sat holding an olive branch. According to tradition, the oracle – a woman who could be young or old, aristocratic or common, the only requirement being that she had to be a native of Delphi – fell into a sort of trance and received inspiration from sweet-smelling fumes emerging from a crack in the ground. After centuries of debate, the recent discovery of traces of inebriating gas coming from a geological stratum beneath the archaeological site has proved the veracity of the ancient Greek and Roman sources.

Although the site is still very beautiful, Delphi is but a shadow of what it was during its period of greatest splendor, or until the year AD 191 when it was conquered by the Romans. Until that time, it had been visited by people from around the Mediterranean basin who brought gifts to give thanks to Apollo and his oracle. High quality objects found during excavation can be seen in the museum next to the site, but little remains of the many buildings, votive temples, and 3,000 statues that lined the Sacred Way leading to the Temple of Apollo. The only building that archaeologists have been able to reconstruct is the Treasury of the Athenians, dating back to the end of the fifth century BC, which was built following the victory over the Persians at the battle of Marathon (490 BC). The ruins of the black and white marble Altar of Chios (fifth century BC) are clearly distinguishable in the Ionic Stoa of the Athenians (478 BC) as well as the two monumental fountains from the early

84 left The Sphinx of Naxos (at the Delphi Museum) honors the oracle and was donated by the islanders towards the middle of the sixth century BC. It has a woman's face and the body of a winged dog.

84-85 This view of the Marmaria, the "marble quarry," shows the tholos, the sanctuary of Athena Pronaia (fourth century BC), and the remains of a previous temple of Athena, presumably constructed towards the end of the sixth century BC.

85 top left Built in about 380 BC, the tholos was partly rebuilt in 1938. Its functions are unknown, but given its refined overall elegance it was indubitably an important building, possibly a sanctuary dedicated to Gea.

85 top right The Stoa of the Athenians was built in 479 BC to house the booty from the naval battle of Salamis, which marked a dramatic defeat for the Persians.

Roman period that adorned the fountain of Castalia, where pilgrims purified themselves before proceeding to the oracle. Also of great interest, as well as being better preserved than the religious buildings, are the theater (fourth century BC, but rebuilt by the Romans in the imperial age) and the stadium that was built in the fifth century BC to hold the Pythian Games (second in importance only to the Olympic Games) and remodeled in the second century AD by Herod Atticus. Once they had conquered Delphi, the Romans were more interested in its wealth and sporting fame than its religious value, though oracles were allowed to continue dispensing prophecies there for another two centuries. However, in AD 393, the Roman emperor Theodosius abolished the "vile rites and pagan games," marking the demise of the site forever.

86 top The Archaeological Museum of Delphi houses much of the rich statuary from the site, as well as valuable works from the treasuries and sanctuaries, and "secondary" objects like this gold button, which came from a ceremonial garment.

86-87 A splendid example of mature Archaic art, the bas-relief on the treasury of the Siphnians is decorated with representations of the gigantomachy, or the war the Olympian gods waged against the Giants. The treasuries housed the "tenths," tributes the Hellenic city-states paid to Apollo.

87 top left A griffin of Asiatic origin decorates this small votive plaque, held at the Delphi Museum. The local museum was inaugurated in 1903 but was expanded a number of times; a new hall was added in 1974 to house gold and ivory objects.

87 top right This natural-sized head made with the chryselephantine technique – using gold for the garments and ivory for the flesh – probably portrays the god Apollo.

The Acropolis in Athens
GREECE

ATTICA
REGISTRATION: 1987
CRITERIA: **C** (I) (II) (III) (IV) (VI)

88-89 The area was first settled during the Neolithic period, and in the Mycenaean era the Acropolis was a fortified citadel. During the sixth century BC the tyrant Pisisatrus started the work that would ultimately give the Acropolis its monumental layout. The view is dominated by the Parthenon, or temple of Athena Parthenos.

88 bottom Shown here is the western side of the Parthenon, which was built between 447 and 432 BC. The originals of the three

statues from the west tympanum, depicting the contest between Athena and Poseidon, are now at the Acropolis Museum.

89 bottom Three young hydriaphoroi (water-bearers) carry their hydriae on their left shoulders, in a detail from the north frieze of the Parthenon. As a whole,

this section depicts a sacrificial procession. Some of the blocks, which average 4 feet in length, are housed at the Acropolis Museum, while others are at the British Museum.

Sublime wisdom in times of war and peace was the characteristic of Athena, the goddess of the most splendid and powerful city in Greece. According to myth, she was victorious over her brother Poseidon in the struggle to possess Attica, which she then consigned to king Cecrops, having appeared to him in all her magnificence on the top of the hill on which the Acropolis was to be built. On that occasion, she offered him the gift of an olive tree, as opposed to the gift of a horse – an efficient instrument of war –, which had just been offered by Poseidon. The king's wisdom led him to accept the apparently modest symbol of hard, honest work and the oil trade that was related to it, but, above all, of the peace and justice that were necessary for the city to progress.

Although the construction in the seventh century BC of the temples dedicated to Athena, Zeus, Artemis, Heracles, and even the defeat of Poseidon was attributed to this legendary event, the site on which they were built – the steep rocky hill which was to become the religious heart of the Athenian *polis* that today dominates the chaotic capital of Greece– had in fact been inhabited since the Neolithic period, and the Mycenaeans had built a fortified citadel on the spot. The first to give the Acropolis a monumental appearance was the tyrant Peisistratus in the sixth century BC, the same leader who instituted the Panathenian Games, held in August every four years in honor of the goddess Athena. One hundred years later, after the interlude in which the Persians invaded Athens and placed their own idols on the Acropolis, the ruler Cimon commissioned the architect Kallicrates to design a magnificent temple dedicated to Athena Parthenos.

The year 449 BC marked the point at which the Acropolis was to be transformed into the most extraordinary and beautiful architectural complex in the Classical world. It would represent the meeting point between philosophic conceptions, ethical and religious values, political will, and the technical skills of the proud Athenian *polis*. There were two main personalities behind the development: Pericles, the city leader personifying Athenian democracy, and Phidias, his close friend, who may have been the greatest sculptor in history.

Construction of Kallicrates' temple dedicated to Athena Parthenos – universally known as the Parthenon – had suffered an interruption but was completed under the direction of the architect Ictinus. He turned the original plans into an extraordinary Doric octastyle peripteral temple in which every measurement, proportion, and form was simply the translation into stone of the arithmetical, geometric, and philosophical theories of Pythagoras and Plato. Even today, the numerous techniques incorporated to influence the observer's perspective and create optical illusions to harmonize and mitigate individual

elements of the monument are astounding.

In addition to the architectural expertise of the construction, the decoration of the Parthenon, completed by Phidias his skilled workshop – the greatest masters of the era – transformed the monument into what has been rightly described as an "experiment in perfection." Unfortunately the gigantic statue of Athena executed by Phidias in ivory and gold using the chryselephantine technique has been destroyed, and a good part of the friezes that adorned it can no longer be admired *in situ* as they are scattered among the museums of Europe, in particular the British Museum in London. However, when one is standing beside the Parthenon, the imagination easily relocates the sculptural masterpieces on the pediments of the temple. They were originally painted in bright colors and portrayed the birth of Athena from Zeus's head and the contest between the goddess and Poseidon for supremacy over the city.

Carved decorations on the 92 metopes (41 of which are still in place) depict allegories of the struggle between Good and Evil, such as the war between the Greeks and the Trojans (an epic image evoking the still-smoldering conflict with the hated Persians) and battles against Amazons, centaurs, and giants. The absolute masterpiece of Phidias was the Ionic frieze in the *naos* (the abode of the goddess Athena inside the temple) depicting the long and solemn procession of Athenian citizens during the Panathenian festivities. The astounding plasticity of the figures, the richness of the details down to the thinnest garment, and the care lavished on individual jewels, hairstyles, facial expressions, and gestures, which provide an immediate understanding of the psychology of the various figures in the procession, demonstrate Phidias' exceptional awareness of the human figure, both physically and philosophically.

With the Parthenon almost complete, in 437 BC Pericles inaugurated construction to provide the Acropolis with a worthy entrance, harmonizing proportions, elegance, and stateliness. The challenge was enormous but one that another great architect, Mnesicles, accepted enthusiastically. Construction was concluded in record time – just four years. The splendid *propylaea* were the result of this project, devised by Mnesicles with an

90 top The Porch of the Caryatids, on the south side of the Erechtheum, was built in the Ionic style in about 420 BC. Five of the six original graceful caryatids, which have been attributed to Alcamenes, are now at the Acropolis Museum; the sixth one is at the British Museum in London.

90 center The east façade of the Erechtheum is decorated with six elegant Ionic columns. According to tradition, it was built over the site of the contest between Athena and Poseidon, which decided who would be the patron of the city. Nearby is the olive tree said to be sacred to Athena.

90 bottom Built in the Ionic style by the architect Kallicrates towards the end of the fifth century BC, the little temple of Athena Nike is an amphiprostyle building, meaning that it has a rectangular layout, with two columned porticoes on the short sides.

93 bottom left The
Hephaisteion (temple of
Hephestus) is also known
as the Theseion as the body
of the hero Theseus was
supposely buried there.
Theseus's remains were
found in the fifth century

BC by the politician and
general Cimon on the
island of Skiros, where
he fought the Persians.
The temple is famous for
its excellent condition and
is unique in that it still
has its original roof.

"ascending" perspective that perfectly overcame the problem created by the "contrast" with the Parthenon. The elegant colonnaded structure with porticoed wings lines a steep flight of steps, emphasizing the sacredness of the Acropolis. A dozen or so years later, Kallicrates was once more called on to design a small, elegant, and original temple dedicated to Athena Nike to be constructed on a rocky spur beside the *propylaea*. It was decorated with allegories of Victory by an excellent but unfortunately anonymous pupil of Phidias' school.

The last building to be raised on the Acropolis, at the end of the century, was the Erechtheum. The temple stands to the north of the Parthenon near the sacred olive tree that was traditionally recognized as being the gift of Athena to the city, but

the city's atmospheric pollution.

Despite the decline of Athens, the Acropolis continued to be venerated for a long period, and not just for its religious significance. To the Romans, the Acropolis was a museum representing the essence of the philosophy, politics, and aesthetics of ancient Greece. In other words, it was a model for Rome to follow.

In later epochs, the Parthenon was transformed into a Byzantine church and later a mosque, but it and the other buildings on the Acropolis have survived the darkest eras almost unharmed. The first wound suffered by the Acropolis occurred in 1687; at the time, the Turks, who had turned the ancient temple of Athena Parthenos into a munitions store during the Venetian siege of the city, occupied

93 center right and bottom
right Perhaps representing
a triton, this colossal but
fragmentary statue (top)
was found near Agrippa's
Odeon. The building stood
opposite the Stoa of Attalus
(at the bottom of the
photograph) and was
restored to seem a
contemporary building.
Today it houses the Agora
Museum.

its designer is unknown. It was dedicated to earlier cults linked to the divine figures of Poseidon and Hephaestus. A distinctive element of the temple is the loggia in which the supporting columns were replaced by six slender female figures called the Caryatids; they were probably the work of Alcamenes, another of Phidias's pupils. Today, the loggia is supported by copies of the statues, and what remains of the originals has been stored in the site museum safe from the damage caused by

the hill. The Venetians fired an incendiary bomb, causing a tremendous explosion and destroying a section of the temple.

The most serious attack on the monument took place at the start of the nineteenth century and was apparently peaceful in intent. Perhaps for love of beauty or perhaps for envy, Lord Elgin, the British ambassador in Constantinople, removed Phidias' masterpieces from the pediments and shipped them back to England.

Olympia
GREECE

PREFECTURE OF ELIS, PELOPONNESE
REGISTRATION: 1989
CRITERIA: C (I) (II) (III) (IV) (VI)

The ancient Olympic Games were instituted in the year 776 BC by Pelops, the son of Tantalus, king of Peloponnese. From that date on, the games were held every four years on the first day of the full moon after the summer solstice and became the cornerstone of the calendar for the entire Greek world. Initially, the athletes competed only in running races, then, over time, the Olympics came to last five days as the number of sporting disciplines increased. Eventually, they included boxing, wrestling, the discus, the javelin, long jump, pentathlon, various equestrian events, and the *pankration*; this last sport was a mixture of boxing and wrestling and was the fighting technique used by Theseus to defeat the Minotaur.

The games held at Olympia for 1,500 years were not, however, simply sporting events: victory was the greatest achievement possible for an athlete, and the only one that could raise him to the level of the gods, if only for an instant. Moreover, it also brought glory to the city from where the athlete came, and, perhaps paradoxically, the Olympics were always a symbol of peace and union between the Greek *poleis*.

Even the choice of the site of the games was not a casual one. Situated on a hill shaded by pine and olive trees where the rivers Alpheus and Cladeus joined, Olympia was linked to Kronos, the father of Zeus. The hill, called *Altis*, had been inhabited since prehistory and, since the tenth century BC during the flowering of the Mycenaean civilization, had been dedicated officially to the cult of the king of the gods.

Though it never became a proper city, Olympia contains one of the most spectacular sets of monuments from Greek antiquity. The most important building, considered the model of the Doric temple, was dedicated to Zeus. Designed by the architect Libon of Elis in 470 BC, it was made of marble, with six columns on the short side and 13 on the long side, each 36 feet high and a minimum of seven feet five inches in diameter. The metopes were carved with bas-reliefs illustrating the twelve labors of Hercules. The *naos* contained one of the seven wonders of the ancient world: the statue of Zeus. This was executed by Phidias from wood and then covered with ivory and gold in the technique known as

94 The famous statue of Hermes with the infant Dionysus, sculpted by Praxiteles between 340 and 330 BC, was discovered near the temple of Hera (Olympia Museum).

94-95 Considered one of the most important sanctuaries of antiquity, Olympia owes its fame to the Olympics, the athletic games organized here every four years starting in 776 BC.

95 top left Laconian master builder (i.e. from the region of Sparta) built the Doric temple of Hera in the seventh century BC. It was originally also dedicated to Zeus.

95 top right At the stadium (which is 695.5 feet long and 93.5 feet wide), this stone platform was for the Hellanodikes, the judges of the competitions.

chryselephantine. It stood 39 feet tall and portrayed the god seated on a throne holding a scepter in his right hand and the effigy of Nike (winged Victory) in his left. Next to the temple lay the sacred olive tree whose branches were used to prepare the crowns worn by the victors of the games.

Other important religious buildings on the site included the Doric Temple of Hera (seventh century BC) and the Treasuries, which were small temples built by the various cities participating in the games. Of the sporting arenas, the most famous is the stadium, which could seat 45,000 spectators. Two stone platforms, facing south and north, overlooked the field; the first was where the *hellanodikes* – the judges of the games – sat, and the second held the altar tended by the priestess of Demeter, the only woman allowed to be present at the Olympic Games. Also of particular interest are the ruins of the *Prytaneion*, where the eternal flame burned, the *palaestra*, the gymnasium, and the *Philippeion*. The latter was a sanctuary

celebrating the Macedonian athletes, construction of which was begun by Philip II in 338 BC and completed by Alexander the Great.

The Olympics survived the Roman conquest of Greece, lasting until AD 393 when Emperor Theodosius, who considered them an example of depravation and paganism, abolished them. Olympia was later sacked by the barbarians and ultimately buried by two earthquakes. The memory of the games survived in sculptures, decorations on Attic vases, paintings, and odes dedicated to the athletes by generations of artists.

The German archaeological expedition to Peloponnese led by Ernst Curtius returned the magnificent ruins of Olympia to the light in 1875, whereas the French baron Pierre Fredi de Coubertin revived the games. On April 6, 1896, the Parisian aristocrat organized the new Olympics in Athens, which lasted ten days and were participated in by 13 countries and 245 athletes. That day is remembered as the birthday of modern sport.

Mycenae

GREECE

DISTRICT OF ARGOLIS, PELOPONNESE
REGISTRATION: 1999
CRITERIA: C (I) (II) (III) (IV) (VI)

"Exultant, I announce to Your Majesty that I have discovered the tombs that, according to tradition, belong to Agamemnon, Cassandra, Eurymedon, and their companions. In the tombs, I found immense treasures, which alone would make the finest of museums famous." This was the message sent by Heinrich Schliemann to king George I of Greece on December 6, 1876. The German archaeologist was in a state of extreme excitement: he had only begun to excavate the site of Mycenae three months earlier and had already achieved phenomenal results supporting his intuition. He had followed to the letter the indications given by Pausanias (the Greek geographer of the second century AD) who had identified Mycenae as the city of the Achaeans, the people that declared war on Troy, as narrated by Homer in *The Iliad*.

That day Schliemann had held in his hands a marvelous gold leaf mask, which he had found in one of the tombs. "I have seen the face of Agamemnon!" he exulted. Though he was considered by many a coarse autodidact and a shady figure embodying the worst characteristics of a tradesman, Schliemann had the undoubted merit of opening up a new world to archaeological studies and paving the way to an understanding of the most important civilization in Greek prehistory, one that flourished between the sixteenth and twelfth centuries BC.

The exact location of Mycenae had been known, in fact, for thirty or so years. Part of the cyclopean walls between 20 and 26 feet thick that run for nearly a mile and the stately, monumental Lion Gate (named after the two stylized animals carved in bas-relief on columns supporting the triangular architrave) had been found on a flat area between two mountains in Euboea in

Argolis. Yet, Schliemann was not interested in the walls or gate and did not even consider the ruins of the royal palace, places of worship, houses, or granaries of importance. He dug large trenches through them, ruining important archaeological data from the middle and late Mycenaean periods. However, he did discover Grave Circle A (with 19 graves) inside the city wall, and

98 *Set in a desolate and narrow spot between two peaks of the mountains of Euboea, in Argolis, the city of Mycenae founded one of Greece's most important prehistoric civilizations, which flourished between the sixteenth and twelfth centuries BC. Its walls, which were 20-26 feet thick, were over half a mile long.*

99 top *This death mask in repoussé gold is also known as "Schliemann's Agamemnon," due to the*

fact that the Greek archaeologist discovered it on December 6, 1876 in Tomb V of Grave Circle A in Mycenae. Dating from the second half of the sixteenth century BC, it is now at the National Archaeological Museum in Athens.

99 bottom *A noblewoman is portrayed in this fresco fragment from a Mycenaean palace. It is now at the National Museum in Athens.*

Grave Circle B (with 25 graves, of which 14 were royal tombs) just outside the Lion Gate. Grave Circle B included the grave Schliemann believed to be that of Agamemnon.

The two complexes date back to the fifteenth and sixteenth centuries BC respectively. Some are shaft graves dug out of the rock, and some tumulus graves. Inside, he found jewelry, masks,

100 top The tholos (a round or pseudo-ogival domed structure) of the tomb of Clytemnestra, one of the nine beehive tombs in Mycenae, dates from the end of the fourteenth century BC.

100 center left and bottom right The most beautiful royal Mycenaean tombs (top, the treasury of Atreus; bottom, the tomb of Clytemnestra) are preceded by a long dromos, or sacred way.

100 center right Mycenaean dwellings are not well preserved, perhaps due also to Schliemann's work. In searching for the necropolis, he dug wide trenches through them.

100 bottom left The great ramp, which also had sections of steps, led from the Lion Gate to the royal palace of the Atrids.

101 Framed by four colossal monoliths, the Lion Gate consists of a flat triangle with two stylized lions sculpted in bas-relief on opposite sides of a column. Somber and severe, the gate represents the height of Mycenaean architecture.

and vases made from gold and silver, decorated mostly with abstract motifs; there were also fragments of clothing and goods from far away places like Nubia, Anatolia, Syria, and Mesopotamia, demonstrating the high level of civilization and wealth achieved during the Mycenaean period.

Carried along on a wave of enthusiasm, and using the Homeric myths as his "guide," Schliemann undertook a new excavation in Argolis in 1884, helped by Wilhelm Dörpfeld, in which he unearthed the lost city of Tiryns, which, in The Iliad, was ruled by king Diomedes. Tiryns boasted extraordinary walls, nearly 800 yards long and up to 26 feet thick, that enclosed cells and corridors. Inside the walls, he found a vast royal palace and a city laid out in a manner linking it indissolubly to Mycenae from the earliest days of the Mycenaean civilization.

To the visitor, the ruins of Mycenae and Tiryns do not have the same charm as more refined and "recent" archaeological areas in Greece, but for archaeologists they are of fundamental importance to understanding the subsequent Hellenic civilization, offspring of the earlier Mycenaean one. And, even if they do so through gritted teeth, they are obliged to thank that "visionary" Schliemann.

102 left The tombs of Grave Circle A have yielded a variety of everyday objects, such as this long pin in silver and gold, found on the body of a woman buried in Tomb III.

102-103 Grave Circle A contained six royal tombs that were between about 3 and 13 feet deep, enclosed in a double circular wall. There were 19 bodies buried in them and the funerary treasures found there included nearly 31 pounds of gold.

102 bottom Far less elaborate than "Agamemnon's Mask," this specimen dates from the fifteenth century BC and is now preserved at the National Archaeological Museum in Athens.

103 bottom left A lion-hunting scene in gold and silver decorates the blade of this bronze dagger, discovered in Grave Circle A. The work dates back to the sixteenth century BC.

103 bottom right Found in Tomb IV of Funerary Circle A, Nestor's Cup, 5.7 inches high, features handles ending in two animal figures that look as if they are either biting the edge or drinking from the cup.

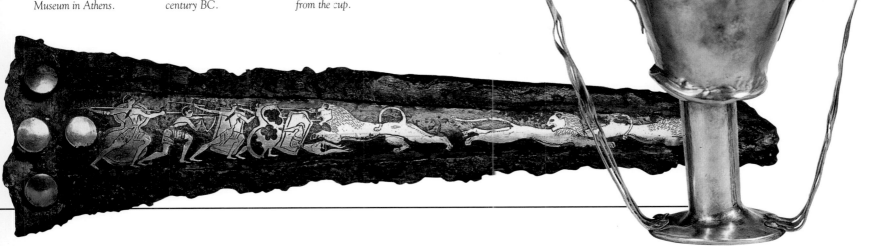

Epidaurus
GREECE

District of Argolis, Peloponnese
Registration: 1988
Criteria: C (i) (ii) (iii) (iv) (vi)

Asclepius, the Greek god of medicine better known by the Roman name Aesculapius, belongs to the ranks of the "non-Olympian" gods. It is still under debate whether he was originally a divinity of the underworld or a real man who was deified as a result of his ability to work wonders. According to Homer, Asclepius was simply the father of Machaon and Podalirios, two minor figures in the *Iliad* who fought alongside Agamemnon and were praised for their healing powers. According to Pindar, Asclepius was the son of Apollo and a mortal named Coronis. He was educated by the centaur Chiron and, as an adult, healed the Proetides of madness, the Phineides of blindness, and Heracles of wounds. However, Asclepius' became overly ambitious and attempted to resuscitate the dead, so Zeus killed him with a lightning bolt. Another legend sees Asclepius as beloved by the king of the gods, married to Epione, and the father not just of Machaon and Podalirios but also of four daughters: Hygieia, the personification of health, Panacea, who could cure all ills, Iasos, who brought them on, and Aegle, who was believed to be the mother of the Three Graces. It is said that Asclepius was the founder of the line of Asclepiads, of which Hippocrates, the most famous doctor of antiquity, was a member.

Asclepius was portrayed as a mature man in vigorous health, with a thick beard and tranquil expression, holding a scepter and a book in his hands. He was associated with the serpent that caressed wounds with its coils and the cock, which was a symbol of daytime and rebirth. In antiquity, the most famous representation of Asclepius was the statue in the temple dedicated to him at Epidaurus and designed by Trasimedes.

Situated on a rise overlooking the bay of Metana in Argolis, Epidaurus was a florid city-state that became the principal center of healing in the Greek world during the fourth century BC. The sanctuary of Asclepius was built over a previous temple dedicated to Apollo in this verdant place full of fresh-water springs. On the site, there were also a theater, a gymnasium, an *adyton* (the clinic), a *tholos* (a round building ringed by columns with a crypt divided into concentric corridors, and probably where the sacred serpents were housed), a stadium, and various lodgings for pilgrims.

Little is known of the healing methods used at Epidaurus. It is supposed that no particular medical science was practiced so much as a series of empirical therapies that were magical or symbolic in nature (today called holistic), culminating in "incubation." This involved patients spending the night in the *adyton* during which they fell into a deep sleep, perhaps achieved with the help of potions, and Asclepius visited them in their dreams, after which they would wake miraculously cured. The cult of Asclepius lasted until the third century AD under the Romans, who called him Aesculapius, and the large number of visitors to Epidaurus stimulated many local service industries. Every four years the Asclepiad games were held in which poetry and singing competitions were followed by sports contests.

The only building on the site to have survived until today in good condition is the theater. Designed by Polyclitus the Younger in the fourth century BC, it was admired by the geographer Pausanias for its perfect symmetry and the harmony of its forms. Today it is considered the most beautiful building of its kind in the Greek

world. It has a round orchestra measuring 66 feet across, a proscenium decorated with 14 half-columns resting on pillars, two side corridors (*paradoi*) for the actors, and a cavea with 34 tiers of seats. In the middle of the second century BC, a further 21 tiers were added, separated from the first 34 by a passageway (*diazoma*), allowing for a total of 12,300 spectators to be seated. The perfect acoustics and "magical" atmosphere of the site mean that it is still a superb venue for musical and theatrical performances.

104-105 The archaeological complex of Epidaurus was devoted to the cult of Asclepius, the god of medicine, better known by the Roman name of Aesculapius. A thriving city-state of Argolis, starting in the fourth century BC Epidaurus became the chief location of curative treatment in the Greek world.

105 top The cavea of the theater is composed of two sections. The lower one has 12 cunei with 34 rows, while the upper one has 22 cunei with 21 rows. At its widest point, the construction, which could seat 12,300 spectators, had a radius of 190 feet.

105 center This portion of a statue of Nike is from the sanctuary of Asclepius in Epidaurus: Nike holds a rooster, the symbol of the new day, in her right hand. The statue is now at the National Archaeological Museum in Athens.

105 bottom left These marble seats on the south side of the temple of Asclepius are arranged in a semi-circle of an exedra and were once part of a votive offering to the god.

105 bottom right Built in two phases between the fourth and second century BC, the theater of Epidaurus has been well preserved due to the fact that it was covered with dirt for centuries (until 1881).

Delos

GREECE

CYCLADES ARCHIPELAGO
REGISTRATION: 1990
CRITERIA: C (II) (III) (IV) (VI)

106-107 In this partial view of the site, the intricate residential districts come after the theater (bottom right), and in the upper section of the photograph, we see the orderly and spacious sanctuary area.

107 top left The circular monument dedicated to Hermes, the god of trade, is located in the main and best-preserved agora of Delos, frequently visited by Roman merchants.

107 top right The crepidoma (in this case, from a temple dedicated to Apollo, in the sacred area of Delos) was the base of a Greek temple, and acted as a transitional element between the soil and building.

107 bottom Originally sculpted in bronze by Polycleitus around 450 BC and found at Delos, the Diadoumenos (the one shown here is a Roman copy) depicted an athlete victorious in the Olympic Games.

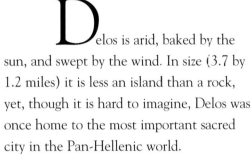

Delos is arid, baked by the sun, and swept by the wind. In size (3.7 by 1.2 miles) it is less an island than a rock, yet, though it is hard to imagine, Delos was once home to the most important sacred city in the Pan-Hellenic world.

The more pragmatic believe that its fortune was due to the fact that it offered the safest harbor in the Aegean Sea, situated at the center of the Cyclades Archipelago (the name Cyclades comes from the Greek word *kiklós*, meaning circular). Others sustain it was due to the legend in which Leto, the lover of Zeus, was given hospitality there and gave birth to the twins Apollo and Artemis, far from the jealous wrath of Hera, Zeus's sole legitimate wife. Whichever is the right theory, since the third millennium BC Delos had been a city-sanctuary dedicated to Apollo, a cultural center, a trading center, a theater of war and peace treaties, a site for sports competitions, and a holiday resort for important individuals. Some documents attest that even Cleopatra had a house on the island.

At the start of the fifth century BC, Delos was under the influence of Athens and became the political seat of the Delian-Attic League formed by Athens and other *poleis* against the Persians. It also had the honor of safeguarding the riches of the League's allies. Under the protection of Apollo, the city was able to extend its influence across the Aegean to the extent that, to ensure the perpetuation of his divine benevolence, in 426 BC an edict was issued prohibiteing anyone from being born or dying on the island. A century later, the city became independent and remained as

108 top left *The marble lions dedicated to Apollo by the residents of Naxos at the end of the seventh century BC are aligned to face east, towards the sacred lake. There were originally 16 of them, but only five complete ones have survived alongside the remains of three others. Another, however headless, lion decorates the Arsenal in Venice.*

108 top right *Divided by arches into nine collection chambers, the enormous cistern next to the theater was used to collect rainwater. During heavy storms, the water would run from the terraces to the orchestra pit.*

such until 166 BC when an agreement was signed with the Romans.

The Roman conquest of Greece occurred at the time of Delos' greatest splendor but it also marked its subsequent decline. The Romans declared the city a free port, turning it into a bustling commercial center where no duties were paid (the market in front of the port saw the buying and selling of 10,000 slaves a day), however its success drew the most desperate of peoples to the island. At that time, Delos had a population of 30,000 inhabitants, which was completely out of proportion to the tiny size of the island by the demographic standards of antiquity. When the island was at its peak, King Mithridates of Pontus declared war on the Romans and, in 88 BC, landed on Delos and pillaged it irremediably. Although most of the refined sculptural works of art in the temples of Apollo, Artemis, Hera, and the Stoivaderión, dedicated to Dionysus, can now be seen in museums throughout Greece, the past wealth of the city is still apparent in the layout of city and the number of its buildings. Surprising constructions are the theater, which could seat 5,500 spectators, and patrician houses like that of Dionysus, which takes its name from the mosaic portraying the god riding a panther. The cosmopolitanism of the city is reflected in its commercial guilds such as the association of Syrian merchants, which built several temples dedicated to Poseidon, Heracles, and Roma, or by the temple built in honor of the Egyptian gods Isis and Anubis, and a later, but very curious, addition of a synagogue.

The most famous sight on Delos is the Lions' Terrace, built to protect what was once the Sacred Lake of Apollo. Originally, there were believed to be 16 but only five are still intact, whereas three are in fragments. The rest have been lost except for one, which is found in Venice. Altered by an anonymous sculptor to resemble the lion of St. Mark, it now watches over the entrance to the Arsenale.

108-109 Built on three levels to follow the slope, the House of Hermes, part of which can be see in the middle of the photograph, was one of the most sumptuous buildings in Delos. Because of its size, it is thought to have been a public building erected by a group of foreign traders, rather than an aristocratic home.

109 top The theater of Delos was built in the third century BC in place of a previous wooden structure. The new one, which could seat 5,500 spectators, was divided into two orders of seats. The lower part had 26 rows and the upper order, or epitheatron, had seventeen.

109 bottom The headless statues known as "Cleopatra" and "Dioscurides" stand in the courtyard of a splendid residence located near the port and named after these two figures. There is nothing to prove that the queen of Egypt owned a residence at Delos. In any event, she clearly had nothing in common with Dioscurides, as the Greek physician lived a century after Cleopatra.

110 top left In the House of Hermes, the columns of the atrium on the first floor, like those of the peristyle on the second floor, have been restored.

110 top right Part of the central peristyle has been preserved in the building that was the headquarters of the league of Syrian merchants, bankers, and traders. Built towards the middle of the second century BC, it included various halls for civic use and three temples dedicated respectively to Poseidon, Hercules, and Rome.

110 bottom left There is a squared-based column decorated with friezes at each end of the Stoivadeion, the rectangular platform northwest of the sanctuary of Apollo. The one shown here sustains the remains of an enormous phallus, the symbol of Dionysus. The structure, which was used for theatrical performances, dates back to 300 BC and was built by Karystios, a wealthy resident of Delos.

110 bottom right This floor mosaic with marine subjects decorated a house in the Theater Quarter. The side panel shows an anchor with a dolphin around it. Dolphins were a common subject in Delian mosaics.

110-111 East of the theater there is a vast complex with four dwellings, the most important of which is the House of the Masks, shown in the center of the photograph. The most elegant houses of Delos followed the style of Hellenistic residences and were laid out around a central patio, often surrounded by columned porticoes.

111 bottom left Two surviving columns indicate the site of the temple of Hera, built towards the sixth century BC. It is uncertain who was responsible for its construction: perhaps Polycrates, the tyrant of Samos.

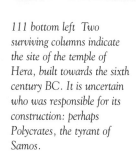

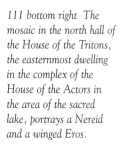

111 bottom right The mosaic in the north hall of the House of the Tritons, the easternmost dwelling in the complex of the House of the Actors in the area of the sacred lake, portrays a Nereid and a winged Eros.

Samos

GREECE

District of the Southern Sporades
Archipelago
Registration: 1982
Criteria: C (II) (III) (IV)

The son of a gem cutter, Pythagoras was born on the island of Samos around 580 BC. From a very early age he showed he had a curious and brilliant mind, so his father did everything in his power to send him when an adolescent to the best schools in the Hellenic world. Pythagoras returned to his native island after twenty years of study and travel, but, despite his fame having reached every corner of Greece, his relations with his compatriots were anything but idyllic. Indeed, Polycrates, the tyrant of Samos, did everything possible to impede Pythagoras. The great philosopher and mathematician felt obliged to abandon Samos and so moved to the distant city of Croton. No trace of Pythagoras remains on the island, and it was only in 1955 that the inhabitants decided to right the wrong he suffered and change the name of the hamlet of Tigani to Pythagoreion (today a lively tourist resort), which stands over the earliest settlement on the island and was known in ancient times as being the best landing place from which to reach the sanctuary of Hera. Despite having been described by Homer as the rather colorless wife of Zeus, Hera had become a figure of major importance in the realm of the Greek pantheon as early as the sixth millennium BC, much earlier than the advent of the Hellenic civilization. Hera had been worshiped as the "mother goddess" and was associated with the cult of fertility. According to legend, she was born in the shade of a willow tree on the plain bathed by the Imvrassos River in the place where, between 538 and 522 BC, the Heraion was erected. The Heraion was an Ionic temple described by Herodotus as being the largest in Greece, measuring 356 feet four inches by 180 feet eleven inches. A portico with 155 columns supporting a wooden roof surrounded the naos and pronaos, which followed the layout of an earlier place of worship. Today only one column remains, which stands majestically on the plain and can be seen from such a great distance that the people of Samos have named the place Kolona.

The Heraion and the Great Altar, which had already been used for sacrifices as early as the Bronze Age and which stands in front of the entrance to the Heraion (only the foundations remain but

fragments of the building show it was decorated with geometric patterns alternating with sphinxes), are connected to the port of Pythagoreion by the Sacred Way. Perfectly straight and nearly four miles long, this road was lined by a series of monumental statues. The bust of a kouroi (a representation of a young man) was found here that must have stood at least 16 feet tall.

Although the Heraion never rose to the status of a Pan-Hellenic sanctuary, for a long time it was an important place of pilgrimage. Its fortunes declined, however, soon after the death of Polycrates when Samos was devastated by the wars against the Persians. The island regained its importance as a maritime port much later with the Roman conquest. In 31 and again in 20 BC, Emperor Octavian Augustus spent the winter there, having the Sacred Way paved and renovating the religious complex in the process. Upon the death of his wife, Livia, he had a temple dedicated

to her there, and her cult continued to be associated with that of Hera until AD 262 when an earthquake completely destroyed the buildings and the site was abandoned.

In addition to the Heraion, the island is famous for the Samos Tunnel, which was designed by the architect Euphalinus of Megara. It was an aqueduct that carried water 1,133 yards through solid rock to supply the settlement that grew up around the port. Construction of the tunnel, which was dug by thousands of prisoners from the island of Lesbos, began in 550 BC and lasted for more than ten years. Today it is considered to be one of the greatest achievements of engineering in ancient Greece.

112-113 Herodotus described the Heraion of Samos as the largest in Greece. Today, of the portico's 155 original columns only one remains, hence the local name for this site: Kolona.

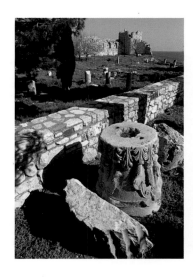

112 bottom left The perimeter defined by the bases of the columns of the Heraion, which pertain to four different styles, measure 356.4 by 181.97 feet.

112 bottom right The remains of a large caldarium have been preserved in the Roman baths west of the Heraion. According to several Roman historians, these facilities were used by Antony and Cleopatra.

113 top This marvelous view shows the archaeological area of Samos near the sea. Visible in the foreground are a Byzantine capital and the large fragment of the fluted drum of a column, reutilized in the construction of a basilica.

113 bottom The three statues from the votive offering of Gheneleos (copies of the originals are in the Vathy Museum) are portraits of the family of the priestess Phileia, a devotee of Hera.

The Megalithic Temples of Malta

MALTA

VARIOUS LOCALITIES ON THE ISLANDS
OF MALTA AND GOZO
REGISTRATION: 1980, 1992
CRITERIA: (IV)

It was in 1913 that the Maltese archaeologist Themistocles Zanmit heard the curious complaints of a farmer regarding the presence of huge rocks in his field near Paola. When he went to see, he found he was looking at the megalithic temple of Tarxien. Ten years earlier, another fortuitous circumstance had revealed the entrance to another extraordinary hypogean temple, that of Hal Saflieni. On that occasion, workers excavating a well had had to interrupt their digging when they came across a layer of rock that hid, they later discovered, three underground chambers. Excavated in the rock as much as 6,000 years ago, the chambers contained a chamber that had probably been used as the ceremonial room, and a series of catacombs found to contain almost 7,000 graves, amulets, statuettes, vases, and other objects.

At the start of the twentieth century, Malta and Gozo figured prominently in the interest of many experts, in particular British scholars, who set about performing a series of digs, attracted by the puzzle of the many megalithic monuments scattered across the two islands. Some of these were even older than Stonehenge, having been built between 4,000 and 2,500 years ago by a people that had probably reached the islands from Sicily, though their civilization later disappeared completely, perhaps at the hands of conquerors or an epidemic. Even today, only hypotheses can be made about the culture and fate of the people responsible for the temples. They were a peaceful people (no defensive works or weapons have been found at any of the sites, not even rudimentary ones) whose livelihood was based on agriculture; they owned domestic animals and developed remarkable skills in their production of handcrafts. As for their "spiritual life," the discovery of a great many statuettes, both large and small, of the Mother Goddess, a figure common to all the Mediterranean area, indicates that they practiced cults linked to fertility.

It is not yet possible to determine whether the priests of the cult were men or women, or whether the priests were the heads of the community or simply performed a ceremonial role. The main temples on Malta – Tarxien and Hal Saflieni, Hagar Qin and Mnajdra, Skorba and Ta' Hagrat, Tal Qadi and Bugibba – as well as the Ggantija

GGANTIJA

LA VALLETTA
HAL SAFLIENI
TARXIEN

MNAJDRA
HAGAR QIN

114 top left One of the entrances of Tarxien in the village of Paola. This enormous complex was discovered by chance in 1913 by the Maltese archaeologist Themistocles Zanmit.

114 bottom left This looks like the lower section of a colossal effigy of the Mother Goddess at Tarxien. The many images linked to the cult and the remains of animal sacrifices

demonstrate that the megalithic temples on Malta and Gozo were temples.

114 top right Known as the "Sleeping Woman of Malta," this terracotta statuette was found in the hypogean temple of Hal Saflieni. It is one of the most refined images of the Mother Goddess, who was associated with the cult of fertility throughout the Mediterranean.

114-115 Of the megalithic monuments on the island, Tarxien represents the highest point of artistic expression by the early Maltese people. The decorations on the stones are inspired by nature: dominant motifs are spirals and fish.

115 top left Only an aerial view allows the observer a complete understanding of the megalithic complex of Tarxien. Covering 5,000 square yards in all, most of

its structures date back to 3000-2500 BC, but its earliest nucleus was built around 3600 BC.

115 top right One of the rooms inside Hal Salfieni. Excavated from the rock starting about 6,000 years ago, the rock tomb is formed by a large and probably ceremonial chamber and catacombs in which the remains of roughly 7,000 people have been found.

complex on Gozo were built in pairs, a short distance from one another, suggesting to scholars that they may have been used respectively by male and female priests. Each of the megalithic complexes was built with a half-dome roof and it is thought that animal skins furnished the rest of the covering.

Despite their enormous size (Tarxien covers 5,000 square yards), the temples –built on a cloverleaf plan– have a central chamber just 16 feet across and ten feet tall. This means that no more

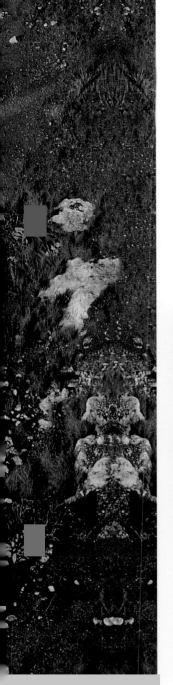

116 top Hagar Qin, situated on a plateau in the south part of Malta. There is no evidence that the temples had a stone roof, and it is supposed that they were covered by a canopy made of animal skins.

116-117 A view of Mnajdra, Malta's oldest temple, built around 4000 BC. Note the cloverleaf plan that was characteristic of all the megalithic complexes on the island.

116 bottom left Dug out of a massive monolith, this entrance to one of the temples at Hagar Qin is called the "Gate of the oracle." The complex was built in several stages between 3600 and 2700 BC.

116 bottom right Although the megalithic complexes of Malta are very large, the chambers dedicated to worship did not allow many people inside at the same time, to be suggesting that the rites were not open to the people.

117 top One of the passages that leads to the ceremonial chambers at Hagar Qin. Little or nothing is known of the Maltese Neolithic people, nor of their demise, which may have been due to war or epidemic.

than a dozen people could enter at one time, which suggests that the people did not indulge in rituals. Traces on the walls, however, indicate that the chamber was entirely lined with ocher-colored stucco featuring spiral decorations and pictures of animals painted with great artistic skill.

In some temples, the central chamber contains a niche (called the "niche of the oracle") in the wall opposite the entrance that the sunlight enters on the days of the equinox. Many of the megaliths stand in positions aligned with the sun, suggesting to some that history's first calendar may reside on Malta. This could even make Malta the next place to become fashionable among New-Age enthusiasts.

117 center In the archaic Maltese language, Hagar Qin means "standing stones" and takes its name from these menhirs on the edge of the complex. Each one weighs about 70 tons.

117 bottom The temple of Ggantija on the island of Gozo. According to an ancient legend, this mysterious place was the abode of a giantess with superhuman strength named Qala.

Paphos
CYPRUS

NICOSIA

PAPHOS

118-119, 118 bottom, and 119 top left The necropolis at Nea Paphos was used between the third century BC and third century AD, and later provided refuge to Christians during an era of persecution. Still later, the Ottomans used it as a quarry for building materials.

119 top right Though there is no evidence that rulers were buried here, the tombs in the necropolis of Nea Paphos are called "royal" due to their magnificence. The burial chambers were dug out of the rock around a colonnaded atrium; some of which are Doric in style.

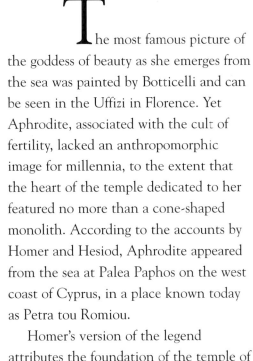

The most famous picture of the goddess of beauty as she emerges from the sea was painted by Botticelli and can be seen in the Uffizi in Florence. Yet Aphrodite, associated with the cult of fertility, lacked an anthropomorphic image for millennia, to the extent that the heart of the temple dedicated to her featured no more than a cone-shaped monolith. According to the accounts by Homer and Hesiod, Aphrodite appeared from the sea at Palea Paphos on the west coast of Cyprus, in a place known today as Petra tou Romiou.

Homer's version of the legend attributes the foundation of the temple of Aphrodite (and the city of Palea Paphos) to Agamemnon. Another version, of Cypriot origin, claims that credit goes to king Kynras, the father of Adonis, who became the temple's first priest. In reality, what was to become one of Classical Greece's most important sanctuaries was built in the twelfth century BC, on a site that had been inhabited since the Bronze Age. The few remains of the building are the result of many renovations that culminated in the Roman era, though the archaic architectural concept was respected throughout.

In the year AD 69, the emperor Trajan stopped in Palea Paphos on his way to Palestine and stole the temple's treasure. At that time, only ruins surrounded the temple, since Palea Paphos had been sacked and burned by the Persians in 499 BC. A century later, king Nikokles founded the city of Nea Paphos a short distance away from the old city.

Although the more ancient city is a mass of rubble – the ruins of the temple, the foundations of a royal palace, and fragments of the wall that ringed it – Nea Paphos boasts magnificent remains.

Shortly after the new city's foundation, Ptolemy, the Egyptian king of Greek-Macedon origin, took Cyprus. Under the Ptolemaic dynasty, the city grew rapidly to become the island's capital in the second century BC, thanks to the port connecting it to Alexandria, and to the copper resources in the nearby mountains of Troodos. During this period, construction of a splendid necropolis was begun. The tombs dug out of the rock are today given

119 bottom The Doric peristyle in one of the "royal" tombs. The most monumental are decorated with frescoes and lie at the north end of the necropolis. They provided family burial chambers for several generations of the city's nobility.

the epithet "royal," though there is no evidence that this is the case. They consist of several frescoed rooms laid out around an atrium with Doric columns.

Nea Paphos retained its capital status even after the Roman conquest of the island in 58 BC. It was given public buildings, like the Odeon and the Forum, embellished with fine statues. Its greatest

center, and a panel of a Dionysian procession at the entrance. The other rooms contain mythological decorations, featuring scenes such as the Rape of Ganymede and Apollo and Daphne.

Though fragmentary, the mosaics in other houses are even more sophisticated. Two deserving special mention are the House of Orpheus and the House of

period coincided with the Severan Age, from the second half of the second century to the beginning of the third century AD. During this period, most of the patrician residences were built, in which the superb decorations demonstrate that the city was one of the main centers of mosaic art in the Roman world.

The most famous is the House of Dionysus, in which mosaics cover more than a quarter of its 2,400 square yards of floor space. The largest room (38 by 28 feet) has a floor mosaic showing the grape harvest and hunting scenes at the

Aion, which are interesting for the clear syncretism between pagan and Christian iconography. This is not surprising, given that they date to the fourth century AD, the age in which Cyprus became definitively Christian. However, as early as AD 45 the island was the first colony in the Roman Empire to have had a Christian governor, as Lucius Sergius Paulus had recently been converted to the new religion by the apostle Paul. After the fourth century, even Aphrodite became Christian and the cult of the goddess was assimilated to that of the *Virgo lactans*, that is to say the Virgin suckling the Child.

120-121 The largest mosaic panel in the portico of the House of Dionysius is of Icarus and Dionysius. On the left, the Athenian king holds the reins of a chariot loaded with goatskins of wine; on the right we see the god drinking with the nymph Akme. The mosaic tells the story of the start of viticulture.

121 top The ruins of a patrician house in Nea Paphos. The archaeological area has interesting remains of Hellenistic, Ptolemaic, Roman, and Byzantine architecture.

121 bottom left The most recent and monumental section of the sanctuary of Aphrodite in Palea Paphos dates to the Roman era.

121 bottom right Built at the start of the second century AD by the Romans and recently restored to its ancient splendor, the odeon in Nova Paphos could seat 3,000 people in 25 rows.

OIΠΡΩΤΟΙ
ΟΙΝΟΝΠΙΟΝΤΕϹ

List of the Sites

Africa

Contemplating the many radically different African worlds as one glances down the archaeological sites in the World Heritage List, one is prompted to ask – Which Africa?

First and foremost, Africa is the land in which the evolution of man separated from that of the first anthropomorphic primates. Judging by the most recent paleo-anthropological discoveries in the Chad desert, that step forward might have occurred between seven and five million years ago, but the scarcity and fragility of the evidence overall hinder scientific study and speculation.

Everyone has heard of Lucy (*Australopithecus afarensis*), who lived three and a half million years ago and was discovered by Donald Johanson and his colleagues in 1974 in the Awash Valley in Ethiopia. During the last few decades, an extraordinary collection of finds made in East Africa (in particular the Rift Valley) and southern Africa have made it possible to at least partially reconstruct man's evolution over the last three million years. Therefore, UNESCO decided to add two further sites of interest (in addition to the place where Lucy was found) to the World Heritage List: the Omo Valley in Ethiopia and the complex of Sterkfontein, Swartkrans, and Kromdraai in South Africa.

There is also the Africa that was the cradle of *Homo sapiens* and his first experiments with figurative art, as seen in the rock paintings of Tsodilo in Botswana, on the edges of the Kalahari, where proof of 20,000 years of human history has been discovered. A little closer to the present day, the art of the Tassili in Algeria and the Akakus in Libya reiterates that the Sahara was not always the expanse of sand that exists today.

It is undeniable, however, that African archaeology achieved its highest expression in the Nile Valley, where the majestic monuments of the Ancient Egyptian civilization line the banks of the river. Starting in the north at Memphis, the vast necropolises of Saqqarah and Dahshur, and the pyramids of the pharaohs of the Fourth Dynasty, they continue south through Thebes, the country's second capital, and end in Abu Simbel with the magnificent temples built by Ramses II.

Along the north coast of Africa, where the remains of Carthage, Cyrene, Leptis Magna, and Timgad – just to name a few – still stand, African archaeology merged with its European counterpart and with the history of the Mediterranean civilization, dominated by the splendor of the ruins of the Roman colonies.

More authentically African was the kingdom of Aksum, which flourished in Ethiopia from the first to thirteenth centuries AD and left behind highly sophisticated sculptural masterpieces. The kingdom was associated with the Queen of Sheba, and it was while following the traces of this legendary monarch than Carl Mauch happened upon the Great Zimbabwe, a fortified city that prospered between the eleventh and fourteenth centuries. The only monumental complex south of the Sahara, it is the most enigmatic legacy of the African civilizations.

Volubilis

MOROCCO

MOULAY IDRISS ZERHOUN
REGISTRATION: 1997
CRITERIA: **C** (II) (III) (IV) (VI)

Volubilis stands at an altitude of 1,312 feet on a three-sided plain bounded by two rushing torrents, the Oued Fertassa and the Oued Khomane. The Berbers call it Oualili, after the flower that vividly colors the fields around the city. It was this bucolic setting and the fertility of the land that must have led the Romans to assassinate its king, Ptolemy, and take the city for themselves in 40 BC.

Although Volubilis is famous for its Roman remains (though, to create some confusion, the Arabs gave it the name Ksar Pharoun, the "Palace of the Pharaoh," due to the magnificence of its monuments), it was actually founded by the Mauritanians in the third century BC, long before the start of the Roman conquest of northern Africa. Of the more than two centuries during which it was independent, little remains except a few fragments of temples of Punic cults and a mysterious tumulus. The Romans even altered the surrounding landscape, cutting down trees to make space for

what would become the westernmost section of Rome's immense granary.

In a short period, emperor Claudius extended Rome's dominion over a vast region that included what is today Morocco and part of Algeria. This was then divided into two sections, a western one with the capital Tingi (today Tangiers), and the other in the east governed by Caesara. Volubilis, which eventually boasted a population of 20,000 composed of Romans, Carthaginians, Syrians, Berbers, and Jews, was raised to the rank of

124

VOLUBILIS
RABAT

municipium and, until AD 285, grew exponentially.

Excavation operations, begun during the French protectorate of Morocco, are still underway. Currently, they have unearthed over half of the 100 acres that the city once covered. The greatest alterations of the city's layout date back to the first century AD, when the streets were paved, and baths and temples were built. In AD 168–169, the emperor Marcus Aurelius ordered the city to be given a defensive wall with eight gates. The most important public buildings, however, were constructed during the Severan dynasty (AD 193–235): the forum (covering 1,560 square yards), the *capitolium*, and the basilica dedicated to Jupiter, Juno, and Minerva. To thank emperor Caracalla for having conceded the inhabitants of Volubilis the rank of Roman citizens, in 217 the city built a triumphal arch in his honor.

The residential area of the city features a number of bread ovens, oil presses, and luxury houses. The houses on the *decumanus maximus* deserve special mention, in particular the House of the Ephebus, which has a mosaic of Bacchus on a chariot pulled by panthers, the House of the Columns, named after the columns in various styles in the portico, some of which are spiral, and the House of Venus, which was decorated with the most elegant mosaics in the city.

124 bottom A wide staircase leads to the capitolium, whose face features four columns. The important public building was built in 217, during Macrino's principality.

124-125 The basilica, built in the third century AD with two apses and a two-aisle nave, looks onto the forum of Volubilis, also added in the Severan age. Some of the spaces placed around the building may have been administrative offices.

125 top Two avant-corps columns rose at the sides of the only barrel vault in the remarkable arch of Caracalla to frame two niches for statues. At the base of these niches, water basins can be seen, perhaps related to fountains.

126 top *The House of the Columns owes its name to these elegant spiral columns, part of the elaborate decorative apparatus of its portico, also characterized by an unusual circular impluvium.*

Unlike most of the cities in the Roman province of Africa, Volubilis was not abandoned when the empire collapsed, and the population, which embraced Christianity *en masse* around 600, continued to speak Latin until the arrival of the Arabs in the eighth century. For a short time, the city was the capital of the first Muslim dynasty in Morocco, led by Idriss I. Upon his death, his son Idriss II moved the capital to Fès, and the fortunes of Volubilis waned until it was finally abandoned shortly after 1000.

126 center and 126-127 The splendid panel portraying the courting of the goddess of beauty is part of the mosaic decoration in the House of Venus. The building, covering 12,900 square feet, is the most luxurious patrician residence in Volubilis.

126 bottom The symbolic theme of the mosaic of "Dionysus and the Four Seasons" alludes to the inevitability of time. In fact, in this octagonal medallion, the god is portrayed well into adulthood, whereas in another detail he appears nude as a young man.

127 bottom An overall view of the extraordinary mosaic of "Dionysus and the Four Seasons." Archaeologists that have done excavations at Volubilis agree on the theory that, in the third century AD, mystery rites related to the Dionysian cult were widely practiced by members of the city's nobility.

Timgad
ALGERIA

DAIRE DE BATNA
REGISTRATION: 1982
CRITERIA: C (II) (III) (IV)

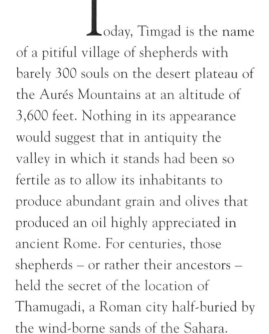

128 top *The forum, at the
intersection of the* cardus
and decumanus, *was built
on a platform. The square
covered an area of 164 by
141 feet and was entirely
surrounded by columned
porticoes.*

Today, Timgad is the name of a pitiful village of shepherds with barely 300 souls on the desert plateau of the Aurés Mountains at an altitude of 3,600 feet. Nothing in its appearance would suggest that in antiquity the valley in which it stands had been so fertile as to allow its inhabitants to produce abundant grain and olives that produced an oil highly appreciated in ancient Rome. For centuries, those shepherds – or rather their ancestors – held the secret of the location of Thamugadi, a Roman city half-buried by the wind-borne sands of the Sahara.

Not incorrectly, ancient Timgad is considered the "Algerian Pompeii." It was founded in AD 100 by emperor Trajan with the purpose of housing the veterans of the *Legio Tertia Augusta*. For a long time it was the largest Roman outpost in Numidia, a region conquered during Caesar's reign and inhabited by nomads who had little inclination to bend to the customs of their dominators. Built on the traditional layout of a Roman *castrum* and originally covering an area of 30 acres, in just a few decades it grew to cover 125 acres and become a defensive base populated by coarse soldiers in a city of 20,000 inhabitants, whose ambition was to lead the refined life typical of thriving cities elsewhere in the Roman province.

The traditional grid pattern based on the two main streets of the *decumanus* and *cardus* features a curious variant in Timgad, as the latter intersects with the former at the sixth block and does not continue on the other side. The heart of the city lay around this intersection;

there was an elegant forum built on a platform with a colonnaded passageway leading diagonally away from the intersection to the 4,000-seat theater. The houses of the patricians were built along the *cardus*, all of which were preceded by a portico. The *decumanus*, lined by columns, led southwards to Trajan's Arch, the most majestic of Timgad's ancient monuments. The arch had a façade with three barrel-vaulted passages, two false windows, and four Corinthian columns, but the attic that once existed on top of the arch has been destroyed. Grooves left by the wheels of chariots

can still be seen in the street paving stones by the gates of the arch.

The remains of the "market of Sertius" lie a short distance from the arch. Decorated with motifs reflecting the city's commercial and agricultural economy, it was a covered market with a central square lined by the stone counters of the shops. Like many of the columns supporting the market roof, many of the shops are still intact, and carvings of the products they sold can still be seen on them. Nearby, two of the five Corinthian columns in the façade of the temple dedicated to Jupiter, Juno,

128 center Connected to the forum by a diagonal column-lined street, almost all of the theater's stage has been lost. Fortunately, a good part of the cavea, which could hold 4,000 spectators, has been preserved.

128 bottom Founded in AD 100 by Trajan to accommodate the veterans of the Tertian Augustan Legion, Thamugadi was built according to the model of the Roman castrum, but soon grew to contain 20,000 inhabitants.

128-129 The most majestic Roman monument in Timgad, the Arch of Trajan (early third century AD) is adorned by two elegant blind windows on its façade and four Corinthian columns placed on tall pedestals.

129 bottom Two human figures and a ram, sculpted in relief, emphasize the importance of sheep-herding for the people of Numidia, a region of North Africa that corresponds to present-day Algeria.

and Minerva are still standing.

The excavation of Timgad begun by the French in 1881 is far from finished. Still undiscovered are those buildings that were essential to every Roman city: the amphitheater and the circus. However, the remains of 14 public baths have been cleared and found to contain, in addition to the *calidarium, tepidarium,* and *frigidarium,* a room where visitors were massaged with olive oil. Like some of the houses, these buildings were decorated with mosaics that can now be seen in the site museum, along with votive stelae dedicated to Saturn and decorative furnishings.

After the fall of the Roman Empire, Timgad was occupied by the Byzantines, who, in 534, built a fort there. From this period, there is a necropolis containing 9,000 sarcophagi. Once on the road of inexorable decline, Timgad became a refuge for Donatists, a Christian sect that found a large following among the Numidian population. In the sixth century, a fire, the cause of which is unknown, destroyed almost the entire city and, two hundred years later, when the Arabs arrived in Numidia, Timgad was forgotten by all but the local shepherds.

Carthage
TUNISIA

DISTRICT OF TUNIS
REGISTRATION: 1979
CRITERIA: C (II) (III) (VI)

130-131 Of the Antonine Baths, today only their base remains, where the storerooms and furnaces for heating water were located. The thermal salons were found on a raised floor supported by giant columns. One of the columns, visible on the right in the photo, has been reconstructed in recent years. It is almost 50 feet tall and crowned by a Corinthian capital.

In 218–217 BC, the young Carthaginian general, Hannibal, crossed the Alps at the head of an army of 38,000 soldiers, 8,000 cavalry, and 40 or so elephants. His plan was to attack the heart of his enemy, conquer Rome, and take over control of the Mediterranean. The first battles were fought on the Trebbia River, at Lake Trasimeno, and at Cannae and seemed to support Hannibal's strategy, but once arrived at the gates of Rome, he delayed because his army was tired, with the result that the enemy had time to reorganize, thus carrying the conflict back to Africa. In 204, after fifteen years of uninterrupted warfare, Scipio the African inflicted a very heavy defeat on the Carthaginians at Zama and the city of Carthage was obliged to surrender.

The history of Carthage is mostly famous for the episode when its troops challenged the hegemony of Rome in the three Punic Wars, but the city dates back to at least six hundred years earlier, officially from 814 BC. Legend has it that Carthage was founded by Dido, who escaped from Tyre after Pygmalion, her brother, killed her husband in order to take the throne. In reality, it was probably a group of exiles who, after unsuccessfully trying to take the Phoenician city, built a new settlement on the coast of what is today Tunisia.

Few ruins actually remain of Punic Carthage, destroyed first by the Romans and then definitively by the Arabs around AD 700. The most interesting are found on Birsa Hill where the acropolis stood, which was ringed by defensive walls at the time. A few graves have been found there but none of the public buildings and houses survived the conquests. Some ruins mark the sanctuary of Tophet, the place

used for sacrificial burials, where there was a temple dedicated to the Phoenician gods Baal and Tanit. To these gods, the children of the Carthaginian noblemen were immolated. Identified in 1921, a number of stelae have been unearthed that have helped in part to understand the customs of the era. A pool beside the sea a little to the north of the city is all that remains of the two large ports – mercantile and military – that had made Carthage great.

From the Roman era there is more to see, such as the vestiges of the large baths of Antoninus built between AD 146 and 162. Today, it is only possible to see the base, which was the location of the servants' rooms and the furnaces for heating the water sent to the baths on the

130 bottom Built on the seashore between AD 146 and 162, the Antonine Baths must have been one of the most impressive architectural complexes in Carthage. The frigidarium alone is estimated to have occupied an area of 154 by 72 feet.

131 top left The majority of the remains of ancient Carthage, like those seen in the image, are from the Roman era. The original Punic settlement was destroyed by the Arabs between the seventh and eighth century.

131 top right Seen here in the background of some Roman-era finds, the Museum of Carthage, in Arabesque style, holds collections belonging to three important periods: Phoenician-Punic, Afro-Roman, and Arab.

131 center The House of the Aviary (a name attributed to the building for a mosaic portraying numerous birds) features a splendid peristyle.

131 bottom Of particular interest in observing the structure of the houses, the park of Roman villas stretches as far as the sea. Excavations here have identified a large number of patrician dwellings, whose mosaics are held in the Bardo Museum.

132 top and 132 bottom left Nearly seven feet in diameter, the monolithic support columns of the Antonine Baths must have weighed over 70 tons. One of the capitals – recently discovered – is over three feet tall and weighs over four tons.

132 center left Hailed as one of the most majestic in the Roman world, the amphitheater in Carthage was famous as far as the extreme reaches of the empire for its battles between beasts and gladiators, well

before it became a site of martyrdom for thousands of Christians. Admired until the Middle Ages for the elegance of its arches, it was gradually stripped bare by stone scavengers. Today, only a few remnants remain, hidden among the green of the pine trees.

132 center right Hadrian's theater, a mighty structure that has preserved its elegance intact, still hosts an international music, song, and dance festival, held between July and August.

132 bottom right A mosaic portrays a horseman against the background of a luxurious palace with tropical vegetation found on the hill of Borj-Jedid. The slopes of this rise are still today yielding remains belonging to various periods, among which some Punic-era graves.

133 The terrace of the House of the Aviary is covered by a vast floor, originating in another residence, that features an alternation of square mosaic panels, portraying horses and their riders, with others in marble. Of the original 98 pieces, 62 have been preserved.

upper floor, in turn supported by columns almost seven feet in diameter, each of which weighed 70 tons. One of these columns has been reconstructed in recent years and reaches a height of 49 feet, whereas the vault of the *frigidarium* (which is being rebuilt) should be over 66 feet high. A short distance away is the basilica of Damus el-Karita, the name of which is probably a distortion of the Latin Domus Charitatis, where Saint Augustine preached between 399 and 413.

The amphitheater was used to hold shows featuring gladiator battles and fights between wild animals. It was famous throughout the Roman world and was celebrated as being one of the largest amphitheaters in the empire, but today it is only just visible among the pine trees as most of the stone blocks were taken away over the centuries and used to construct other buildings. Northeast of the amphitheater, there is a series of gigantic cisterns that provided the main water source for the city in the Roman period. Very little remains of the theater built by Hadrian or of the temples and houses of the ancient Mediterranean power.

Fortunately, memory of the city's greatness is preserved in the collections of the national museum, housed in the White Fathers Seminary next to the cathedral of Saint Louis built by the French in 1890. The museum has vases, sculptures, inscriptions and ceramics discovered during excavation; these are the last tangible remains of Carthage – whether Punic, Roman or Arab – and the vestiges of a lost empire.

Dougga
TUNISIA

GOVERNORATE OF BEJA
REGISTRATION: 1997
CRITERIA: C (II) (III)

134 top Built between AD 168 and 169 in a natural hollow on the hill of Dougga, the theater could hold up to 4,000 spectators. Next to it, there was also a small circus for horse races, which has been completely destroyed.

134 bottom Framed by the leafy branches of olive trees, the Arch of Alexander Severus, today renamed the Bab el-Roumia, was built between AD 222 and 235 to celebrate privileges conceded Dougga by the Romans.

Dougga has been called the Rome of Africa, yet the city that was awarded the title of *municipium* by Septimius Severus in AD 205, and the even more flattering one of honorary colony in AD 261, was not a true Roman city. Situated at an altitude of 1,800 feet above sea level, it covers an area of 60 acres and looks more like a Mediterranean village. The grid layout typical of an imperial city was discarded in favor of a tangle of alleyways lined with houses built to fit the twisting lie of the terrain.

The layout and architecture of the city are a reflection of its fate, which was

linked to the man who was the first to make it great. First documented by Diodorus Siculus in his series *Bibliotheca Historica* as the capital of a Libyan-Punic kingdom named Thukka in the fourth century BC, it leapt into history thanks to Massinissa (ca. 238–149 BC), the leader of the Massyli people and king of Numidia, who built one of his residences there. A courageous soldier and skilled diplomat, Massinissa grew up in Carthage and, after fighting for the Carthaginians in Spain against the Romans, switched sides. The famous battle of Zama in 202 BC won by the Romans with the help of his cavalry marked the end of the Carthaginians' expansionist ambitions. Although he was an admirer of Rome, Massinissa was more inspired by Carthage in his transformation of Numidia into a strong and compact kingdom. He conceded vast territories to tribal chiefs and introduced Punic techniques both in land administration and the cultivation of grain and oil. In a short period, Dougga, which eventually numbered 10,000 inhabitants, found itself at the center of Rome's flourishing breadbasket.

The wealth of the city is demonstrated by many residences, first and foremost the House of Dionysus and Ulysses, which was named after the mosaic showing the Ithacan exile surrounded by sirens. Today the mosaic can be seen in the Bardo Museum in Tunis. The House of the Trifolium seems to have been the city bordello, at least judging by the phallic statue at its entrance, which was recently removed by the Tunisian authorities so as not to offend the sensibilities of Muslim visitors.

134-135 Located 1,805 feet high on a hill dominating the fertile valley of Wadi Kralled, the archaeological area features an irregular layout, unusual for a Roman city.

135 top The affluence of the patrician class of Dougga is demonstrated by the presence of numerous baths. The Licinian Baths (in the photo), which were used in winter, are in very good condition.

135 bottom left The largest residence in Dougga, named after the House of the Trifolium because of the numerous clovers illustrated in the mosaics and on the marble staircases, was the city brothel. A phallus-shaped statue, recently removed by the Tunisian authorities, was found at the entrance.

135 bottom right A mosaic in the House of Venus extended towards the southwestern corner of the ruins of the capitolium, seen in the background. The full name of the colony, Lincinia Septima Aurelia Alexandriana Thuggensis, concluded in the proper original place name in the local language, coming from Thucca, or "rock."

TUNIS

DOUGGA

136 top The ship of Ulysses, with the hero tied to the main mast in order to resist the Sirens' bewitching song, is the theme of this detail from the magnificent mosaic in the House of Dionysus and Ulysses, today in the Bardo Museum in Tunis.

136-137 The paved streets and the ruins are dominated by the capitolium, seen in the background. At the time of its maximum splendor around AD 200, when it was at the center of Rome's flourishing granary, Dougga boasted up to 10,000 inhabitants.

*137 top The temple of
Juno Caelestis, the
Romanized version of the
Punic goddess Tanit, was
the most opulent in
Dougga: it enclosed a silver
effigy of the deity and
featured sculpted symbols of
all the Roman provinces.*

*137 bottom left Jupiter,
Juno, and Minerva were
the titular gods of the
elegant, somber
capitolium. Built between
AD 166-167, the*

*construction features a
portico with six fluted
Corinthian columns and
contained a statue of the
king of the gods.*

*137 bottom right Datable to
around the mid-second
century BC, the tomb of
Prince Ataban is one of the
very rare pre-Roman
monuments in Numidia. Its
pyramidal roof culminates at
69 feet tall and is decorated
with Ancient Egyptian and
archaic Greek motifs.*

However, what is most striking about the
city is the elegance of the public religious
and civil buildings.

At the center of the city lies the
Square of the Rose of the Winds, whose
name is derived from the carving of three
concentric circles on the paving stones in
which the names of the 12 winds are
engraved. Roads lead from this square to
the forum, market, baths, theater,
hippodrome, triumphal arch in honor of
Alexander Severus, and to 12 temples.
One of these is the Capitolium, which
was built in AD 166–167. Its cella is
enclosed by a Corinthian portico that
contained a statue of Jupiter over 21 feet
tall and two smaller statues of Juno and
Minerva. The most elegant temple,

however, was dedicated to Juno Caelestis,
a Romanized version of the Punic
goddess Tanit.

Dougga still holds one of the very rare
pre-Roman Numidian monuments: the
Libyan-Punic mausoleum of a prince
named Ataban. Dated to around the mid-
second century BC, it stands 69 feet
high, culminates in a pyramidal roof, and
is decorated with bas-reliefs of archaic
Greek and Egyptian motifs. The bilingual
epitaph of the tomb in Libyan and Punic
is no longer there: it was removed in
1842 by Sir Thomas Reade, the British
consul to Tunisia, who took it to London
so that the ancient Libyan script could be
deciphered. The object of that "theft" is
today exhibited in the British Museum.

The Amphitheater at El Djem

TUNISIA

EL MAHDIA
REGISTRATION: 1979
CRITERIA: C (IV) (VI)

The austere but majestic Roman amphitheater that stands on the semi-arid plain of inland Tunisia today could be considered to be either a cathedral in the desert or a monument to ambition and vanity. It is crowned by a huddle of houses that together compose El Djem, but the past of this Berber village with 7,000 in habitants was a glorious one, to which the remains of many noble Roman houses attest, each decorated with elegant mosaics, built when the name of the place was Tysdrus.

Founded on an existing Punic settlement at the time of Julius Caesar at a junction of roads that fanned out towards the main ports in the province of Africa, after AD 117 the city became a trading center for olive oil. Its inhabitants were

businessmen and estate owners of Roman and African origin who accumulated enormous wealth. They were so rich that in AD 238, when Rome was attempting to cope with a financial crisis, Emperor Maximinus of Thrace decided to levy heavy taxes on the province. This move struck Tysdrus a heavy blow and the city rebelled. The city's

proconsul, the eighty-year-old Gordianus, took the title of emperor in opposition to Maximinus, but his reign was a short one: the revolt was put down bloodily, and Gordianus committed suicide to avoid being taken to Rome in chains.

The ephemeral African empire would have been lost in the mists of history if Gordianus had not begun, soon after his proclamation as emperor, to build an amphitheater rivaling the Colosseum in magnificence and size. The elliptical building has a perimeter of 467 yards, is built on three levels of round arches, and could seat 35,000 spectators: a number much greater than the entire population of Tysdrus ever was. Its underground level was divided into sections reserved for gladiators, storerooms for stage equipment, and cages for animals, all of which could be raised into the arena at the start of the performance by an elaborate system of hoists. The extravagance of the amphitheater in terms of cost and labor was increased by the fact that the stone used for its construction was quarried 19 miles from the city.

The wish to erect a monument of this type in a situation of serious political instability could be considered rash, if not absurd, yet the explanation lies in the unconfined love of fights between gladiators and wild beasts that united subjects of the Roman Empire.

The organization of increasingly cruel games allowed governors to establish a paternalistic relationship with their people in order to maintain their loyalty.

The victim of events beyond his power, Gordianus was never able to watch, from the imperial platform, more than ten thousand spectacles, and the amphitheater itself was never completed. After the revolt was quelled, the fortunes of Tysdrus quickly took a dive, and Gordianus' largest monument would probably have been dismantled and its stones

138 top Second in size only to the Colosseum in Rome, the amphitheater has an elliptical shape and measures 1,401 feet around its perimeter. It rises in three levels composed of round arches, and its terraced benches could accommodate up to 35,000 spectators.

138 bottom The eighty-year-old proconsul Gordianus, who named himself emperor in AD 238 in rebellion against new taxes levied by Rome, commissioned the amphitheater. However, the luck of his little empire soon ran out, to the extent that the coliseum's construction was never completed.

138-139 The massive amphitheater overwhelms the modest buildings of the modern-day village of El Djem, which has barely 7,000 inhabitants, many fewer than the Roman monument could have held. Nevertheless the population would not have been sufficient to fill it to maximum capacity even back when the city was ancient Tysdrus.

139 top The Romans nurtured a great if not unhealthy love for the struggles between gladiators and beasts, the purpose for which the amphitheater was built. The atmosphere there has completely changed since 1985, when the building became the stage for an internationally acclaimed symphonic-music festival held in August.

TUNISI

EL JEM

used as building materials by later arrivals in the area over the following centuries had a legend not grown up around it. In the seventh century, the theater was the setting for the strenuous resistance put up by Kahina, a Berber heroine, who succeeded in fighting off the Arab invasion by barricading herself in the arena.

Sabratha

LIBYA

DISTRICT OF ZAWIA
REGISTRATION: 1982
CRITERIA: C (III)

Although Italo Balbo, governor of Italian Libya during the 1920s, did not pass into history for his talent as a military planner or administrator, anyone who loves ancient times will be grateful to him for having restored the theater in Sabratha to its past splendor. Enchanted by the beauty of the ruins, Balbo drew abundantly on the coffers of the Italian state to sponsor a colossal operation of excavation and restoration.

The archaeologists Giacomo Giusti and Giacomo Caputo were commissioned to authentically rebuild the largest theater in Africa, which was constructed in AD 190 for the emperor Commodus. With a stage almost 50 yards long, the auditorium could seat 5,000 spectators and measured just over 100 yards across. Lining the back of the stage was an amazing *frons scenae* composed of three semi-circular niches and a triple order of 108 Corinthian columns made from differently colored marbles with elaborate decorations on the capitals. Also magnificent were the high reliefs in the niches carved with dance scenes, mythological figures, and allegorical celebrations of the relations between Rome and Sabratha.

Nevertheless, the theater was not the only marvel in Sabratha. This port city in Roman Tripolitania – founded by Punic colonists in the fourth century BC – enjoyed a period of great wealth between AD 138 and 210 thanks to the export of African animals and ivory to Rome. During that golden century, Sabratha saw the construction of monumental buildings in marble and stucco-lined sandstone. One of these, standing in a magnificent position overlooking the sea, was the Temple of Isis, whose cult had

spread from Egypt to the Roman cities and who was worshiped as the protectress of sailors. Others were the Capitolium, the Sanctuary of Serapis, the Temple of Liber Pater, and the building referred to as Mausoleum B. Also rebuilt by the Italian archaeologists, this last monument features a pyramidal roof and merged Punic, Egyptian, Hellenistic, and Roman architectural elements. Particularly outstanding are the high-relief decorations on the metopes, bounded by lions supporting ten-foot-high male figures. Though many statues and mosaics have been destroyed or moved to the museum at the border of the archaeological area, the public buildings, such as the Forum, Curia, and the three

140 top and bottom The border of the theater's stage is decorated with a series of niches and panels, with bas-relief and high-relief figures representing divinities, dancers, thespians, and historical scenes attesting to relations between Rome and Sabratha.

140 center The imposing theater, the most important in Roman Africa, was built by Emperor Commodus around AD 190. The structure was returned to its original splendor thanks to a skillful restoration project dating back to the era of the Italian colonization of Libya.

140-141 *The elegant frons scaenae of the theater of Sabratha recalls the façade of a royal palace. 148 feet long, it features a triple order of 108 Corinthian columns in different-color types of marble with elaborate decorations on their capitals. The sides are closed in by the versurae, or "angles" where the rectilinear line of the stage connected to the cavea.*

TRIPOLI

SABRATHA

elegant baths complexes, still exude an aura of magnificence.

The decline of Rome in the third century AD also marked the decline of Sabratha, which, in any case, was struck by an earthquake in 365. The city had to wait almost two centuries before it reacquired any importance under the Byzantines, when the defensive walls and superb Basilica of Justinian were built.

In fact, Sabratha already had a basilica (today only the foundations remain), which had been a law court and a place of worship for the cult of the Roman emperors in the first century AD, before being transformed 300 years later into a Christian church.

In AD 158, the building had been the site of an event that resounded throughout the Roman world. It was there that the trial of the philosopher Apuleius was held, accused of having used magic powers to seduce and marry a rich, old widow in order to inherit her money. The author of the *Golden Ass* defended himself in person: his summation lasted four full days, at the end of which he was exonerated. This masterpiece of oratory, later transcribed, not only brought great fame to its author but remains a precious source for understanding daily life in Sabratha in the second century AD.

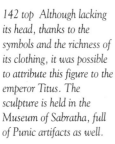

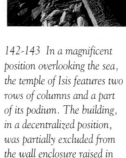

142 top Although lacking its head, thanks to the symbols and the richness of its clothing, it was possible to attribute this figure to the emperor Titus. The sculpture is held in the Museum of Sabratha, full of Punic artifacts as well.

142 bottom left Not far from the outstanding main theater, the amphitheater of Sabratha was erected between the end of the second century and the beginning of the third. In addition to its spacious cavea, it features intact the corridors by which beasts entered the arena.

142 bottom right A panoramic view of the residential area along the sea. Thanks to its favorable position, since the Phoenician era Sabratha prospered on maritime trading in African goods.

142-143 In a magnificent position overlooking the sea, the temple of Isis features two rows of columns and a part of its podium. The building, in a decentralized position, was partially excluded from the wall enclosure raised in the fourth century.

143 bottom left The columns of the temple of Isis, carved in rather poor-quality local sandstone, still feature part of the abundant plastering used in efforts to protect the monuments.

143 bottom right Almost double natural proportions, this bust of Jupiter, possibly part of a statue from the capitolium, is one of the highlights of the Museum of Sabratha.

*144 top left An octagonal
pool opens in the middle of
the lovely mosaics
decorating one of the main
rooms in the sumptuous
baths near the sea. From
here, a splendid view of the
coast and the ruins of the
warehouses of the city's
ancient port can be
enjoyed.*

*144 top right The god of
the ocean, with his thick
green beard and a crown of
fruit on his head, is
portrayed in this octagon
from a mosaic adorning a
room in the seaside baths.*

*144 center A meeting
place for the senatorial
class, the curia of Sabratha
still contains a good number
of its columns, on which
rested Corinthian-order
capitals in white marble.
The building faces the
forum, the hub of city life.*

*144 bottom This supple
marble statue portrayed a
naiad, a nymph considered
to be the protector of fresh-
water springs. It once
adorned one of the
numerous fountains in
Sabratha.*

144-145 *A view of the ruins over which Mausoleum B looms. The funerary monument has a pyramidal roof and mixes Punic, Egyptian, Hellenistic, and Roman stylistic elements. Extraordinary features are the high-relief decorations on the metopes, framed by lions that support male figures 10 feet tall (now in the Sabratha Museum).*

145 top *This refined mosaic panel portrays a Christian saint and dates back to the era of Sabratha's revival during Byzantine times. The important mosaic, like others found at the site, is held in the Sabratha Museum.*

Leptis Magna

LIBYA

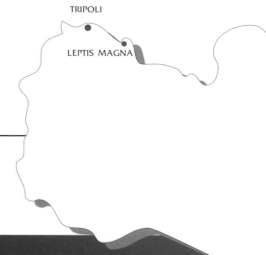

TRIPOLI

LEPTIS MAGNA

DISTRICT OF AL-KHOMS

REGISTRATION: 1982

CRITERIA: (I) (II) (III)

146-147 One of the livelier places devoted to business and trade in the Roman Empire, the market at Leptis Magna consisted of a series of octagonal kicsks, porticoes, workshops, and a majestic central pavilion.

146 bottom Decorated with Corinthian columns and precious marble bas-reliefs and about 66 feet tall, the Arch of Septimius Severus was built at the intersection of the cardus and decumanus in AD 203, on the occasion of the emperor's fifty-seventh birthday.

147 top A staircase and an arch lead into the area of the fruit and vegetable market. The excellent-quality sandstone used in the construction of the main monuments in Leptis Magna came from the Ras el-Hammam quarry, about a dozen miles south of the city.

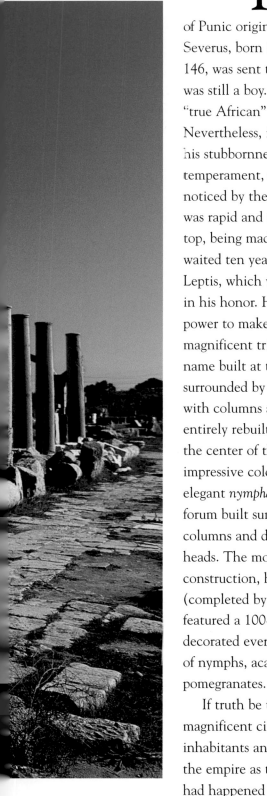

T he son of rich merchants of Punic origin, Lucius Septimius Severus, born in the city of Leptis in AD 146, was sent to Rome to study when he was still a boy. At that time, he was a "true African" and spoke Latin badly. Nevertheless, in the space of a few years, his stubbornness, courageous temperament, and eloquence got him noticed by the imperial court. His rise was rapid and took him straight to the top, being made emperor in 193. He waited ten years before returning home to Leptis, which was given the title *magna* in his honor. He did everything in his power to make it great. He had the magnificent triumphal arch bearing his name built at the entrance to the city, surrounded by four fountains decorated with columns and bas-reliefs. He then entirely rebuilt the port and joined it to the center of the city by means of an impressive colonnade, inaugurated an elegant *nymphaeum*, and had a huge forum built surrounded by a forest of columns and decorated with Medusa heads. The most outstanding construction, however, was the Basilica (completed by his son Caracalla), which featured a 100-foot-tall main hall and was decorated everywhere with elegant reliefs of nymphs, acanthus leaves, grapes, and pomegranates.

If truth be told, Leptis was already a magnificent city. It had 80,000 inhabitants and was known throughout the empire as the "pearl of Africa." As had happened to Septimius Severus, the city flourished upon coming into contact with Rome. Founded by Phoenicians from Tyre, it had for centuries been under the rule of the Carthaginians, but this state of affairs ended in 146 BC when the Romans defeated their historic rival across the sea and took possession of the city. It became the most important city in

Tripolitania, and later the entire province of Africa. Thanks to its port and the skill of its merchants, Leptis got rich by trading gold, ivory, ebony, slaves, and wild animals for the games in the circus. The expansion of the wharves and markets was matched by construction of increasingly impressive civil and religious buildings. These were financed by the families of the merchant class who competed in importing the loveliest

marbles and most skilled artists and decorators. The wealthy Hannibal Tapapius Rufus amazed his fellow citizens by sponsoring the construction of the Theater – adorned with statues, it may have been the jewel of the city – and the Market, which had two elegant octagonal kiosks at its center surrounded by a

147 center Bounded by pink-granite columns, the palaestra *of the luxurious baths commissioned by Emperor Hadrian was inaugurated in AD 127 and stood in the forum. The complex lies near the stream in Wadi Lebda, from which the water required for the baths was channeled.*

147 bottom Sixty-nine feet wide and still impeccably paved, the decumanus maximus *led to the port. The route was marked by the monumental Arch of Septimius Severus and the more modest arches of Tiberius (AD 37) and Trajan (shown in the photo), erected in AD 109-111.*

148 top The extraordinary Severan Forum, separated from the basilica by a tall sandstone wall, covers an area of 328 by 197 feet. Originally, it was constructed with precious materials: green cipolin for the arches, Egyptian pink granite for the columns, and bright white marble for the floor.

148 center The inscription on the portico of the forum praises Lucius Septimius Severus. Lucius, born in Leptis in AD 146, was elected emperor at 47 years old, and after a decade returned to the city, which received the title of "Magna" in his honor.

multitude of counters for goods to be displayed. The Flavini family, on the other hand, were responsible for the construction of Leptis' most unusual building, an immense amphitheater dug out of the ground on the seashore.

Even before the advent of Septimius Severus, other emperors had judged Leptis worthy of particular attention. Hadrian had provided it with a magnificent baths complex, two large temples facing the port, and a city wall. Further back in time, Nero helped to protect the port with the digging of a

148 bottom Once an ornament on the portico, this is one of about 70 medusa heads that today rest on the open ground of the new Severan Forum, now badly stripped. In the sixteenth century, the French consul Claude Lamaire brought back 200 columns and decorative marble pieces with him to France.

148-149 The grandiose Severan Basilica was initiated by Septimius Severus and completed, in AD 216, by his son Caracalla. Later, in the sixth century, the building was transformed into a Christian church by Justinian.

149 bottom left In this detail, two capitals resting on pink-granite columns in turn support the winged griffins on the only remaining piece of the pediment, which faces the apse of the Severan Basilica.

149 bottom right Rendered even more vivid by the warm light of the sun, the decorations on one of the columns in the north apse of the Severan Basilica portray numerous mythological characters, gods, and demigods among acanthus leaves and bunches of grapes.

150 top A forest of columns faces the port of Leptis Magna. The city was founded between the seventh and sixth century BC by Phoenicians from Tyre, who chose the site because there was an inlet providing the only safe landing point on the tract of coast between Alexandria and Carthage.

150 bottom left, right, and 151 bottom right The Museum of Tripoli holds some statutes from the theater of Leptis. From left to right, there is Athena with a Corinthian helmet, lance, and shield at her feet, a nymph, and a portrait of Marcus Aurelius. All the sculptures date back to between the first and second centuries AD.

dike, but this worsened the port's operations as it impeded the currents and caused the port to silt up gradually.

The mistake made by Nero's engineers occurred just as Leptis was reaching its greatest splendor, and marked the first, although immediately almost imperceptible, inkling of its decline. Around the year 250, with the end of the Severian dynasty, it quickly lost prestige and business dropped off. The end came in 365 when, along with all the cities of Tripolitania, it was destroyed by an earthquake.

Under Diocletian and Constantine, the city may have seen a glimmer of light shortly before the end. Nonetheless, perhaps having received a presage of the disaster, a treasurer buried 100,000 coins to the west of the city, during the rule of Constantine. Discovered in 1981, this haul was the most sensational numismatic find from the ancient world. Today some of these coins are on display together with other treasures in the museum next to the lovely archaeological site of Leptis Magna.

150-151 Situated in a panoramic position, the theater in Leptis was, and still is, one of the most magnificent in the Roman world. Its construction between the first and second centuries AD was financed by the merchant Hannibal Tapapius Rufus, an influential member of the city aristocracy.

151 bottom left A portico of columns with Corinthian capitals, accessible via an archway, surrounds a thermal bath in Leptis Magna. On its short side, narrow steps that "facilitated" entering the water can be noticed inside the pool.

152 With his shoulders
wrapped in the lion skin, or
leontea, that constituted
one of his symbols, this
scowling Hercules from
Leptis Magna is on display
at the Museum of Tripoli.

153 Apollo the Bard, the
divine lyre player, is
portrayed in yet another of
the sophisticated sculptures
found at Leptis Magna.

The Tadrart Akakus

LIBYA

Fezzan
Registration: 1985
Criteria: C (III)

TRIPOLI

AKAKUS

154-155 Covering 155 miles in the southwestern region of Libya as far as Algerian border, the Akakus chain is one of the richest locations in the world in terms of rock drawings. On its rocks, and above all in its inner cavities, is written a history recording 10,000 years of the population of and climatic evolution in the Sahara Desert.

154 bottom Above all, hunting and sheep-herding are the main characters in the Akakus rock paintings, as this complex scene in which armed human figures alternate with animals demonstrates.

155 top left The Bubalic Period takes its name from the Bubalus antiquus, a long-extinct bovine species. In this scene, hunters armed with bows confront the animal.

Near one of the rare *ghilte* (wells of collected rainwater) in the Wadi Sughd, hidden in the twists and turns of the Akakus, lies the "Sahara post office." It is a wall of basalt worn smooth by the wind on which generations of Tuareg, the nomadic people of this desert, have left messages for the future caravans that would pass there. Some of the messages have been made with chalk and others scratched in with a piece of metal. A few of them are just a few days old, some have been there for centuries, and all of them are written in Tifinagh, the written version of Tamashaq, the Tuareg language.

This "post office" is no more than an introduction to the human history of the region, which is more than 10,000 years old and narrated by the many rock paintings and engravings found in sites scattered across the Tadrart Akakus. The Tadrart Akakus is a mountain chain (in Tamashaq, the world *tadrart* is the plural of *adrar*, meaning mountain) stretching for 150 miles in southwest Libya as far as the Algerian border. Paradoxically, the most recent traces of man also seem to be the least refined, as if artistic sensibilities had waned as the climate became more inhospitable. Apart from the Tifinagh hieroglyphs, the most recent paintings and incisions date back to 2,000 to 3,000 years ago to an era that experts refer to as the "camel" period due to the prevalence of dromedaries in the pictures painted. At that time, the Sahara must have been more or less like it is today: a maze of black rocks and deep sandy valleys in which life was hard, despite the beauty of the landscape.

In the period before this, between 3,000 to 4,000 years ago, desertification

was already at an advanced stage, but in the Akakus there were still vast oases and the distances between them could be covered by horse. In fact, during this period known as the "horse" period, people drew and incised four-legged animals and humans, often in stiff poses on strange-looking carts, with great artistic skill.

During the 4,000 years before this period, the Saharan civilization was pastoral and partially sedentary. The drawings made during this earliest arc of time were either carved using hammers or painted with red ocher, ferrous oxide and other mineral substances that were fixed

155 top right The pastoral subjects narrate a past of transition between the "pre-desertic" period and total desertification.

155 center The Wan Amil Cycle dates back to the first Pastoral Period. This detail shows the final scene. Possibly a wedding, it portrays the reconciliation of two warring tribes, the "Yellow Hairs" and the "Red Hairs."

155 bottom Two large human figures, a bovine, and an ostrich. The drawings from the Pastoral Period were etched with small hammers or painted with red ochre, iron oxide, and other minerals.

with egg white and urine. The herds of
cattle and groups of humans illustrated
attest to an organized society that enjoyed
a relative, though primitive, well-being
that fostered artistic expression. One of
the most impressive rock sites from the
early pastoral period is Wan Amil in the
south of the Akakus. With a careful use of
colors, a scene shows a battle between
two factions distinguished by red and
yellow head coverings. Next to it, a
cartoon-like scene is found that has been
interpreted as a wedding, celebrated to
sanction peace.

In the even more primitive phase
before this, referred to as the "roundhead"
period (9,000 to 8,000 years ago), the
Saharan civilization left the most
interesting and "magical" records of itself.
During this time, man first began to
understand his power compared to other
living creatures and expressed the
concept of the divine. In fact, the large
anthropomorphic figures seen, for
example, in the ravines of Wan Tabu and
Wan Amillal have a sacred dimension.
Ten thousand years ago, the Sahara was
still green and populated by animals like
giraffes, elephants, large predators, and
above all, an extinct species of buffalo
defined as *Bufalus antiquus*, which used to
dominate the earliest paintings.

Though described by Herodotus in the
fifth century BC, Saharan rock art
remained almost unknown until the mid-
nineteenth century when, thanks to
German explorer Heinrich Barth, the
work of studying and cataloguing the
paintings and incisions began, still in
progress today. Wide-ranging and
systematic efforts to complete this
undertaking have been made by the
Italian researcher Fabrizio Mori.

156 top left The close proximity of a bovine to a palm tree may allude to the watering of the animal, in a territory in which water was increasingly scarce. Desertification, which began around 4000 BC, would only reach present-day levels one thousand years later.

156 top right The great crescent-shaped horns of the bovines illustrated recall those of the livestock still raised today by the shepherd peoples of the Sahel.

156-157 Some of the anthropomorphic figures are quite enigmatic, endowed with features that suggest a person with a mask, costume, and ritual horn, as in the case shown here (in which the human character overlaps animal figures).

157 top Works from the Pastoral Period all relate to nature. Of an elegant line and especially colorful, they generally describe the life of the shepherds, sometimes even down to the tiniest detail.

157 bottom The earliest examples of the rock art of the Akakus date back to the so-called Bubalic Period (10,000 years ago), when the desert was green and populated by large mammals such as giraffes, elephants, and big predators.

Cyrene

LIBYA

DISTRICT OF GHEBEL AKHDAR
REGISTRATION: 1982
CRITERIA: C (II) (III) (VI)

Cyrene was a beautiful, graceful wood nymph with an adventurous tomboy temperament. One day Apollo saw her as she was fighting a lion, fell desperately in love with her, and abducted her, fleeing on a gold chariot to Africa, where together they founded a city named after her.

Mythology aside, the story of the foundation of Cyrene passed down by Herodotus also involved Apollo as a main character. The famous Greek historian recounts that the city was founded by a group of Greek colonists from Thera (the present-day island of Santorini), who came to Libya according to instructions given them by the Pythia, the oracle of Apollo at Delphi. The first stone in the Temple of Apollo – which stood at the center of what was to become the most important city in the Greek Pentapolis – was laid in 631 BC. Battus, the expedition's leader, became king and established the Battiad dynasty that was to number eight monarchs (just as the oracle had predicted). The dynasty ended in 440 BC when a democracy was instituted on the Athenian model.

The fourth century BC coincided with Cyrene's heyday, when it prospered economically thanks to its agricultural exports to Greece. The city also became famous for breeding horses and cultivating *Cachrys ferulacea*, a wild plant that grew abundantly on the nearby plateaus and which was sold by weight at the same price as gold for its presumed magical and thaumaturgical powers. During that successful period, in which the city became distinguished for its rich cultural life, promoted by famous citizens like the philosopher Aristippus, the astronomer Theodorus, and the mathematician and physicist Eratosthenes, a number of extraordinary architectural monuments were built.

The Temple of Apollo was originally a simple open space, but was enclosed by a double row of six columns on the short sides and eleven on the long ones; the pediment, of which only fragments survive, was carved with a bas-relief of the nymph Cyrene strangling the lion. Standing in front of the temple was the monumental altar, a limestone structure 72 feet long lined with marble. The sacred complex was adorned with a so-called *Greek propylaeum* (the temple's monumental entrance), thermal baths,

158 top and 158-159 The archaeological site extends over three terraces that descend towards the sea and is dominated by the remains of the temple of Apollo. Founded in 631 BC by colonists from Thera (present-day Santorini), Cyrene grew rich through trade, becoming the most important city in the Greek Pentapolis.

158 bottom The theater near the Odeon is the best preserved of the theaters in Cyrene. The city became famous for being a center of art and culture and was the birthplace of illustrious personalities like the philosopher Aristippus, the astronomer Theodorus, and the mathematician and physicist Eratosthenes.

159 top A view of the remains of the propylaea. Although they had already taken possession of Cyrene by 96 BC, the Romans did not make any architectural alterations until two centuries later, when a massive restoration of the buildings became necessary, having been heavily damaged during the Jewish revolt of AD 117.

and a theater. The importance of Cyrene was heightened in that period with the construction of the Temple of Zeus, which today is one of the loveliest monuments in the vast archaeological site. Begun in the fifth century BC, it was bigger than the Parthenon and contained an enormous statue of Zeus modeled on the one made by Phidias for the Temple of Zeus at Olympia.

In 331 BC, the city was conquered by Alexander the Great and, upon the collapse of his empire, passed to the Ptolemaic dynasty that governed Egypt.

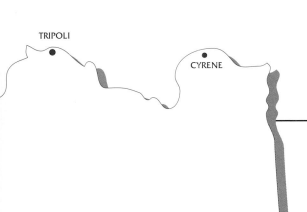

TRIPOLI

CYRENE

159 bottom left The temple of Apollo, the city's main sanctuary, was enclosed by a double row of six columns on its short sides and eleven on the long ones. On the pediment, the nymph Cyrene was portrayed in the act of strangling a lion.

159 bottom right The temple was dedicated to Apollo Archegetes, meaning the "progenitor" but also the "guide," an epithet that made him the divinity par excellence for the colonists that had left Hellas for these foreign lands.

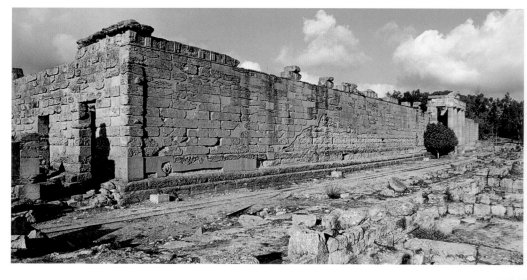

160 top The Caesareum, opposite the theater, was a vast public area enclosed by a wall (a good part of which has been preserved), access to which was gained through two propylaea on the south and east sides.

160 center In front of the temple of Apollo stood a terrace with a monumental altar, a 72-foot-long

limestone structure covered with marble slabs.

160 bottom The agora was surrounded by porticoes, temples, and public buildings, among which the market. In the middle of it, there was the only funereal monument allowed within the city walls, the cenotaph of Battus, leader of the Greeks who founded Cyrene and its first sovereign.

In the third century BC, a large public gymnasium was built, which was later turned into the forum dedicated to the Caesars when the Romans arrived. The Skyrota, which ran past the gymnasium, was the city's main street. A century later, the monumental agora took on its definitive form. It was lined by the circular Temple of Demeter and Kore (Persephone), and by an amazing monument raised to celebrate a naval victory. It contained a marble statue of Victory (today headless, but its elegant female forms perfectly carved in marble are still visible), which rises like a figurehead on a ship's bow. The cenotaph of Battus stands behind this monument.

The Romans took Cyrene in 96 BC but respected the Greek city and adapted to its traditions. No Roman alterations were made until AD 117 when a revolt of the Jewish community seriously damaged many of the buildings. Emperor Hadrian attempted to restore the city with monuments suited to its rank, as well as typically Roman luxury houses decorated with splendid mosaics. His contributions, however, were reduced to dust by the disastrous earthquake of AD 282, and so Cyrene, just a shadow of what it had once been, was rebuilt as a Christian settlement, before fading away forever with the arrival of the Arabs.

160-161 The big House of Jason Magnus, built in the second century BC along the street that went east from the forum, Caryatid Street, contains remarkable architectural ruins and a part of its original decorations, including some outstanding draped, and unfortunately, mutilated statues.

161 top An archaic theater that most likely dates back to the fifth century BC was erected west of the temple of Apollo. In Hadrian's times, the Romans made it into an amphitheater to hold exhibitions with gladiators.

161 bottom Everywhere among the fascinating ruins of Cyrene, numerous – and remarkable – statuary works by the city's artists can be found. Unfortunately, they all lack heads due to the revolt of the Jews, who destroyed them out of iconoclastic fury.

163 top Comparable in beauty and size to the Parthenon in Athens, the temple of Zeus, or the Olympieion, is a mammoth Doric peripteros with 17 columns on its long side and eight on its short one. Its construction began in the fifth century BC.

163 center Part of the sculptural decorations in the house of Jason Magnus, the master skill with which the draping of the robe on this statue was sculpted is admirable. Cyrene is famous for what are called its "faceless women"; they are actually headless statues or portrayals of Persephone, the goddess of death, whose face is always featureless.

163 bottom The entrance propylaea to the baths, commissioned by Emperor Hadrian. The complex, located a short distance to the east from the sacred terrace of the temple of Apollo, represents the most "invasive" of the Roman constructions at Cyrene.

162-163 A view of the gymnasium. Its original purpose altered by the Romans, it is a vast square-shaped space delimited by Ionic-order columns, next to which are the remains of an exercise track, restored during the 1930s by an Italian archaeological mission.

162 bottom left In an excellent state of preservation, the monumental entrance to the big gymnasium, erected by the Greeks in the second century BC, was later transformed into the Forum of the Caesars with the annexed basilica in the first century AD.

162 bottom right This precious flooring of marble mosaics is found in one of the 83 rooms in the opulent house of Jason Magnus, an illustrious personality who held the office of high priest in the temple of Apollo around the mid-second century AD.

Memphis and its Necropolis. The Pyramids from Giza to Dahshur

EGYPT

GOVERNORATE OF GIZA
REGISTRATION: 1979
CRITERIA: C (I) (III) (VI)

In the beginning, there was *Inbw-hdj*, or "white walls," which probably referred to the appearance of the fortified palace, though it was but a part of the city that most likely lay in the area now occupied by the town of Abusir. Later, the name was changed to *Hwt-ke-pth* after one of its temple enclosures, from which the Greek name *Aigyptos* was derived, and finally the modern version of Egypt. However, the most suitable name may have been *Ankh-tawy*, which more or less meant "the place that links the two lands." Located at the apex of the Nile Delta, at the

confluence of the commercial routes joining the East and West, the ancient city is best known today as Memphis, which is derived from *Mennefer*, the name of the pyramid built by the pharaoh Pepi I. *Mennefer* was transformed into the Copt *Menfe* and then the Greek *Memphis*.

Memphis was the royal residence and capital of Egypt during the proto-dynastic period and the Old Kingdom (3100–2184 BC), and for at least another two millennia, it was one of the most populated and famous cities in the region. Indeed, Herodotus, Strabo, and Diodorus Siculus all described its magnificence in

their writings. Modern evidence of its greatness, besides the few remains of the city itself excavated at Mit Rahina and Saqqarah, is found in the enormous necropolises stretching for 19 miles along the edge of the desert on the west bank of the Nile. In addition, there are the pyramids of Helwan, Dahshur, Saqqarah, Abusir, Zawyer el-Aryan, Abu Rawash, and of course, Giza. According to William Matthew Flinders Petrie, a nineteenth-century British archaeologist, Memphis must have measured about seven miles long by four miles wide and lain around the temple of Ptah in the area of the modern city of Mit Rahina. Ptah was the principal god of the city at the start of the dynastic period, if not earlier, and the first temple built in his name may rest hidden beneath a knoll called Kom el-Fakhry. Of the more recent temple, built during the reign of Ramses II, only the western section has been excavated, which is formed by a massive pylon and a colonnaded hypostyle room. Remains of foundations nearby indicate the presence of an earlier temple attributed to Thutmosis IV (Eighteenth Dynasty, 1419–1386 BC). The grandeur of Memphis begins to become apparent a little to the west, where the field containing the pyramids of Dahshur lies at the southern tip of the necropolis. A point of reference is the pyramid of Snefru, the founding father of the Fourth Dynasty who was pharaoh from 2630 to 2606 BC, and whose reign marked the transition from stepped pyramids to smooth-faced constructions. At Dahshur, pharaohs of the Twelfth Dynasty, Amenemhat II, Amenemhat III, and Sesostris III built another three pyramids. Next to the royal tombs are two groups of noble tombs,

called *mastabas*. They are rectangular with their sides slightly inclined and composed of two rooms: the burial chamber and a chapel. Buried in them were the princesses Iti, Khnemt, Itiwert, and Sitmerhut, all daughters of Amenemhat II, and other members of the families of the Twelfth-Dynasty pharaohs. Further north at Saqqarah, the entire history of Ancient Egypt can be embraced in a single site. It covers the period from the first unbaked brick *mastaba* of Menes, the legendary pharaoh of the First Dynasty considered the founder of Memphis, to the Greco-Roman period. The tombs of the royal families,

164 *The awesome "Red Pyramid" at Dahshur was named for the color of the granite at its core. It was built by Snefru, a pharaoh of the Fourth Dynasty. Standing 345 feet tall, it is the third largest pyramid after those of Khufu and Khafre.*

164-165 *Djoser's funerary monument at Saqqarah is the most complete example of a stepped pyramid. Its concept was derived from the overlaying of simple, ancient "bench tombs," called mastabas.*

165 top *The foundations of the funerary temple of Sahura, the second king of the Fifth Dynasty, precede what remains of the king's funerary temple at Abu Sir. Originally the monument was a "true" pyramid, i.e. with smooth rather than stepped sides.*

165 center *The imposing nucleus is all that remains of Snefru's pyramid at Meidum. Begun as a stepped monument, it was later fitted with smooth sides.*

CAIRO
MEMPHIS - GIZA

nobles, and high dignitaries of the First Dynasty run along the east edge of the desert plateau. Dominating Saqqarah is the stepped pyramid of Djoser, the oldest of the 97 known Egyptian pyramids, which was built in the middle of the twenty-seventh century BC and surrounded by temples and buildings used to celebrate the royal jubilee. There are at least 13 other royal pyramids at Saqqarah, of which the most notable are those of Sekhemkhet (the successor to Djoser in the Third Dynasty), Unas and Teti (Fifth and Sixth dynasties, twenty-fourth century BC), Pepi I (Sixth Dynasty, ca. 2300 BC), and

165 bottom *With the Twelfth Dynasty, the era of the pyramids came to an end. The funerary monument of Senusret, shown here, at Illahun was never completed due to the king's premature death, and it later collapsed completely.*

166 top left Bearers carry offerings in the tomb of Ti, a supervisor of the pyramids and sun temples at Saqqarah, and chief hairdresser at court.

166 top right The nobleman Ptahotep faces his own name in finely carved hieroglyphs on a wall in his mastaba at Saqqarah. The meaning of the name is "(the god) Ptah is pleased."

Didufri (Fourth Dynasty, 2583–2575 BC) in the northernmost area of the necropolis. To the north of Djoser's pyramid lies the largest area of non-royal tombs from the Old Kingdom, besides an unknown number of more recent graves. There are hundreds worth mentioning, either because they were of people of a particular rank or because of their architectural, structural, or decorative aspects. Recently archaeologists in the field have found new leads for excavation.

166 bottom On the great mastaba at Saqqara, Mereruka, on the right, is portrayed with his mother and his wife, sculpted in small size at his feet, whereas he appears with one of his two sons on the left.

167 The vizier Mereruka advances towards the offerings' table standing on a stepped dais. The tombs of the great dignitaries, as was customary, stood near the pyramid of the king they had served. In this case, the pharaoh was Teti.

168 top *Enormous, gradually overlapping blocks of granite form the Great Gallery at the heart of Khufu's pyramid. This extraordinary passage is 154 feet long and 28 feet high.*

Further north there are the most famous monuments, those that the Ptolemies (the Macedon governors of Egypt that took power in the fourth century BC) wished to see included as one of the Seven Wonders of the World. They are the pyramids of Giza built by Khufu, Khafre, and Menkaure, the three pharaohs of the Fourth Dynasty that governed Egypt for almost all of the twenty-sixth century BC. In fact, the Giza plateau (which lies about 130 feet higher than the plain and from which the greenery of the Nile Delta can be seen) had already been used as a necropolis since the proto-dynastic period, but it was with these three pharaohs that the royal tombs reached their greatest glory. Construction of the pyramid of Khufu (*Cheops* in Greek) required 35 years of work and two and a half million blocks of stone weighing between two and 75 tons each. It originally stood 481 feet four inches tall and its square base measures 755 feet nine inches on each side. Today, after

millennia of being worn away by erosion, it still stands 452 feet ten inches high. The entrance lies at a height of about 56 feet where a narrow corridor enters the rock and continues for more than 110 yards inside the monument to the first chamber. This was where the pharaoh was to be laid in the first plan, but in fact, to reach his real burial chamber, it is necessary to take an ascending side corridor 35 yards from the entrance that leads up to a junction. From here, one passageway leads to an intermediate chamber referred to as the Queen's Chamber, whereas the Great Gallery – almost 160 feet long and 28 feet high – leads to the pharaoh's real place of burial. Here, in a chamber measuring about 33 feet by 16, stands Khufu's simple granite sarcophagus. Khafre (*Chephren* in Greek) built his funerary monument just a little to the south of his father's. It measures 689 feet on each side and, being more inclined, reached a lower height of a little over 470 feet.

168 bottom *The steep angle of the sides of Khufu's pyramid (51° against the 45° of Snefru's, the first "real" pyramid to have survived without collapsing) gave it an overall height of 482 feet as opposed to its 456 feet today.*

168-169 *It is not know for certain why Menkaure's pyramid is so small in comparison to the "giants" of Giza, but probably construction of the earlier two was so demanding on the nation that it could not be repeated.*

169 bottom left *These large niches in a wall inside the pyramid of Menkaure, the fifth pharaoh of the Fourth Dynasty, may have been used for offerings.*

169 bottom right *The burial chamber of Khafre is roofed with sloping slabs of pink granite: this placement made it possible to redistribute the enormous weight of the upper part of the pyramid, which would have crushed an empty room with a flat roof. On the left wall, the budding invasion of archaeologists at the beginning of the 1800s is heralded in the triumphant words etched by Belzoni as he made his discovery in 1818.*

To the side of and downhill from Khafre's pyramid, two temples are found in a better state of conservation than those of Khufu. To the west is the enigmatic and gigantic sculpture of the Sphinx, about 180 feet long and 66 high. It was carved out of a single block left remaining from the quarries used to provide the materials for Khufu's pyramid. Unique in Egypt, its date oscillates between the reign of Khufu and Khafre, though it was almost certainly attributable to the former. In the symbolism of Ancient Egypt, the sculpture represented the pharaoh in whom the strength of wild animals combined with the intelligence of man. The last of the pyramids built at

Giza was that of Menkaure (*Mycerinus* in Greek), the son of Khafre, on the remaining space on the south side of the plateau. At just 343 feet per side and a height of 213 feet four inches, and with a layout of burial chambers the same as that of Khufu's pyramid, it marked the last of the colossal funerary monuments of the Fourth Dynasty. The temples also feature a simple layout and were ornamented with fine statuary made from a variety of materials. With these constructions, the era of the great pyramids closed forever.

Ancient sources provide us with almost no information on the techniques used to construct the three monuments, but it is

probable that they were assembled using many small ramps to transport the blocks of stone up heights of 80 to 100 feet and these were then combined to form a single ramp for the higher sections of the construction. However, any theory is pure speculation. What is certain is that the pyramids of Giza are the only wonder of the ancient world to have survived until the present day almost unaltered and to have raised astonishment and admiration for 4,500 years. Even the great Napoleon, on the eve of the battle of Giza, admonished his soldiers saying, "from the tops of these pyramids, 40 centuries of history gaze down upon you."

170 top The identity of the king portrayed on the Sphinx is unknown: it was once believed to be Khafre, due to the monument's connection to the ramp of his pyramid, but more recently some experts have associated its construction with Khufu.

170 bottom A vast sanctuary lay in front of the Sphinx, built in various stages as part of Khafre's burial complex. The ramp that ran up to this pharaoh's pyramid can be seen bottom right.

171 The inconsistent stratification of the rock that forms the Sphinx is revealed in the different colors of its parts. The head is darker and the most resistant section, whereas the paws seem well preserved but are in fact "artificial," having been lined with limestone that is easily restored or replaced.

Ancient Thebes and its Necropolis

EGYPT

GOVERNORATE OF QENA
REGISTRATION: 1979
CRITERIA: C (I) (III) (VI)

About 420 miles south of Cairo, where the Nile River rounds a tight bend and is lined by a low range of mountains, tourism is certainly not a novelty, nor is the uncontrollable desire of visitors to leave a sign of their passage on the monuments and works of art. In Thebes - the capital of the Egyptian dynasties during the New Kingdom, from 1570 to 1070 BC - the scrawls of the tourists have also become a piece of history. The first to pass through were Greek and Roman travelers during the Ptolemaic age, and they left at least 2,000 graffiti scribblings on the walls of the tombs of the pharaohs in the Valley of the Kings. In addition to these, there are messages in Phoenician, Cypriot, Lycian, Coptic, and other languages. All of these are proof that the greatness of Egypt was already legendary before the start of the Christian era.

The ancient Greek writers Pausanias, Strabo, and Diodorus Siculus described Thebes – *Waset* to the Egyptians – as a city of marvels, so the richer inhabitants from the other side of the Mediterranean ventured to Egypt to admire the magnificent temples, spectacular Colossi of Memnon, and the endless necropolis of the Valley of the Kings. It was the opinion of Diodorus that "the tombs do not leave to posterity the possibility of producing anything more beautiful."

Today, Luxor, the city that stands on the left bank of the Nile on the site of the ancient capital, in an area inhabited for at least 250,000 years, is the most extraordinary open-air museum in the world. A few miles north of the modern city stands the temple of Amon-Ra at Karnak, consecrated to the sun god, one of the most important in Ancient Egypt. Built around 1900 BC by Sesostris I, a pharaoh of the Twelfth Dynasty during the Middle Kingdom, it did not cease to expand and change until the fourth century AD. Each pharaoh wanted to leave his own mark because the temple of Amon-Ra reflected the Ancient Egyptians' conception of the world. Its structure was spread along two axes: the east-west axis mirrored the trajectory of the sun, which symbolized the divine nature of things, whereas the north-south axis ran parallel to the course of the Nile and was linked to the territory and the function of the sovereign, in which the pharaoh represented the fusion of everything divine and human and whose existence ensured the prosperity of the kingdom.

Further south, in the heart of the city on the east bank of the Nile, stands the temple of Luxor, built during the reign of Amenhotep III (1386–1349 BC) and connected to Karnak by a long paved processional way (*dromos* in Greek) lined by sphinxes. A stretch of this can still be seen in front of the temple. Also called the "southern harem of Amon," it was started by Amenhotep III but concluded by Ramses II.

According to accounts on papyruses, the cult of Amon in the Great Temple at Karnak had no fewer than 20,000 priests. Once a year, on the occasion of the feast of Opet, the priests removed the statue of Amon from its shrine and carried it in procession to the temple of Luxor on a simulacrum of a boat made from gilded wood.

172 top The colossal statue of Ramses II stands in Luxor Temple.

172 bottom The Great Hypostyle Hall in the temple of Karnak contains 134 sandstone columns divided into 16 rows that staand in an area of 53,800 square feet. The shafts in the central nave stand 79 feet tall.

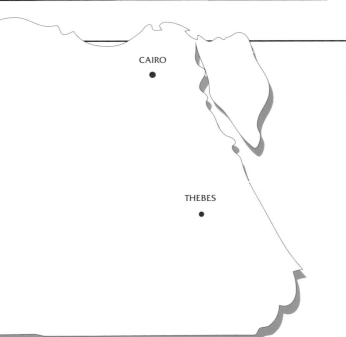

CAIRO

THEBES

172-173 Sixteen centuries (from roughly 1950 to 350 BC) were needed to build the extended temple of Amon-Ra at Karnak. On the left, towards the river, stands the pylon built by Ramses II and Horemheb; in the foreground, beside the sacred lake and Hatshepsut's eighth pylon, lie the ordered foundations of granaries and temple storerooms.

173 top left The ruins of the temple of Luxor stand a few yards from the Nile east side of the "bank of the living." The Great Colonnade (center), built by Amenhotep III, was once enclosed by a parallelepiped building.

173 top right The pylon of Ramses II is flanked by two colossi of the pharaoh. It leads to the temple of Luxor (Ipet-Resit or "Residence of the South" to the Ancient Egyptians) where the statue of Amon was carried once a year during the great Opet festival held in the season of the flooding of the Nile.

On the other side of the river, as though to underline the distance between the government of the divine world represented by the priests of Karnak and the government of the earthly world, Amenhotep III built his palace. Of all those belonging to the pharaohs, this is the one that has survived in the best condition. Like other residences in Egypt, it was built from mud bricks (which is why so many of them have been lost). It was not only home to himself and his queen Tiy, but also the 317 Hittite concubines he received as a gift for having married a Hittite princess. Malkata (the palace's Arab name) was also the pharaoh's administrative center, and nearby a village developed where the craftsmen and servants who served the pharaoh lived.

A mile away stand the Colossi of Memnon, the two gigantic quartzite

statues of Amenhotep III that are each 75 feet tall and weigh a thousand or so tons. They stand at the entrance to the original funerary temple of the pharaoh. Here, at the foot of the limestone cliff of Deir el-Bahari and behind the first majestic temple, another 14 "temples of the millions of years" stand in line. These are the funerary temples of 14 other pharaohs, including Ramses II, Amenhotep II, and Seti I to mention the most famous. They were built to last for eternity so that the pharaohs could always be remembered by their subjects.

Nevertheless, today as in antiquity, the fame of Thebes is owed principally to the

175 center The ruins of the "migdol" (a kind of tower borrowed from Mesopotomian architecture) in Medinet Habu lie in front of the pylon and ceremonial palace of the temple of Ramses III, the last great Egyptian pharaoh, who lived roughly a century after the illustrious Ramses II.

175 bottom The portico that faces onto the second court of the temple of Ramses III is in excellent condition. It is supported by papyriform columns carved entirely with reliefs and painted. On the right, the pharaoh receives the homage of the god Atum "the Whole."

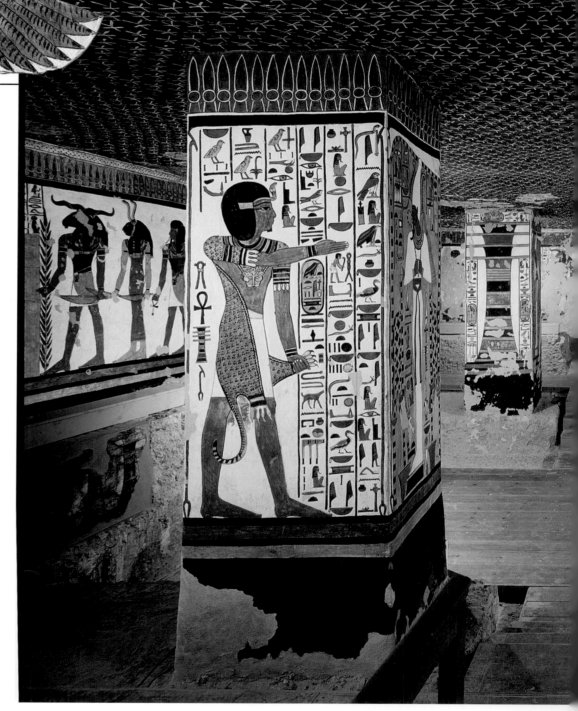

Valley of the Kings and, to a lesser degree, the Valley of the Queens, the two necropolises located on the other side of the cliff. Between the two stretch the civilian necropolises incorrectly called the "Tombs of the Nobles." This is a complex of 500 graves that can be distinguished from the royal tombs by their architecture and the modesty of their decoration.

The Valley of the Queens contains between 75 and 80 tombs from the Eighteenth, Nineteenth, and Twentieth dynasties in which not only the wives but also the children and family members of the pharaohs were buried. They include the tombs of Queen Titi of the Twentieth Dynasty, young Khaemwese, the fourth son of Ramses II, and Amenhikhopeshef, son of Ramses III. However, the most famous of all, and considered one of the most beautiful in all of Ancient Egypt, is unquestionably that of Nefertari, the favorite wife of Ramses II. The walls and ceiling of the tomb are completely covered with scenes in which the queen, "the most beautiful of all," dressed in a white garment and gold crown adorned with vulture's plumes, is accompanied by Egyptian gods and goddesses.

176 top left The goddess Ma'at accepts offerings from Nefertari (not visible). The queen died before her husband, Ramses II, but nothing is known of her demise. After being honored with monuments like the Small Temple at Abu Simbel, she disappeared from recorded history.

176 top right Ta Set Neferu, "Place of the royal children," lies southwest of the Valley of the Kings. At first it was the burial place of the princes and princesses of the Eighteenth Dynasty, but over time, queens like Nefertari (Ramses II's principal wife) were also buried there.

176-177 A ceiling adorned with a myriad of stars on a blue background covers the magnificently decorated burial chamber of Nefertari, "House of Gold." In the background, facing north, the door that led to the "abode of Osiris," the god who oversaw resurrection, can be seen.

177 top Nefertari makes food offerings to Atum and Osiris (left), the god who rose from the dead, shown here as a mummy with green flesh. The provisions include the bodies of decapitated oxen and loaves of bread.

a burial chamber holding the sarcophagus of the pharaoh. In this chamber, according to the Ancient Egyptian religion, the king was transformed into a divine entity. The walls were lined with multicolored bas-reliefs of the afterlife and the journey that the pharaoh had to make to get to the kingdom of Osiris.

At the time of its greatest splendor, Thebes represented the triumph of Egyptian power and was to the Greeks and Romans a place of wonder, but after the Arab conquest of the country, it fell into oblivion. It was only rediscovered at the start of the eighteenth century by the Jesuit Claude Picard, who came there in 1726. One of the first Europeans to draw pictures of Thebes was the Danish artist Frederik Ludwig Norden, followed by Richard Pococke, who drafted a detailed map of the Valley of the Kings. In the nineteenth century, as the Ancient-Egyptian "style" raged across Europe, the monuments of Thebes attracted archaeologists, scholars like Prosper Jollois and Edouard de Villiers, artists like David Roberts, not to mention many unscrupulous visitors seeking easy profit through the contraband of ancient objects.

Though many of the treasures in the Valley of the Kings were pilfered, European scholars contributed decisively to the deciphering of hieroglyphs and the excavation of the Egyptian capital throughout the nineteenth and twentieth centuries. Finally, in 1922, after a decade of hard work, Howard Carter discovered the last tomb, undeniably one of the most fascinating and mysterious, in the Valley of the Kings: the burial place of Tutankhamon, the boy pharaoh.

179

178-179 Various gods (with Hathor in the foreground) are present in the life of Amenhotep II, who wears the nemes headdress in the paintings on the six pillars in the burial chamber of the Eighteenth Dynasty pharaoh's tomb.

179 top The small dark smudges on the floor of the Valley of the Kings are the entrances to tombs. This new design was developed during the New Kingdom, and was based on long, downward-sloping corridors that led to the burial chamber. Tutankhamon's tomb lies in the light-colored area at the center of the photograph.

179 bottom The goddess Nephthys spreads her wings to protect a corner of the outermost sarcophagus of Tutankhamon, made from finely carved red quartzite. The fame of this tomb is due to the fact that it has been basically the only one to be found almost intact, but in fact it was small compared to those of other Egyptian kings.

180 top and bottom left
Craftsmen working in the
Valley of the Kings could
afford fine graves. The
photograph above shows the
ceiling of Sennedjem's tomb,
and the one below that of
Pashedu.

180 bottom right
Representing the promise of
eternal life – but also of
eternal work – the Fields of
Iaru have welcomed
Sennedjem, who, in this
painting in his tomb in West
Thebes, is helped in the
agricultural work by his wife
Ineferti.

181 A decoration painted to
imitate brightly-colored mat
linings adorns a ceiling in the
tomb of Sennefer, the
chancellor of Amenhotep II
of the Twelfth Dynasty
(fourteenth century BC).

180 center left Pashedu
kneels beneath an udjat eye
that bears a brazier of
offerings to the gods. This
picture of the deceased is
painted on the wall over the
sarcophagus.

180 center right Lacking the
grandiosity of the royal
monuments, the workers'
village excavated near the
Valley of the Kings has
provided interesting
information on life in
Ancient Egypt.

The Nubian Monuments from Abu Simbel to Philae

EGYPT

GOVERNORATE OF ASWAN
REGISTRATION: 1979
CRITERIA: C (I) (III) (VI)

It took twenty years to complete the campaign launched by UNESCO in 1960 to save the magnificent temples of Abu Simbel. Built on the left bank of the Nile River over 3,250 years ago by Ramses II and completely dug out of a rock wall, the temples stand a full 175 miles south of Aswan, but not far enough away from where the High Dam on the Nile was constructed. As the water of the Nile built up behind the dam, it became apparent that Abu Simbel was in danger. It was therefore decided to section the temples, dismantle them, and reconstruct them 200 meters away from their original location.

To perform this complex operation, the 15,000 tons of stone were cut into 1,036 blocks and carefully numbered, removing 300,000 tons of the surrounding rock in the process. Then the structures were reassembled, reconstructing the ring of mountains surrounding the temples as well. The same fate fell upon the less famous but equally important temple of Philae, situated between the High Dam and the Aswan Dam, as well as the temples of Gerf Hussein, Dakka, Amada, Derr, Kalabsha, Qasr Ibrahim and Wadi as-Sabua, originally known as the "house of Amun."

Bearing in mind that Egypt donated several minor temples to various countries in gratitude for help provided in the rescue operation, it is clear how much that twenty-year period altered the geography of ancient Nubia. The temple of Debod, donated to Spain, now stands in Madrid; the temple of Dendur is in the Metropolitan Museum in New York; the temple of El-Lessiya is in the Egyptian Museum in Turin; the portal to the temple of Kalabsha traveled to the Egyptian Museum in Berlin; and, the temple of Taffa is in the Rijksmuseum van Oudheden in Leiden in the Netherlands.

The history of Nubia – the vast desert region spread along the banks of the Nile that occupies all of southern Egypt and a part of the Sudan – goes back almost six thousand years. Habitation of the region began around 3,800 BC by semi-nomadic peoples that gradually settled on the fertile banks of the river, giving rise to a fairly sophisticated civilization. Between 2000 and 1559 BC, the nearby kingdom of Kerma governed the region, but the Egyptians began to exercise their influence over a part of Nubia by the start of the second millennium BC and eventually dominated it around 1100 BC. The region interested the pharaohs for a number of reasons, but most importantly, it was rich in precious metals and building stone. Secondly, it

182 top Consecrated to the god of writing and knowledge, Thot, the small Nubian temple of Dakka (Selqet to the Egyptians) was built in the third century BC over an Eighteenth Dynasty building (sixteenth to twelfth centuries BC) and was renovated by Meroitic kings, the Ptolemies and the Romans.

182 bottom A remarkable façade precedes the hypostyle atrium of the temple of Kalabsha, built for Octavian at the southern boundary of the nascent Roman Empire. This is the largest Nubian temple built as a completely free-standing structure and not partially dug out of the rock.

182-183 The temple of Wadi es-Sabua was built in the fourteenth century BC in what was – and still is – the extreme south of Egypt. Moved in the 1960s to protect it from the rising waters of Lake Nasser, it is approached via an avenue of sphinxes with human and falcon heads that earned it the name of "Wadi of the Lions."

CAIRO

PHILAE

ABU SIMBEL

represented the corridor through which the Egyptians could trade in incense, myrrh, ivory, ebony, oils, resins, the skins of leopards and panthers, and other exotic articles from Central Africa. Finally, it rapidly became a region where Egypt could readily find a labor-force. During the fourth dynasty, for example, a campaign was carried out to put down a revolt resulting in the taking of 7,000 slaves, deported to Egypt to build royal palaces back in Egypt.

183 top The temple of Amada was consecrated to Amon-Ra and built by Thutmosis III in the fifteenth century BC. It was later restored by various rulers, including Ramses II.

183 bottom The island of Philae is one of the most famous sites in Egypt, even though its buildings are neither especially monumental nor old (the larger temple in the picture, dedicated to Isis, was Ptolemaic, and the kiosk on its right was built by Trajan).

Despite its long history and the region's strong ties to the Egypt of the pharaohs, almost all the most important temples in Nubia were built during the New Kingdom, in particular during the Eighteenth and Nineteenth Dynasties (1548–1186 BC). Various pharaohs contributed to their construction but artistic perfection was reached under Ramses II, who reigned from 1279–1212 BC along with his five or six wives, one of whom was the famous Nefertari. The temples of Derr, Gerf Hussein, and Wadi as-Sabua were all built on the orders of Ramses or his dignitaries.

The most impressive is, of course, the extraordinary temple of Abu Simbel, constructed in the thirty-fourth year of his reign (1245 BC) together with another, smaller temple consecrated to Nefertari and the goddess Hathor. The immense façade of the main temple cut in the rock stands 100 feet high and 120 wide; it is decorated with four 67-foot-high colossal statues of Ramses himself seated on his throne and wearing the double crown of Upper and Lower Egypt. Smaller statues stand next to Ramses' legs portraying the pharaoh's closest family members. One of these bears the features of Nefertari, while the others depict Ramses' mother, three daughters, and two sons. Bas-reliefs on the thrones represent the kingdoms and peoples conquered during the pharaoh's military campaigns. Above the center of the entrance to the temple, there is the falcon-headed image of the god Ra, or Ra-Harakhti the sun god. On the upper cornice of the façade, there are 22 statues of baboons.

184 top The waters of Lake Nasser lap the new site of the temples at Abu Simbel, the relocation of which in the 1960s represented an unprecedented feat of engineering. Even the hills in which the temples were excavated were reconstructed in every detail.

184 bottom The two colossi on the right stand against the natural rock wall from which they were carved. The holes left by the scaffolding used by the ancient stonecutters can be clearly seen along the edge of the stone.

184-185 The façade of the great temple at Abu Simbel is like a pylon: it is decorated with the four colossi of Ramses II and tiny statues of some of his daughters, his mother, and his wife Nefertari. The second colossus from the left collapsed due to an earthquake during Ramses' reign.

185 top left The façade of the small temple (the temple dedicated to Nefertari just north of the great temple) has two unusual features: the queen appears in two out of the six statues and, strange yet, in the same size as those of the pharaoh.

185 top right Nubian prisoners bound together at the neck are carved to the south of the entrance of the great temple at Abu Simbel. Similar images are found in Egyptian sculpture from as early as the pre-dynastic period.

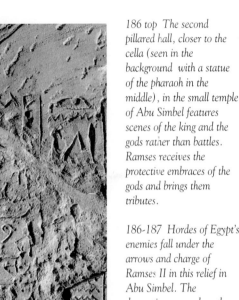

186 top The second pillared hall, closer to the cella (seen in the background with a statue of the pharaoh in the middle), in the small temple of Abu Simbel features scenes of the king and the gods rather than battles. Ramses receives the protective embraces of the gods and brings them tributes.

186-187 Hordes of Egypt's enemies fall under the arrows and charge of Ramses II in this relief in Abu Simbel. The decorations carved on the walls of the big hall of the great temple include rituals and various battle scenes especially dedicated to the victory at Qadesh.

187 top Ramses II was not afraid to replace images of the gods with those of himself. The eight statue-pillars in two rows in the big hall of the great temple of Abu Simbel portray him and not Osiris, as was customary. At the back of the hall, two of the four statues in the cella, portraying Ptah, Amon-Ra, Ra-Horakhti, and the king can be seen.

187 bottom Queen Nefertari pays homage to three seated gods, presenting offerings on two tables and carrying two lotus flowers on a wall in the small temple. Relations between sovereigns and the gods was seen as a sort of family relationship, with the pharaoh and his most important queens receiving the gift of eternal life in virtue of this bond.

Just past the vestibule inside, there is an enormous hypostyle hall supported by eight Osiriac pillars that leads into a second, smaller hypostyle hall, and then a second vestibule preceding the *cella*. In this, on a small altar, stood the statues of the four most important gods of the era: Ptah of Memphis, who was linked with the kingdom of the dead, Amon-Ra of Thebes and Ra-Harakhti of Heliopolis (both sun gods), and Ramses himself, to whom was attributed a divine origin. The position of the temple was calculated so that twice a year – at dawn on 20 February and 20 October – the rays of the sun, adored by the baboons, entered the central hall of the building as far as the *cella* and illuminated the statues of the pharaoh and sun gods Amon-Ra and Ra-Harakhti. The statue of Ptah was only slightly brushed by the sunlight and never completely illuminated.

For centuries, the site of Abu Simbel

was lost from memory until, in March 1830, the successful Swiss traveler and explorer, Johann Ludwig Burchardt, stumbled across it. Just a year previous Burchardt had rediscovered Petra in Jordan, the legendary capital of the Nabataeans. At Abu Simbel, however, Burchardt was only able to admire the monumental façade from the exterior as the entrance had been blocked by sand. Two years later, another traveler, the English antiquarian William John Banks, accompanied by the Italian Giovanni Finati, succeeded in entering the small temple consecrated to Nefertari. It took another two years until on August 1, 1817 another Italian explorer, Giovanni Belzoni, working for the English consul, Henry Salt, succeeded in removing the mass of sand blocking the entrance after a month of backbreaking work and freed the marvels of Abu Simbel from their "prison."

Aksum
ETHIOPIA

REGISTRATION: 1980
CRITERIA: C (I) (IV)

Until 1998, when David Phillipson published his book *Ancient Ethiopia*, atlases of ancient history hardly mentioned the kingdom of Aksum, and in exhibitions on great African civilizations in the world's great museums, the ancient Ethiopian culture was relegated to a corner and represented only by a few coins and bits of pottery. Yet, the *Periplus of the Eritrean Sea*, written in the first century AD by an anonymous Greek merchant tells of Zoskales, the ruler of a vast territory that stretched from the coast of the Red Sea to the highlands, which had its capital in the *metropolis* of Aksum.

Local tradition claims that the first settlement at Aksum stood on Beta Giorgis Hill, and then the legend gets lost in epic tales of the legendary riches of the kingdom of the Queen of Sheba, whose love for Solomon resulted in the birth of Menelik. The founder of the dynasty of Abyssinian negus, Menelik is supposed to have visited his father in Jerusalem and, as he was leaving the city, stolen the Ark of the Covenant, the wooden urn inlaid with gold supposed to contain the Ten Commandments given by God to Moses. Today, it is said, the Ark is held in Aksum in a small chapel standing between the two churches of Maryam Sion (St. Mary of Zion), away from the gaze of the sacrilegious.

The ancient basilica of Maryam Sion was built by king Fasillidas in 1655 and lies at the center of modern Aksum. Despite stories claiming that the city is far more ancient, Aksum enjoyed its greatest period between the second and sixth or seventh centuries AD. A number of remains have survived from that period, many of which refer directly to the legend. The palace of Gondour, dating back to the sixth to seventh centuries, would have been the residence of a nobleman, though it is improperly referred to as the "Palace of the Queen of Sheba." With 54 rooms and covering 30,000 square feet, it provides astounding evidence of the city's past magnificence, which was surrounded by solid walls and had an amazing drainage system.

Similarly, the hollow of May Shum is referred to as the "Baths of the Queen of Sheba," though in fact this large manmade pool was built to collect the scarce rainwater and is still used as a reservoir for the city. Unsurprisingly, this is where the processions of the Coptic epiphany, the Timkat, end up. A short distance from the pool lies the graveyard of the Aksumite kings Kaleb and Gebre-Meskel, two tombs formed by a small maze of graves in which the members of the kings' families were buried. Huge stones seal the sarcophagi, though the sarcophagi themselves have long been emptied of their treasures.

The most extraordinary evidence of Aksum's importance is the Stelae Park containing immense blocks of granite probably carved in the third and fourth centuries. In fact, the city as a whole contains hundreds of stelae in different states of conservation. Some of them are finely sculpted while others were left as unfinished columns. At one time, seven gigantic obelisks dominated the Park, situated at the base of Beta Giorgis Hill, but today only one has been left standing. It is 43 feet tall and has been carved in the shape of a nine-story tower with a monkey's head on the top. The largest stele, with 13 stories and 108 feet tall, has fallen heavily to the ground. Legend attributes its destruction to the will of the pagan queen Judith, but according to archaeologists, it fell because it lacked a foundation. Since ten graves have recently been discovered at its base, the obelisks are now considered to have been funerary monuments.

Another stele from the park has a controversial history. Stolen by the Italian Minister of the Colonies, Alessandro Lessona, to be given as a gift to Benito Mussolini, the obelisk is still found in Rome, where it has remained for more than 60 years despite the agreement signed in 1947 stipulating its restitution to Ethiopia. Recently, in response to concerns over its supposed fragility, the Italian government has made plans for the obelisk to be dismantled.

188 top A formidable example of ancient engineering, the hollow of May Shum (which traditionally is called "the baths of the Queen of Sheba") is a vast artificial basin built to hold rainwater. It is still used as a reservoir today.

188 bottom left The tomb of King Kaleb, who died in AD 542, is flanked by that of his son Gebre-Meskel, who succeeded him on the throne of Aksum. Small mazes of tombs, the two burial places contain sarcophagi covered with slabs of stone weighing dozens of tons. This, however, has not impeded the pillaging of their treasures over the centuries.

188 bottom right Found a few miles from the city, this rock bearing the sculpted face of a lioness may have been the work of an Aksumite artist, but its origin is still a mystery.

189 Legacy of Aksum's greatness, the Park of the Stelae is packed with giant granite monoliths raised between the third and fourth century as funereal monuments.

AKSUM

ADDIS ABABA

The Great Zimbabwe

ZIMBABWE

SOUTHEAST ZIMBABWE
REGISTRATION: 1986
CRITERIA: C (I) (III) (VI)

HARARE

GREAT ZIMBABWE

In 1871, Carl Mauch, a young German adventurer, set off to search for the legendary mines of Ofir from which the queen of Sheba was supposed to have mined the gold used to build the throne of King Solomon. Once he arrived at the heart of Africa, he learnt of the majestic ruins belonging to a city that "could never have been built by the local peoples." On September 5, 1871, Mauch was the first European to set foot in the Great Zimbabwe.

Based on the legend nourished in 1552 by the Portuguese explorer João de

Barros in his book *De Asia*, Mauch continued to believe that the gigantic buildings were a relic of the Queen of Sheba's mythical kingdom. The book described a fort built with gigantic blocks of stone that, according to the narrator, must have been the palace of Axum, the kingdom's capital.

During the golden period of European colonialism, under the ideological drive of Cecil Rhodes, the founder of Rhodesia, innumerable attempts were made to demonstrate that the Great Zimbabwe was the work of Mediterranean peoples, and it was in turn attributed to the Phoenicians, the Greeks, and then the Romans. It was only in the 1930s that David Randall-MacIver and Gertrude Caton-Thompson finally deduced that Zimbabwe – the greatest work of architecture in sub-Saharan Africa – was the most advanced example of an African civilization, which had then disappeared under mysterious circumstances.

The most widely accepted hypothesis argues that the word Zimbabwe is derived from an expression used by the Shona (a Bantu-speaking people) meaning "houses of stone," but some experts prefer the meaning "worshiped houses" to indicate either the religious buildings or rulers' residences. Whichever it may be, the Great Zimbabwe is all that remains of

an extraordinary city built between the twelfth and fourteenth centuries. This was a period in which this African region enjoyed particular prosperity as a result of trading ivory and gold for goods from the Orient in ports like Safala, in Mozambique.

It is still unclear whether it was the ancestors of the Shona, Lemba, or Venda peoples to build the city, whose ruins cover an area of over 1,700 acres. It is divided into three sets of constructions: the Great Enclosure (which is by far the most impressive), the Hill Complex, and the Valley Complex. The first, which may have been a king's residence, is an elliptical structure with a perimeter of 800 feet, and walls up to 33 feet high and 16 thick that required a million blocks of granite to build. As in other buildings in the Great Zimbabwe, the blocks of stone were perfectly cut and smoothed so that they required no lime to hold them together. This is perhaps the most surprising aspect, as the buildings have remained unaltered for centuries without any material to hold the blocks together.

The Hill Complex is oval shaped (measuring about 330 by 150 feet) and contains rocky spurs and large masses of granite. The largest structure is the Western Enclosure, with walls up to 26 feet high on which there were originally towers and monoliths at regular intervals. The walls in the Valley Complex would have ringed about 50 houses probably belonging to the most important people in the city, given that most of the population had to live in mud huts that have not survived to this day.

Archaeologists agree that at the height of its prosperity the Great Zimbabwe had to have about 20,000 inhabitants, and that it had been abandoned by the fifteenth century without any apparent reason. Although the peoples in the region today are unable to clarify the mystery in any way, and there are no written records, it is certain that the Great Zimbabwe was the work of an African people. Such is the pride in it that, when independence was gained in 1980, the country adopted the name of the city, thus canceling Cecil Rhodes from its history.

190 top The raised position of Hill Complex – a granite block construction enclosed by an oval wall measuring 108 by 49 yards – reflected the social, political, and religious prestige of those who lived there.

190-191 The largest stone construction in sub-Saharan Africa, the Great Enclosure is an elliptical structure with a perimeter of 264 yards. To raise its walls, a million blocks of granite were required, with a total weight of 15,000 tons.

190 bottom The sector in the photo, located inside the Great Enclosure, contains what were probably the quarters of the ruler's many wives. The sovereign himself had his own residence in an area on top of the hill, the Hill Complex.

191 left This detail from the upper part of the outer circle of the Great Enclosure shows its decoration: the zigzag represents a snake, the traditional symbol of fertility among the Bantu.

191 top right Most experts believe that the high walls (seen here from the inside) were not defensive but symbolized the power of the people who were united and faithful to the sovereign.

191 bottom right The perfectly smoothed walls of the Great Enclosure did not require mortar. Each row was laid slightly inwards relative to the one before it, giving the construction greater stability and balance.

List of the Sites

Asia

Man's earliest ancestors in Asia evolved in an isolated context for roughly two million years before succumbing to the waves of migration by *Homo sapiens* from Africa about 50,000 years ago. This hypothesis is supported by finds in two of the most interesting paleo-anthropological sites in the world: Sangiran in Indonesia and Zhoukoudian in China. In the first, the remains of about 50 individuals have been found that were initially named *Pithecanthropus erectus*, and are now known as *Homo erectus*. In the second, a skull dating to half a million years ago was discovered in the 1920s in a cave near the Chinese capital and is therefore known as Peking Man to this day.

Above all, Asia can be considered the cradle of human civilization, the place where man passed from the nomadic life of the hunter-gatherer to the sedentary life of the farmer. Writing was invented in Mesopotamia more than 5,000 years ago, and in the centuries before and immediately after the start of the Christian era, it was in Asia that the crossroads of the great religions were laid. In the Middle East and Arabian Peninsula, the great monotheist faiths were born, thereafter coming into contact, by way of the commercial route of the Silk Road, with the Buddhism and Hinduism of India, the Confucianism of China, and the Shintoism of Japan.

The great religions and the civilizations that prospered from agriculture and trade, despite their eventual decline, were responsible for most of the archaeological heritage of Asia. The early spread of Buddhism stimulated the art of the Gandhara School in Afghanistan and Pakistan, where the symbols of the new religion merged with the forms of Hellenistic art. Hinduism gave rise to places like Khajuraho, Hampi, and Mahabalipuram in India, and Prambanan in Indonesia. Ajanta and Sanchi in India, Borobudur in Indonesia, and Paharpur in present-day Bangladesh were Buddhist centers. But it was in Southeast Asia that this conjunction of religions found its highest artistic expression, as in the temples of Angkor for example, where the architecture altered to follow the change in faith of the Khmer rulers, and in the thousands of sacred Buddhist images in the caves of Mogao, Longmen, and Yungang.

Asia's archaeological heritage also celebrates the early expansion of Islam and short-lived trading civilizations like at Hatra in Iraq, the Nabataean city of Petra in Jordan, and the Phoenician towns of Baalbek and Tyre, not to mention the many ruins of cities on the remote borders of the Roman Empire.

The history of the Asian civilizations is also the history of individuals. Clear traces were left behind by legendary commanders such as Alexander the Great – apparent in the art of Gandhara – and the Moghul emperors. Likewise, the most magnificent tomb in history was built for Qin Shi Huangdi, the founder of the Chinese Empire, which has been protected for over two thousand years by a silent Terracotta Army.

Nemrut Dagi
TURKEY

In February 2003, Turkish archaeologist Mahmud Arslan announced the discovery of the burial chamber of Antiochus I, king of Commagene, inside the stone tumulus on the top of the 7,237-foot Mount Nemrut. Before the arrival of Arslan and his team of forty or so archaeologists and geologists, many scholars had attempted in vain to penetrate the mound of stones 165 feet high and 500 across, but only modern equipment made it possible to reach the four-sided chamber that had been cut out of the living rock and then sealed within it. Inside, three sarcophagi were found containing the remains of Antiochus I, his father Mithridates Callinicus, and another unidentified person.

Thanks to this discovery, a fundamental piece in understanding of one of the most mysterious places in Turkey has been added to the puzzle. In a spectacular position on a peak in the Taurus Mountains in eastern Anatolia, a geologist in the service of the Ottomans drew the megalomaniac personality of King Antiochus I out from the mists of history when he identified the site of Nemrut Dagi at the end of the nineteenth century.

Born in 80 BC out of the fragmentation of the Seleucid Empire, which had in turn come into being with the breakup of Alexander the Great's empire, the kingdom of Commagene acted as a buffer between the Roman and Persian empires. Its founder, Mithridates Callinicus, allied himself with Rome, but when his son Antiochus I came to the throne in 69 BC, the new king believed he could survive independently by implementing a policy in which he would provide information to the Persians though maintaining friendly relations with the Romans. Antiochus I also invented a genealogy that allowed him to claim

descent from Alexander the Great and, before him, from the gods of Olympus, but his boastful parentage brought him no benefit. After him, the kings of Commagene were no more than Roman puppets and, in AD 72, Emperor Vespasian put an end to the foolish situation by incorporating the kingdom into the province of Syria.

To judge by the wonderful temples and tumulus (Hierotheseion) that he had built for himself on Nemrut Dagi, Antiochus I

considered himself a great ruler. He left a long inscription on the site (the *Nomos*, composed of 217 lines of text) from which not only his pretentious claims to be descended from the gods can be deduced, but also those that his kingdom would last forever.

Three platforms were excavated in the rock next to the mound of stones. The one on the north side was used as accommodation for priests; its boundary stones still exist, but the bas-reliefs that

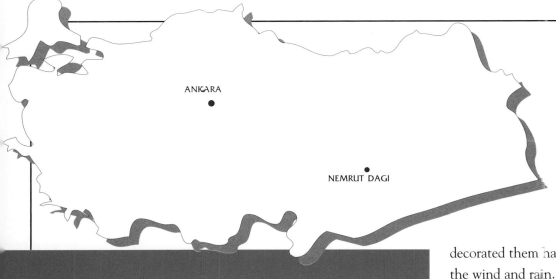

194-195 On the west terrace are the remains of five majestic statues. In the foreground, the head of Zeus sculpted from a single block weighing 8 tons can be seen. Zeus was associated with the Persian god Orosmasdes and is recognizable by his curly beard and stern gaze.

195 top Heracles (left) and Mithridates I greet one another in a bas-relief at Nemrut Dagi. Familiarity between heroes and kings was a common theme in these reliefs; in this case, the Commagene rulers wished to conceal in part their dependence on Rome.

decorated them have been worn away by the wind and rain. However, the two to the east and west are monumental temple complexes, in each of which have been found the remains of five superb statues. Though they are now scattered on the ground, they once stood between 26 and 33 feet tall and were each formed of blocks of stone weighing over eight tons. They are interesting for their iconography in which the syncretism of Greek and Persian deities is evident. On both the platforms, Zeus is associated with the Persian god Ahura Mazda, then Apollo and Mithras, Heracles and Atagnes, Tyche (the Commagenean goddess of fertility), and Antiochus I. The tiaras worn on their heads, which now lie on the ground, are Persian, as are the clothes they wear in the platform's bas-reliefs illustrating Antiochus in the presence of the gods.

The most enigmatic figure in Nemrut Dagi is that of a lion carved on the west platform. On his mane, there are 19 stars, on his neck a crescent moon, and on his back the planets Mars, Jupiter, and Mercury. According to experts, the relief has a precise astronomic significance. Study of the various elements has led to the conclusion that they represent a particular date: July 7, 62 BC. Perhaps that was the day Antiochus I conceived the crazy idea of his immortality.

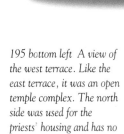

195 bottom left A view of the west terrace. Like the east terrace, it was an open temple complex. The north side was used for the priests' housing and has no statues.

195 bottom right The east terrace in the clear morning light. On the left is the effigy of a lion; further away are the heads of five gods wearing Persian-style headdresses.

Hierapolis - Pamukkale

TURKEY

DENIZLI PLAIN
REGISTRATION: 1988
CRITERIA: C (III) (IV); N (III)

The city of Hierapolis was built to dominate the valley of the Lykos River along the road joining inner Anatolia to the Mediterranean. During the centuries of Roman dominion, it was the most famous baths center in the empire. The noblewomen of the imperial court would make long, tiring journeys to bathe in its beneficent, rust-colored waters. They would lie in them for hours, washing themselves with laurel-scented soap, and then present themselves to their men with their heads encircled with bunches of grapes.

The place where these beauty cures took place was – and still is – as poetic as it is extraordinary, with its natural pools on terraces of travertine that the incessant action of the water has covered with a white calcareous coating resembling cotton wool. In fact, the Turks named the place Pamukkale, meaning "Castle of Cotton."

Under the aegis of UNESCO for its naturalistic characteristics and historic importance, Hierapolis-Pamukkale was founded around 190 BC by Eumenes II, a king of the Attalid dynasty, on the site of an underground spring where the Lydian and Phrygian peoples had long worshiped the mother goddess Cybele. The king called the place Hierapolis in tribute to Hiera, the wife of Telephus, the legendary king of Pergamum. A little less than a century later, Attalus III, another king of Pergamum, ceded the city – which already had some remarkable buildings in the elegant Hellenistic architectural style – to the Romans, who placed it under the jurisdiction of the governor of Ephesus.

Situated in a highly seismic zone, two earthquakes struck Hierapolis in AD 17

and 60, and the reconstruction work, though done over the Greek urban plan, gave the city a typically Roman appearance. The place centered on the underground spring the Romans had dedicated to the god of the afterworld, calling it the Plutonium. From there, as Strabo recounted, toxic vapors emerged that were lethal to anyone except the priests; they demonstrated their powers by making doves fly through the fumes, which died immediately. The city's main street was the colonnaded Plateia, built by the proconsul Sextus Julius Frontinus around AD 80. He was also responsible for the construction of the city's monumental entrance arch dedicated to the emperor Domitian.

Recent excavations along the Plateia have unearthed the remains of a spacious agora lined by shops, and, in a side street, the elegant House of the Ionic Capitals. Little remains of the fabulous marble temple dedicated to Apollo, which was

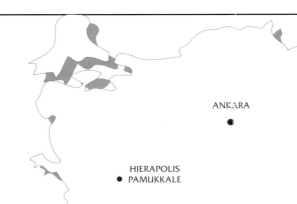

196 top A Roman tomb on one of the travertine terraces. With its covering of white limestone, the site on which old Hierapolis stood earned itself the name Pamukkale, Turkish for "Cotton castle."

ANKARA

HIERAPOLIS
● PAMUKKALE

196-197 The frons scaenae of the Roman theater, which, between 193 and 211 AD, was given an elegant structure with historiated balconies, windows and porticoes with Corinthian capitals in imitation of an imperial palace.

196 bottom The Roman theater is used for performances of music and plays. Recently restored, it still has 46 rows of seats that can hold 6,000 spectators, as opposed to the 10,000 of the original theater.

197 top The baths were built in the second century AD and their excellent state of conservation is due to the fact that 200 years later they were transformed into a basilica. Hierapolis was an important Christian center and the site of the martyrdom of the apostle Philip.

197 bottom A majestic funerary monument (heroon) from the first century BC in the Hierapolis necropolis. The necropolis has more than 1,200 Hellenistic, Roman, and Christian graves and is the largest in Asia Minor.

erected in the third century over a sanctuary built in the Hellenistic era, or of the nymphaeum of the Tritons, which featured a fountain with a 76-yard-long basin surrounded by columns on three sides. The second-century baths, however, are in good condition, as is the theater, built in the reign of Flavius and enlarged and embellished with bas-reliefs of Apollo and Artemis between 193 and 211 by emperor Septimius Severus. The city was experiencing its greatest period at that time, not just because of the completion of its luxurious baths complex, but also owing to the wealth generated by the marble quarries and textile manufacture. From the first half of the first century AD,

Hierapolis was an important center of Christianity, though the apostle Philip was martyred there with his seven children in the year 80. In the fifth century, the Byzantines built the Martyrion, a majestic octagonal basilica, in his honor, though today it is half in ruins.

Yet, the most fascinating feature left behind by the civilizations that uninterruptedly inhabited Hierapolis is the necropolis lying a short distance away from the ancient city. The more than 1,200 graves include Hellenistic tumuli, elaborate Roman sarcophagi, and Christian vaulted tombs, making the Hierapolis necropolis the largest and best conserved in Anatolia.

Aleppo

SYRIA

REGION OF ALEPPO
REGISTRATION: 1986
CRITERIA: C (III) (IV)

Aleppo shares with Damascus the honor of being the longest continuously inhabited city in history. However, it maintains its links with the past to a greater degree than the present-day Syrian capital. It is a city-souk in which the Arab traditions of the Middle Ages seem anything but remote. More than in any other city of the Levant, trade is still governed by rules and conventions unchanged since the age of the Mamluks. In addition, it contains many examples attesting to Arab resistance against the Crusaders. There are fewer examples of the period in which Aleppo was ruled by the Byzantines, and those relating to more ancient periods seem to have disappeared completely, at least to the eye. Despite that, Aleppo has been included in this book on archaeological sites in homage to the opinion of experts who consider the city a jigsaw puzzle as extraordinary as it is complex, given that its innumerable pieces are hidden in the many historical layers of its monuments.

Aleppo was founded about eight thousand years ago. The first written references to it were found in the Euphrates Valley in the archives of Mari, which mention a city named Halap as being the capital of the Amorite kingdom of Yamkhad. In those long ago eras, Halap was more affected by Mesopotamian influence than that of Damascus, which looked more towards the civilizations of Egypt and Palestine. The kingdom of the Amorites remained stable until 1286 BC, the year of the epic battle of Kadesh, when it fell to the power of the Hittites. Not so long after, the Hittites were threatened by the arrival, from the sea, of the Egyptians, and Halap remained at the center of a series of city-states until the eighth century BC when it was taken by the Assyrians. In 539 BC, the Assyrians lost

198 top The hill on which the Citadel of Aleppo stands has been the site of human settlements for the past eight thousand years. The walls seen today were built by the Mamelukes in the sixteenth century to replace the older defensive structures. The Mamelukes also built the monumental bridge, preceded by an imposing tower, that gave entry to the city.

198 bottom Qalaat Semaan Hill on which the basilica and its related buildings were built between 476 and 521 in honor of Saint Simeon Stylite. The hill dominates the plain near Aleppo.

199 The majestic ruins of Saint Simeon, a site important to eastern Christianity found outside the city, conserve the remains of the 40-foot-tall column (visible in the middle of the picture) on which the saint lived and, in 459, died.

out to the Persians, but they too were defeated in 333 BC by the Seleucid troops of Alexander the Great, who gave the city the Macedonian name of Beroia. Under Alexander's rule, the city expanded in size and the first defensive walls were built around the citadel, the ancient heart of the Amorite city standing on a natural hill to the east of the city itself.

The current appearance of the citadel mostly dates back to the period of the Mamluks, who rebuilt it in the fourteenth century after the fortifications erected by the Umayyads (the first Arabs to reach Aleppo) were devastated by Tamerlaine. Nonetheless, the citadel retains two splendid lions carved in basalt that were most probably part of the Hittite temple from the tenth century BC. Before becoming a military bulwark, Aleppo's

citadel had been used for ceremonial purposes dedicated to Hadad, a Mesopotamian god that the Seleucids associated with Zeus when they conquered the city. With the conquest of Syria by Rome in 64 BC, the hill retained its religious functions. Many years afterwards, Julian the Apostate, one of the last pagan emperors of Rome, made a sacrifice there to Jupiter, a highly political gesture in a province that was by then strongly Christian.

The presence of the Byzantines in Aleppo today is almost negligible, though a plethora of archaeological sites are located a short distance from the city, most importantly the fascinating remains of the basilica and column of Saint Simeon Stylite, and those of the Byzantine "dead cities." Archaeologists are agreed,

however, that the Halawiye Madrasa, built by the Umayyads next to the Great Mosque, rests on the foundations of the cathedral of Aleppo founded in the sixth century in honor of Saint Helena, the mother of Emperor Constantine. Ancient columns with Byzantine style capitals can be seen in both the *madrasa* and the Great Mosque, which were taken from the Christian building that, in turn, was built on the site of the agora of Hellenistic Beroia.

Other vestiges of Aleppo's ancient past are waiting to be revealed. They lie beneath the maze of alleyways and caravanserai (the *khan*) that make the city a setting worthy of *A Thousand and One Nights*.

ALEPPO

DAMASCUS

Palmyra

SYRIA

PROVINCE OF HOMS
REGISTRATION: 1980
CRITERIA: **C** (I) (II) (IV)

200-201 *The fascinating ruins of Palmyra are surrounded by desert and overlooked by the hill on which the Qalaat ibn Maan stands, a fort built by the Arabs in the twelfth century.*

200 bottom *A view of the monumental arch and colonnaded street. Originally lined entirely with porticoes, it was divided into four sections and cut right through the city from east to west for 1,300 yards.*

A sumptuous procession with elephants and gladiators parades through the streets of Rome. At its center, the triumphal chariot of the emperor Aurelian is preceded by a woman on foot dressed only in Eastern-style jewelry. Attached to her arms and legs are gold chains so heavy they have to be carried by a slave. This story is recounted in *Historia Augusta*, a monumental work celebrating the military triumphs of Rome. The year is AD 274 and the prisoner is Zenobia, the most beautiful woman in the East, and one who dared to challenge the power of Rome. The *Historia* continues, relating that Aurelian, who conquered her in battle, succumbed to her beauty, made her his lover, and gave her a villa in Tivoli.

Zenobia is one of the legendary women of antiquity. In addition to her beauty, it is known that she was the wife of Septimius Odenatus, ruler of Palmyra and faithful to Rome. We know that she learned from him the skills of government and military strategies, and that she learnt Greek, Latin, and Egyptian at court. She bore Septimius a son but had him assassinated so that she could take power. No one at the Palmyran court suspected Zenobia, with the result that she was able give the title of emperor to her son and that of *Augusta* for herself.

She allied herself to the Persians and began campaigns of conquest in the direction of Turkey and Egypt with the aim of creating an Eastern empire to counter the power of Rome. Nevertheless, her dreams of glory were smashed when Aurelian quickly abandoned his campaign against the Goths in order to send his troops to tame the rebels in Syria.

Zenobia deserved her punishment. Though Palmyra had always enjoyed a large degree of autonomy (it was part of the Roman province *Syria Phoenice*), it had become the most important caravan city in the East thanks to Roman support. In AD 124, Hadrian honored it with the title *Civitas Libera*, and it was the Romans, as consumers of exotic goods, who had permitted the city to extend its commercial traffic as far as India and

China, with the result that it became fabulously wealthy.

The first evidence of the existence of a settlement called Tadmor is found in an Assyrian contract from the nineteenth century BC. The place name, now used again by the modern village found on the edge of the archaeological site of Palmyra, has been interpreted by experts as derived from the Semitic word *tamr*, meaning "date palms" in Arabic. This etymological root coincides with the

201 top The monumental arch was built by Septimius Severus (AD 193–211) when Palmyra enjoyed a period of great construction.

201 center The best-conserved section of the colonnaded street lies between the propylaea of the temple of Bel and the monumental arch. Note the brackets two-thirds of the way up the columns that originally held statues of prominent and wealthy Palmyran citizens.

201 bottom The remains of the temple of Baal-Shamin, lord of the Heavens in the Semitic pantheon believed to be responsible for the rain.

202 top The theater of Palmyra (second century AD) was one of the most magnificent in the Middle East. The stage is 157 feet wide and 34 deep; the backdrop imitated the façade of a palace of which only the ground floor has survived, with colonnades and doors crowned by niches.

202-203 The elegant Tetrapylon was formed by a platform on which four superb buildings once stood, each of which housed a statue. Only one of the original pink Aswan-marble columns remains, the others are faithful copies.

202 bottom left Consecrated in 32 BC, the cella was the real temple of Bel, to which access was granted only to the priests. The statue of the god flanked by those of Yarhibol and Aglibol, the gods of the Sun and Moon were found here.

202 bottom right The imposing cella of the temple of Bel lies at the center of an immense court (230 by 224 yards) lined by high walls. Bel was the principal god of the Semitic pantheon and was associated with the Roman Jupiter.

203 top Standing at the opposite end of the long colonnaded street from the temple of Bel, the funerary temple (third century AD) was in fact a magnificent tomb preceded by a portico with six columns.

203 bottom Situated in the north section of the city on a transversal road that starts at the Tetrapylon, the temple of Baal-Shamin is in excellent condition considering that in the fifth century its cella was turned into a Christian church.

Latin name of the city, also derived from the word "palm." References to Tadmor are made in Babylonian tablets from the age of Hammurabi and, much later, in the accounts of Alexander the Great's war against the Persians.

From the first century BC on, during the Roman era, there is an increase in the number of material and literary references to the growth and development of Palmyra. The city of merchants seemed to enjoy a privileged position between the two major empires, the Roman and Persian. In AD 77, in his *Naturalis Historia*, Pliny the Elder wrote, "Palmyra is a noble city for the site it occupies, for the richness of its soil, and for the pleasantness of its waters. Expanses of sand surround its fields on every side, and it is as though it were isolated from the world by nature."

Despite its population being mostly Semitic, Palmyra gradually embraced the Roman political and social model, though it maintained an Eastern style in its art and customs. The ruins that can be seen today date mostly to the second and third centuries AD and reflect both a mix of styles and the increasing wealth of its citizens. Well-to-do merchants competed to embellish the city with ever more magnificent monuments.

The remains of the ancient city around the Efqa spring, which supplied abundant water for the crops of olives, dates, and pomegranates, cover an area of about four square miles. Though it had no particular city plan and its residential districts were typical of the cities of the East, the growth of Palmyra reflects the Greco-Roman principle of autonomy. Therefore, there was a large colonnaded street 1,300 yards long and 24 yards wide, a theater, a baths complex, and

204-205 With those of Artaban and the "Three Brothers," the tomb of Bolha, son of Nabushuri (AD 89), is one of the most refined in Palmyra. Like the others, it is formed by a gallery topped by a barrel vault onto which the bays face. The bays contained the burial niches decorated with stucco friezes and sculptures.

204 bottom left These tower tombs are among the oldest and most original funerary constructions in Palmyra. They are mostly square, stand on a stepped platform, and are formed by various levels connected by a flight of steps.

205 top right This lady wearing a soft fabric headdress has been immortalized on a funerary effigy. The statues provide valuable information on the clothing and jewelry that were in style in Palmyra.

205 bottom A funerary stele decorated with bas-reliefsis held in the site's archaeological museum. As occurred in this case, stelae often show the dead during real events in their lives.

204 bottom right The tomb of Ehlabel (AD 103) is an elegant tower four stories high. The terrace gives a view over the Valley of the Tombs. The family buried here was one of the richest in the city and responsible for the construction of the temple of Nebo.

205 top left The details and unique facial features suggest that these funerary statues were realistic portraits of the dead. They were referred to as nafsnâ, a word that in Semitic languages means "soul" or "person."

widespread use of Greek architectural orders, in particular Corinthian.

The colonnaded street is divided into four sections. The first runs from the monumental arch to the Temple of Bel. The second continues to the Tetrapylon – composed of four pedestals with four columns each – and was lined by the baths, the Temple of Nebo, the agora, and the Senate, whereas a cross street led to the Temple of Baal-Shamin. The third section cut through the residential quarters and led to the Funerary Temple, and the last section ended at the Gate of Diocletian that gave onto the Valley of the Tombs.

The most impressive temple is the one dedicated to Bel, the supreme Palmyran deity, construction of which began in AD 32. The enormous courtyard measures 230 yards by 224 and had a pool for ritual bathing, a sacrificial altar, a banquet room, and a *cella*. The cella was the most sacred section of the temple and was reserved for use by the priests. It contained a statue of Bel between Yarhibol and Aglibol, the Palmyran gods of the Sun and the Moon. The coffered geometric decorations and rosettes on the

ceiling of the *cella* feature elements that later became typical of Byzantine and Arab art.

The Palmyrans were highly skilled and original in their sculptural art, especially in their carving of bas-reliefs. Those in the best state of conservation decorate the tombs – built in either hypogeum or tower form – of the rich families. Made from limestone, they feature detailed portrayals of the deceased with facial features, clothing, and jewelry. Of the few tombs open to the public, the most interesting are those of the Elahbel family, for the beauty of its sculptures, and of the Three Brothers, for its delicate frescoes.

Following Zenobia's downfall, the city began to languish, and though emperor Diocletian later gave Palmyra a new boost by stationing an immense military camp there, the city's fate was already marked out. It was just ruins when, in the twelfth century, the Arabs built a castle on the rocky spur overlooking the site, but this fort too was soon abandoned. What had once been the magnificent and ambitious Palmyra was soon covered over by the desert.

Bosra

SYRIA

Hauran, Governorate of Deraa

Registration: 1980

Criteria: C (i) (iii) (vi)

206 top A panel from a floor mosaic found in excellent condition inside the theater is yet another indication of the refinement of the building and the wealth of the ancient city's inhabitants.

DAMASCUS

BOSRA

In the center of Bosra a small bakery has been built over foundations, and probably with the very stones, of an ancient Roman shop. Early in the morning, it bakes *khobz*, unleavened Arab bread. The women of the place line up to buy it and, while it is still boiling hot, place it on the columns of the *cardus maximus* to dry. Bicycles pass on this Roman road, and, at midday, encounter the children as they get out of school and,

206 bottom The elaborate Corinthian capitals are all that remains of the decoration on the theater's frons scaenae, once embellished with polychrome marbles, false windows, statues, and bas-reliefs. Many of the columns seen today are copies of the pink granite originals brought from Egypt.

207 top The colonnaded way was the city's main street. On the left, note the superb Roman baths building that was built between the late-second and early-third centuries AD.

207 bottom The remains of the market lined by crypto-porticoes. It was a large commercial area with a row of shops 116 yards long and 13 feet wide.

in the afternoon, head off to play soccer on an improvised field in front of the nymphaeum.

After Palmyra, Bosra is the most important and most visited Roman archaeological site in Syria. However, the definition "archaeological site" is not entirely accurate, as there are still people actually living inside the ruins, thereby increasing, in many opinions, the charm of the place.

Although Egyptian papyruses from the second millennium BC refer to a settlement called Busrana, Bosra only became an important city in AD 70 when the Nabataeans, who had ceded Petra to the Romans, moved their capital there. In AD 106, the Nabataeans were unable to fend off Trajan's troops, and the Romans turned the place into the administrative center of the Roman province of Arabia with the name *Nova Traiana Bosra*. They also designated the surrounding region of *Auranitis* (today Hauran) as an area for the cultivation of grain.

The influence of Rome, and the stable presence of 5,000 legionaries, modified the appearance of the Nabataean city, though the irregular layout typical of Eastern cities was retained. From the second century on,

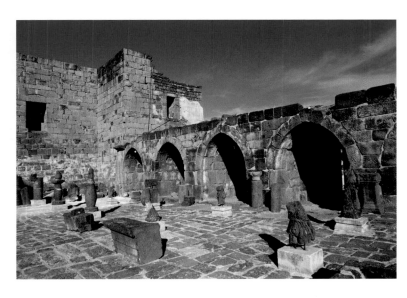

206-207 The jewel of the city is the theater, built in the second century AD and magnificently preserved thanks to the Ayyubids, who filled the cavea with earth and built a fort around it. It is one of the rare Roman buildings of this type not to have been built in a natural hollow, and it boasts superb acoustics.

Bosra was an important stop on the Trajan Way, the commercial route joining Damascus to the Red Sea. It was considered highly by several emperors, most important of whom were Alexander Severus (222–235) and Philip the Arab (244–249), a native of nearby Shabha, who honored the city with the title *metropolis*.

With the growth in its importance, the city was endowed with impressive buildings made from dark basalt. The *cardus maximus*, the main city street, terminated in a monumental arch built at the start of the third century in honor of the Third Cyrenaic Legion. It is still possible to admire the remains of the huge marketplace, a crypto-portico used to store grain, an elegant baths complex, a nymphaeum, a cistern to collect rainwater, and various houses.

The most spectacular of the monuments in Bosra is the theater, one of the best conserved from the Roman world, also representing one of the most outstanding examples of Arab military architecture in Syria. This apparent contradiction is quickly explained: in the twelfth century, when the Ayyubids conquered the city, these newcomers erected a fortification around the theater with lodgings for the troops. They also filled the cavea with earth with the result that the Roman structure survived undamaged to the modern day. Thirty or so years ago, archaeologists removed the soil to reveal a theater that could seat 6,000 spectators in 37 rows of seats. There is also a *frons scaenae* decorated with friezes and Corinthian columns.

The theater, however, is only the most evident example of architectural stratification in Bosra. The town also has a number of mosques, such as the Umar Mosque, built over a pagan temple, and Mabrak Mosque, which stands over the spot where the camel carrying the first copy of the *Koran* to Syria rested. Still an object of veneration for Muslims is the building that was once a Christian basilica (previously a third-century pagan building), as it was there that the prophet Mohammed had a conversation with the wise Nestorian monk Bahira. In the nineteenth century, members of the Druse sect settled around the ancient center of Bosra, after being chased out of Lebanon following religious conflict with Christians.

Baalbek

LEBANON

BEKAA VALLEY
REGISTRATION: 1984
CRITERIA: C (I) (IV)

In spite of its high-sounding name, Heliopolis, the "City of the Sun" founded by the Phoenicians, it was a city of modest wealth when Julius Caesar effortlessly conquered it in 15 BC. As was his custom, the emperor founded a colony there, which he named *Julia Augusta Felix Heliopolitana*, and stationed a legion on the site. At the same time, quite inexplicably, he decided to build there the most magnificent temple in the empire.

Considered one of the wonders of the world by historians of the fifth century, who were among the first to call it Baalbek, meaning "god (*Baal*) from the Bekaa Valley," the temple was dedicated to *Jupiter Heliopolitanus*. The building stands on a rectangular platform measuring 87 by 52 yards, made of stone blocks weighing at least 700 tons, and bordered by 54 columns seven feet three inches in diameter and 66 feet tall. Today only six columns still remain: eight were taken to Constantinople by Justinian to be used in construction of the Hagia Sophia, and the rest were either used to build another Byzantine basilica *in situ* (since destroyed) or were toppled by earthquakes. The temple held a gold statue of Jupiter, which was worshiped by pilgrims who visited from all corners of the Roman Empire.

Construction lasted about 150 years but was never completed, though the capitals and fragments of the architraves decorated with the heads of lions and bulls, acanthus leaves, and roses bear witness to the sophistication of the sculptural work, and many emperors committed themselves to

BAALBEK

BEIRUT

208 left Caracalla (AD 211–217) was responsible for the construction of the elegant propylaea, considered an entrance worth of the religious complex of Baalbek. These consist of a portico with 12 columns flanked by two towers.

208 right A view of the temple of Jupiter. Triliths (blocks of three monoliths each weighing between 750 and 1,000 tons) were used to build the massive platform on which it stands.

209 A fragment of the architrave and the 6 superb columns that remain standing in the temple of Jupiter. Of the other 48, 8 were taken to Constantinople for the construction of the basilica of Hagia Sophia, and the others have been destroyed.

making it as magnificent as Caesar had wished.

Around AD 60, Nero had a tower built in front of the temple that allowed pilgrims to view the statue of the god from a raised position. Trajan (AD 98–117) was responsible for the construction of an enormous entrance courtyard.

Measuring 123 yards per side, three of its sides were lined with 12 exedras, each of which was preceded by a portico with Egyptian pink-granite columns. Inscriptions inform us that the exedras provided shelter to the priests of the various communities and reception facilities to pilgrims of high birth.

In AD 145, Antoninus Pius ordered the construction of the Temple of Bacchus. Standing opposite the Temple of Jupiter, it covers an area measuring 75 by 39 yards. It is still in good condition and its elegant proportions, like the richness of its decorations, make it a masterpiece of Roman art. Inside, there were statues of the entire Roman pantheon that are still recognizable today, even though their faces have been smashed by iconoclastic Muslim invaders.

210 bottom A panoramic
view of the archaeological
site of Baalbek. The
Romans called the city
Heliopolis; the current
name dates to the fifth
century and means "god
[Baal] of the Bekaa Valley."

210-211 One of the
buildings that line the great
court of the temple of
Jupiter, which is reached by
a flight of steps. The
sanctuary was built on a
level 22 feet higher than the
other monuments at
Baalbek to underline its
importance.

211

The third temple at Baalbek was
built by Septimius Severus around AD
200, and its monumental propylaea by
his successor Caracalla. Dedicated to
Venus, the Severan temple is an elegant
pentagonal building surrounded by
columns and niches.

Eusebius of Caesarea, the first
historian of the Christian Church, wrote
horrified that here "men and women
couple without shame, and fathers and
husbands allow their daughters and
wives to prostitute themselves to please
the goddess."
In fact, the Romans had modified
the practice of sacred prostitution taken
from the local Semitic tradition, in the
same way that the divine triad of
Baalbek was the fruit of the syncretism
of the Roman and Phoenician religions:
Jupiter was identified with Baal, Venus
with Astarte, and Bacchus, their son,
with the spirit of nature.

Since 1955, Baalbek has come back
to life and a "new syncretism," thanks to
a music festival of renown. Now the
majestic columns of the Temple of
Jupiter provide a backdrop to artists of
the caliber of Herbert von Karajan and
Mstislav Rostropovich.

Tyre
LEBANON

Sour, Region of South Lebanon
Registration: 1984
Criteria: C (iii) (vi)

The Phoenicians were a people organized into city-states without any concept of overall unity; in fact, we do not even know what they called themselves. The term "Phoenicians" is derived from the Greek word *phoinikes*, which is what Homer called them, and was taken from their most precious product, the crimson dye called *phoinix*.

Worth its weight in gold, *phoinix* was the pride of Tyre, the city owing its foundation to the "discovery" of the dye. Legend has it that the Phoenician god Melqart fell in love with a nymph named Tyre. One morning, while the two were taking a walk on the beach followed by the god's dog, the animal crunched up a shell, staining its mouth crimson as it did so. When the nymph saw it, she told Melqart she would offer him her favors if he would give her a dress of that color, and so Melqart collected as many mollusks as were needed to satisfy the nymph's wishes and, in consequence, his own.

The area close to that beach, where in the meantime Tyre had been established, was visited in the fifth century BC by Herodotus of Halicarnassus, a figure known in the Greek world as the "father of history." The scholar had undertaken his travels due to his desire to know the place to which the Greeks owed their written language, given that they attributed the invention of their alphabet to Cadmos of Tyre. At that time, the cult of Melqart was associated with that of the Greek god Heracles, and Tyre was dominated by a temple dedicated to him. In his *Histories*, Herodotus writes that he asked the priests about the era the temple

was constructed, and that he was told it was 2,300 years old, the same as the city. In truth, the temple – like Solomon's Temple in Jerusalem, which was probably also built by laborers from Tyre – had been built in the tenth century BC by king Hiram I to replace a legendary building that had had a column of gold and another of emerald.

During the era of Hiram I, the city of Tyre, which had become the most important port in the eastern Mediterranean due to its industry and trade in crimson dye, consisted of two parts separated by a strip of sea half a mile long. One section stood on the mainland and the other on two small islands. Both islands were protected by fortifications and boasted temples, palaces, and markets.

Although its commercial monopoly had been undermined since the ninth century BC by the growth of Carthage (which was founded, ironically, by a colony of rebels from Tyre), the Phoenician city continued to flourish and remained unassailable until 332 BC. In that year, Alexander the Great took the city after a siege lasting seven months, the time required for the Macedon army to build a breakwater joining the mainland to the islands and to bring their deadly war machines up against the walls.

Today, only a shadow remains of that fabulous city, today half-buried under sand, as is the stretch of sea that was crossed by Alexander's breakwater. In any case, with the exception of the Phoenician port, which is the object of underwater excavation, the remains are mostly from the Roman period. The most spectacular are those of the hippodrome. Built in the second century AD, it could seat 20,000

spectators and has a U-shaped race track divided into two laps by stone signs (*metae*). To the north of the hippodrome lie the remains of the Roman aqueduct, a triumphal arch, and a street lined with sarcophagi carved with bas-reliefs. On a promontory overlooking the sea, there are the remains of a baths complex and a colonnaded street with fragments of Byzantine mosaics from the fifth century.

After the Romans, Tyre was taken by the Crusaders, who completed the destruction of the ancient Phoenician city. Before a new Arab city came to be built, in the thirteenth century the body of Frederick Barbarossa was buried there, in the false expectation that his royal remains would be transported to Jerusalem.

213

212 The ruins of the Roman baths. Water for the baths, like for the houses in Tyre, was provided by an aqueduct that ran along the north boundary of the city.

212-213 The colonnaded street runs about 550 yards east-west. It is entirely paved and interrupted about halfway by the second-century-AD triumphal arch.

213 bottom left Marble sarcophagi line both sides of the colonnaded street. They are decorated with bas-reliefs, many of which depict bucolic scenes, or episodes from the Iliad and other epic poems.

213 bottom right The ruins of the hippodrome that could once seat 20,000 spectators. Built by the Romans probably in the second century AD, the building remained beneath a thick layer of sand until 30 years ago.

BEIRUT

TYRE

Masada

ISRAEL

REGION OF TAMAR
REGISTRATION: 2001
CRITERIA: C (III) (IV) (VI)

214 top An aerial view of Masada. Begun in 1963, excavation has not only unearthed Herod's buildings but also vestiges of a settlement that seems to date to the Chalcolithic age, around 4000 BC.

214-215 The rock of Masada dominates the desert of Judaea close to the west bank of the Dead Sea and the oasis of Ein Gedi. The top of the mountain is flat and measures 330 by 660 yards in the shape of a diamond.

215 top left Covering 43,000 square feet, the west palace was where the Zealots barricaded themselves against the Roman siege in AD 73. Though they were not captured, they committed mass suicide and their skeletons were found in the fort.

215 top right When Masada was occupied by the Zealots, the furnishings in the west palace and Herod's luxury villa were removed to make space for the poor families of this Jewish sect.

JERUSALEM

MASADA

In the most moving pages of the *History of the Jewish War*, the historian Flavius Josephus reports the words of Eleazar Ben Yair, head of the Zealots besieged by the Romans in the fort of Masada, "while our hands have a sword to grip, they will do us an act of kindness: we will die before our enemies can reduce us to slavery, and as free men we will bid farewell to life with our wives and children." He tells that on that dramatic night in AD 73, the Zealots embraced their nearest and dearest and then committed mass suicide.

The next morning, when the Romans reached the fort, they found 960 bodies and huge quantities of burned household goods. This was not the way in which they expected to tame the rebellion of the handful of Jews who fled Jerusalem following the destruction of the Temple, and who dared to challenge the power of Rome. Yet, this was a bitter victory for the Romans, despite Masada having been considered virtually unassailable.

Masada hill overlooks the desert of Judaea close to the west bank of the Dead Sea and the oasis of Ein Gedi. Like a rocky pedestal, it is topped by a diamond-shaped plateau measuring 325

by 650 yards. The presence of a *wadi* (seasonal torrent) allowed Herod, king of Judaea from 37 BC to AD 4, to construct a permanent military garrison there. He ordered his engineers to dig a network of canals and water tanks that would collect the water from the *wadi*, but then, taken by the beauty of the landscape, decided to use the place as a residence as well.

His ambitious plan is still evident today. In the northern section of the plateau, the palace was built on three terraces connected by steps cut in the rock, with porticoed courtyards, floors decorated with geometric mosaics, and frescoed walls. Next to the palace are the storerooms that could hold an amazing quantity of goods, and next to those are a synagogue and baths building for the use of guests and high officials at Masada.

The most elaborate room in the baths is the *calidarium*, featuring a floor supported by 200 columns and sprinkled with terracotta apertures that allowed hot air to enter from a furnace beneath. The most impressive building in the complex is the west palace, which covered 5,000 square yards and was used as an administrative center. The rest of

215

215 bottom left One of the storerooms to in the south of the baths' complex. Before excavation began, these were not visible as they were covered by earth and debris. They were destroyed by the besieged Zealots to prevent the Romans from plundering their goods.

215 bottom right The pool inside Herod's villa. Water was provided via a system of channels from the wadi to the west of the fort, which conveyed the water into 12 cisterns, that combined with a capacity of over 10,000,000 gallons.

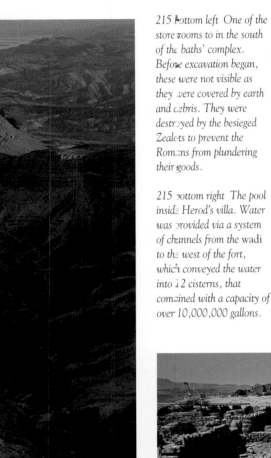

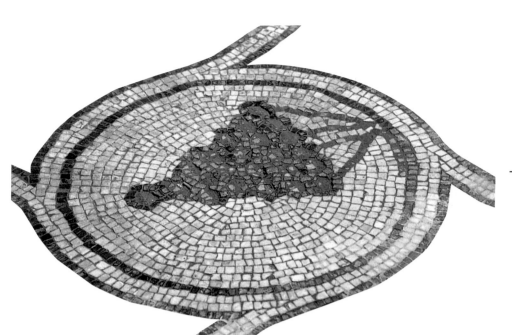

216 top One of the medallions decorated with fruit and geometric patterns from the mosaic floor in the audience room of the west palace. Built by Herod, this was the enormous administrative center of Masada.

217 Laid out on three terraces connected by flights of steps, Herod's royal villa was built on the north tip of the plateau. The size of the building and its elegant interiors are evidence of the man's ambition (king of Judaea from 37 BC to AD 4).

the area was occupied by accommodation for the troops.

Although Masada was identified in the nineteenth century, systematic excavation only began in 1963. In addition to the majestic ruins of the buildings, a great quantity of goods, coins, and skeletons (probably those of the Zealots) have been found. The remains of the fortifications built by the Romans during the siege can be clearly seen at the base of the hill.

Masada is a symbol of the extreme sacrifice made by the Jews for their freedom. Yet, the resistance and suicide of the Zealots does not appear in the Jewish sacred text, the *Talmud*, and the only written record is that of Flavius Josephus, who learnt of it after meeting two women who survived the massacre by hiding in a water conduit. However, Flavius Josephus was a traitor: he was born a Jew but he sold himself to the Romans, and, over the centuries, he was erased from Jewish collective memory. With him, the episode of Masada was also forgotten, until 1920 when the writer Isaac Lamdan composed a poem entitled *Masada*. It was this tale that inspired the revolt of the Jews in the Warsaw ghetto against the Nazis in World War II.

216 center left This small Byzantine chapel was built in the fifth century by monks living in the grottoes near the fort. The mosaics that decorated the floor have been completely destroyed.

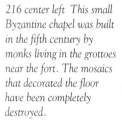

216 center right The lower terrace of Herod's villa overlooks the Dead Sea. To reach the fort, which in the past meant climbing a steep path, today visitors are transported by cable-car.

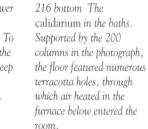

216 bottom The calidarium in the baths. Supported by the 200 columns in the photograph, the floor featured numerous terracotta holes, through which air heated in the furnace below entered the room.

Qusayr 'Amra

JORDAN

REGION OF AZRAQ
REGISTRATION: 1985
CRITERIA: C (I) (III) (IV)

The Arab dynasty of the Umayyads remained in power for a little less than a century, from AD 661 to 750, but their dominion expanded from Damascus, the capital, across North Africa as far as Spain, to central Asia and India. They even made contact with China from where – in exchange for the return of Chinese soldiers captured in battle – they took back the secret of papermaking.

Versed in art as much as war, they produced architectural works of great beauty, including what is known today as the Great Mosque of Damascus, buildings in honor of Allah in Andalusia, and a series of "castles in the desert" scattered across the region of Azraq, a little east of Amman, the modern capital of Jordan.

The exterior appearance of the castles gives the impression they were military constructions or caravan rest stops, but the castles of Azraq were in fact places for relaxation. Situated in or near oases, they were used as the base for hunting parties. They may also have been farms and could be used as retreats during periods when Damascus was scourged by epidemics. Yet, another function they fulfilled was to receive Bedouin chiefs, whose loyalty was of strategic importance for control of the territory. Though modest in size compared to other castles in the region, the Qusayr 'Amra was placed under UNESCO's protection for its exceptional frescoes, which are a unique example of the art of the first Islamic period.

Built by Walid I, caliph from 705 to 715, or, as is claimed by some experts, by his son Yazid II, the Qusayr 'Amra is situated on a natural island formed by the Wadi Butum, one of the seasonal torrents of the region. Originally, the castle was larger than can be seen today, and included a fort with an internal courtyard (of which the foundations remain) and gardens with fountains fed by a waterwheel. The two sandstone buildings that contained the audience hall and the *hammam* (baths) are in an excellent state of conservation. The first is 33 feet long and 20 wide with a barrel-vault ceiling (this form of vault later became typical of Islamic architecture) and three aisles; the two outer aisles end in an alcove, whereas the center one contained the throne.

The ceiling and wall frescoes are extensive. In one, known as the "fresco of the six kings," the figures of Roderick (king of the Visigoths), Krisa (the Sassanid ruler), the emperor of Byzantium, the *negus* of Abyssinia, the Chinese emperor, and the chief of the Turcomans have been identified. These

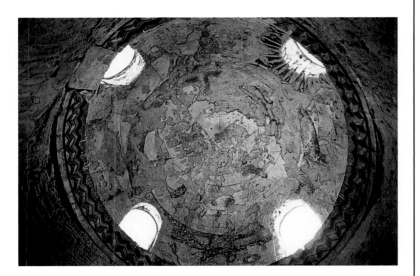

figures may represent either the enemies of Islam or leaders "of equal status" to the Umayyad caliph. The styles and subjects of the other frescoes reveal the influences of Hellenistic, Byzantine, and Persian art. There are hunting scenes in which a wild donkey is pushed towards a net by a group of men on horseback; dancers and musicians in a setting of exotic plants and animals; and scenes that celebrate manly virtues, with athletes competing in a rural setting.

The frescoes in the *hammam* are equally refined. The baths were of fundamental importance to social and religious rituals in the Islamic world, and the three rooms that they were composed of – the *frigidarium*, *tepidarium*, and *calidarium* – had various hunting scenes featuring the caliph, a splendid night sky of the northern hemisphere surrounded by the signs of the zodiac, and a series of scenes derived from classical mythology, with nude female figures representing poetry, philosophy, and history, or perhaps just female grace and beauty.

With the end of the Umayyad dynasty at the hands of the Abbasids of Baghdad, the chapter of figurative Islamic art came to an end. From the year 750 on, the religion prohibited any human or animal representation as sacrilege.

218-219 Qusayr 'Amra from above. The complex was originally larger than what is seen today, and included a fort with an inner courtyard and gardens with fountains powered by a waterwheel.

218 bottom left A niche opens in the audience room where the Umayyad caliph sat on his throne. The walls of this room are decorated with frescoes whose iconography is reminiscent of Persian, Byzantine, and Greco-Roman art.

218 bottom right Covering an area of 33 by 20 feet, the audience room had three aisles and a barrel-vaulted ceiling that was to become a typical feature of Islamic architecture.

219 The dome of the calidarium in the hammam. The refined frescoes suggest that Qusayr 'Amra was more a place of enjoyment than a farm or military complex.

Petra

JORDAN

DISTRICT OF MA'AN
REGISTRATION: 1985
CRITERIA: C (I) (III) (IV)

Incense, saffron, myrrh, cardamom, pepper, ginger, and cinnamon to flavor foods and perfume ointments, balsams, and medicines; muslin and silk that, from the start of the first century AD, became the favorite fabric of the most refined Romans: all these goods – according to the *Periplo del Mare Eritreo*, a manual written by an anonymous Greek merchant – arrived from India by sea at the ports of Hadramauth in Yemen, the legendary kingdom of Sheba. From there, the Nabataeans transported them in caravans across the desert from the Arabian Peninsula to the fabulous city of Petra, where they were divided up for distribution throughout the Mediterranean, Persia, and Mesopotamia.

Little is known of the semi-nomadic merchants who won the respect of the Romans and Persians for their ability to supply such desirable goods. Some scholars identify them with the Edomites who stopped the exodus of the Jews led by Moses. The first written reference to the Nabataeans is much more recent and is found in Book XIX of the *Biblioteca Historica* by Diodorus Siculus (80–20 BC). The events to

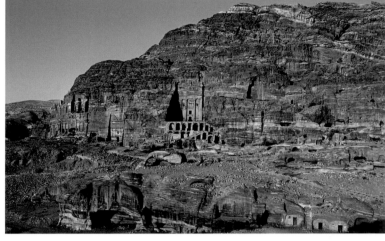

which he refers date to 315 BC and regard the failed attempt by the Diadochs (Alexander the Great's successors) to overcome the Nabataeans living in Petra.

The next news we have of the tribe is from 63 BC when the Romans led by Pompey succeeded in extending their dominion over what are today Syria and Jordan, which were mostly inhabited by the Nabataeans. Nonetheless, they managed to hole themselves up in their capital and maintain their monopoly on goods coming from the Red Sea.

Rome only got the better of them in AD 106, when, upon the death of their king, Rabbele II, the Nabataeans gave their city up to Cornelius Palma,

220 top *Petra at sunset: the low, reddish light makes the buildings look even more extraordinary and brings out the wonderful gradations of color in the rock.*

220 bottom left *A horse-drawn carriage proceeds through the narrow, beautiful gorge called the Siq carved for 4,000 feet out of the sandstone. The Siq provides the only entry to the Nabataean city of Petra.*

governor of Syria under the emperor Trajan. That their surrender was probably the outcome of a diplomatic agreement is suggested by Roman coins minted after annexation, on which, to celebrate the event, the words *Arabia adquisita* were stamped rather than *Arabia capta*, in other words, an indication of a "passage of property" of an administrative nature.

In truth, despite the crushing superiority of their men and arms, the Romans would never have been able to take Petra by force. The Siq – the narrow passage formed over thousands of years by the Wadi Musa (Valley of Moses), one of the seasonal torrents in the zone – was the only means of entry to the city, and the mouth of the passage was practically invisible. From this point for 1,300 yards, there is a series of bends and right-angle turns along sandstone walls up to 330 feet high. It was the only means of taking the city but a suicidal one, even for an army like that of the Romans.

Now that it is no longer an unassailable military obstacle, the Siq is no more than a passage of great beauty on the way to reaching the Khazneh Fir'awn (Treasure of the Pharaoh), the immense building dug out of the rock that is one of the most extraordinary monuments of the ancient world. The

220 bottom right The façade of the Khazneh Fir'awn is two stories high and measures 131 feet tall by 92 wide. Its complex appearance was acheived by recessing the back wall, making it seem as though the building is set in a large frame.

221 The dramatic crevice of the Siq reveals the splendid architecture of the Khazneh Fir'awn (Treasure of the Pharaoh), which was very probably built in memory of Arete III, whose reign (84–56 BC) coincided with the Nabataean people's greatest period of prosperity.

HAMMAN

PETRA

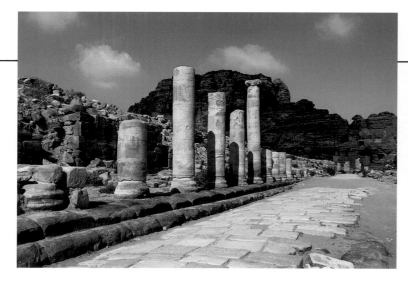

English archaeologist Sir Leonard Woolley wrote, "the Nabataean architects dissected classical architecture and played with the various pieces, arranging them at pleasure with sublime disinterest in the function for which they were originally designed."

The Khazneh Fir'awn has a two-level façade (92 feet wide and 131 feet high) characterized by a very elaborate design. The lower level is formed by a portico with six columns, and the upper level is divided into a round *tholos* with a conical roof topped by an urn. At the sides there are two semi-gables framed by columns and kiosks. Everywhere there are ornamental motifs of very high quality: statues, capitals, and continuous friezes of garlands of flowers and berries reminiscent of Hellenistic models. Like most of the monuments at Petra, the building had a funerary function and was probably carved in memory of King Arete III (84–56 BC), whose rule coincided with the Nabataeans' period of greatest prosperity. The name Khazneh Fir'awn was given to it by the Arabs who were long convinced that the urn on the *tholos* contained a treasure. Their iconoclastic fury led them to destroy the statues on the façade, in the same way that that some Bedouin later destroyed the amphora in search of treasure.

From the Khazneh Fir'awn, the magnificent city opens into a hollow ringed by pink pinnacles where the only surviving building that has not been carved out of the rock has also been named mistakenly: the Qasr al Bint Fir'awn (Castle of the Pharaoh's Daughter). The structure of this vast, richly decorated temple is based on the

architecture of the temples of the Nile
Valley. The origin of the name is derived
from the Egyptian influence on the local
culture that dated back to remote times,
owing to the commerce that took place
between Petra and Alexandria.
Moreover, the mercantile nature of the
Nabataeans ensured that they absorbed
the cultural and artistic characteristics of
the peoples with whom they came into
contact.

The majestic ad-Dayr (the
Monastery) is clearly Hellenistic in style.
It stands on the top of the mountain of
the same name and is reached by endless
steps cut in the rock, a sort of *via sacra*
lined by tombs and votive niches.

224 top This temple tomb from the end of the first century AD is called the Tomb of the Roman Soldier due to the sculpture of a man wearing armor in the central niche. This was an effigy of the high-ranking officer buried inside.

224 bottom The walls of the triclinium in the Tomb of the Roman Soldier are lined with half-columns and niches with large windows. In the middle of the chamber there are stone benches where guests would sit during funeral ceremonies.

224-225 Archaeologists believe that ad-Dayr (The Monastery) was a temple built in honor of a Nabataean sovereign (perhaps Oboda I) who was divinized after his death.

However, many of the tombs in Petra – like the Tomb of the Urn – and the stone triclinia where funeral banquets were held are adorned with stepped decorations typical of Assyrian art.

Nothing has remained of the Nabataean houses, which were probably built with perishable materials. Little is known of the people, who may have been absorbed by the Arabs. After the arrival of the Romans, the city gradually lost its importance, even though individuals like Strabo described it in enthusiastic terms. Then, in the third century AD, with the decline of the empire, the Romans lost interest in Petra. The memory of the city became a secret guarded by scattered groups of Bedouin tribesmen, until August 22, 1812 when it was rediscovered by the Swiss traveler Johann Ludwig Burckhardt.

His account, published in *Travels in Syria and the Holy Land*, found fertile terrain in romantic Europe of the nineteenth century. It persuaded a young Scot of humble origins to set out for the extraordinary city. His name was David Roberts and his roughly 100 sketches and paintings of Petra allowed him to crown his dream of glory. On his return to Britain, Roberts became famous as the greatest landscape painter of his time, and, after his views were published, Petra returned to life.

225 bottom left The tomb of Sextius Florentinus, the Roman governor of the province of Arabia in AD 127, has a female figure on the large central arch. This was probably a Gorgon, a symbol of Hellenistic derivation.

225 bottom right The façade of the Renaissance Tomb. This fanciful name reflects the details on the pediment resembling Italian buildings of that period. Another unusual decorative feature in the tombs of Petra is the bas-relief of a stairway.

Hatra

IRAQ

REGION OF MOSUL
REGISTRATION: 1985
CRITERIA: C (II) (III) (IV) (VI)

226 top A forest of heavy columns in the ruins of Hatra features capitals merging Hellenistic and Persian styles. The city was at its peak during the long reign of Sanatruk II (AD 200–240) when its dominion stretched as far as the Euphrates River.

226 bottom Thick sandstone walls adorned with statues and high-reliefs of human and animal figures frame one of the recesses in the labyrinthine temple of Shamash in the heart of the city.

The war in Iraq alarmed all the world's archaeologists over the fate of the immense historical heritage in the country where man's earliest cultures had flourished. In April 2003, pictures of the looted National Museum in Baghdad raised fear for worst over the 170,000 works of art conserved in its storerooms.

A first estimate suggested that 80 percent of the pieces had been either stolen or destroyed, but a follow-up mission by the College Art Association gave a more precise assessment of the damage, concluding that only around 10,000 pieces, grave nonetheless, were missing. The pillaging of the public galleries was more limited, with "only" 40 pieces gone. These included heads literally detached from the life-size sculptures found in the gallery of the Hatra statues.

A fortress-city in northwest Iraq, halfway between Mosul and Samarra, it is not clear when Hatra was founded. Around 400 BC, it may have originally been a modest Assyrian settlement, but it grew to experience great splendor between the second century BC and third century AD. Situated in a strategic position along the Silk Road, it was one of the most prosperous cities in the Parthian kingdom. Indeed, today it is considered the most important relic from the ancient Mesopotamian cultures. It was later made the capital of the first Arab kingdom after heroically resisting the Roman sieges led by Trajan (AD 116–117) and Septimius Severus (AD 198–199). It was between these two episodes that Sanatruk I (167–190) appointed himself "king of the Arabs" and called Hatra the "City of the Sun" after completing its most impressive building: the temple of Shamash, the sun god.

Circular in layout, Hatra has a diameter of just over one mile and is surrounded by two sets of defensive walls. The first, five miles in length, was built of clay. The inner and second wall enclosure is about three and a half miles long and separated from the clay wall by a deep dike. Its stone walls, up to ten feet thick and seven high, feature 163 defensive towers and are crossed through four main gates from which the same number of streets lead to the heart of the city. The

226-227 The ruins of Hatra lie in a slight depression (called al-Jazirah) in the semi-desertic region between the Tigris and Euphrates, a short distance from the Wadi al-Tharthar and about 60 miles from Mosul.

HATRA

BAGHDAD

227 bottom left The faces of Hatra's outstanding citizens who made large donations for the construction of the great temple were carved on the vaults of the important religious building's eleven entrances.

227 bottom right
A delicate frieze runs above one of the entrances to the temple of Shamash. The building is circled by high walls that give it an almost military aspect. Hatra was famous for its military prowess: its soldiers perfected a sort of incendiary bomb, which was a very innovative weapon in the second century AD.

walls and towers suggest that Hatra had a military role in addition to a commercial one, and explain how it was possible for the city to resist the assaults of the powerful Roman legions.

The city's many temples – all built at the start of the Christian era when Hatra was one of the richest cities in the region – underline its religious function. The most important was that of Shamash, a colossal, four-sided building measuring 478 by 352 yards surrounded by dressed stone walls with one main gate on the east side and eleven secondary ones. Inside there

were a number of chapels dedicated to secondary gods such as Maran, Shiu, Samia, Saqaya, and Alat. On the other hand, the mausoleums, two-story buildings with several burial chambers and vaulted roofs, were found in the east section of the city.

As a commercial crossroads between the Orient and the Mediterranean, Hatra was not a tempting target just for the Romans, and consequently its prosperity did not last long. In 238, it withstood the assault of the Persian king Ardashir I, but just three years later it was taken by the forces of Shapur, the Sassanid king who had no qualms about

destroying the city completely. However, that short-lived period of splendor has left behind extraordinary examples of statuary demonstrating Greek, Roman, and Persian influences. In an unparalleled mixture of styles and cultures, the statues of the divinities of Hatra are mixed with those of Poseidon, Eros, Hermes, Apollo, and Hercules, who is portrayed wearing the Nemean lion-skin over his left shoulder, as well as those of sovereigns and other important figures in the kingdom. Today most of the statues and sculptures are held in the National Museum in Baghdad and the museum in Mosul, where it is hoped that they will survive this new, unexpected assault.

228 top Small and refined, this votive bas-relief plaque depicts the god Nergal with a leashed watchdog. Placed originally on a funerary stele, today the sculpture is in Mosul Museum.

228-229 Hatra's most imposing building is the colossal four-sided great temple measuring 1,568 by 1,155 feet and dedicated to Shamash, the sun god. Built by Sanatruk I (AD 167–190), it also has many chapels consecrated to lesser gods.

229 top A high dignitary is portrayed with an elaborate curly hairstyle.

229 bottom left A delicate female figure with clothes and hair in Hellenistic style stands to one side of a column in the great temple.

229 bottom right The numerous female figures at Hatra were depicted wearing long draped garments, jewels, and elaborate hairstyles, and provide an idea of Parthian clothing in the second century AD.

229

Persepolis

IRAN

PROVINCE OF FÂRS
REGISTRATION: 1979
CRITERIA: C (I) (III) (VI)

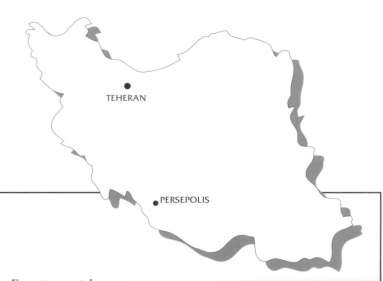

In the procession marking the start of the New Year celebrations, all the representatives of the immense Persian Empire paraded in great pomp. The colorful, festive celebration was a source of great pride for the ruler and entertainment for the spectators. It opened with the solemn march of the army of the Ten Thousand Immortals, then the Medians (who had the honor of opening the parade of Persian subjects), followed by the Elamites with lions on leashes, the Parthians, the Sogdians of central Asia who brought dromedaries and hides as gifts to the emperor, the Egyptians with their standards and a bull, the Sagartians with horses and magnificent clothing, the Bactrians on camels, the Armenians with vases filled with offerings, the Babylonians with cups and fabrics, the Cilicians with rams, the Scythians with their spiked hair, the Assyrians with lances, the Lydians with a chariot, the Ionians with plates, and finally, the peoples of India with dozens of great baskets.

The parade was held in Persepolis. It is recorded in great detail in the magnificent bas-relief a full 330 yards long, divided into various orders, on the walls of the steps of the *Apadana*. This monumental room – supported by 36 columns each 82 feet tall, decorated with capitals in the form of griffins, lions, and bulls – was dedicated to the receptions given by the King of Kings, the ruler of the dynasty of the Achaemenids, who was elected by the supreme god, Ahura Mazda. The superb construction was built on the orders of Darius (522–486 BC) who had made Persepolis his capital.

As soon as he mounted the throne, Darius launched a libertarian policy, instituting satrapies with extensive powers of government in each province. In fact, his "decentralized state" did not need a new seat of government, neither for administrative nor commercial purposes. Therefore, Persepolis was built as a center to hold official celebrations and the imperial coffers that stored the gifts sent to him and his successors from every corner of his empire.

230 top Construction of the city of Persepolis on an artificial platform 1,175 feet long, 984 wide, and 49 high was begun by Darius and continued by his successors with the use of thousands of slaves from every corner of the empire.

230 bottom Sculpted on a massive scale but with carefully executed details, this bull, now hornless, serves as the base for a pillar. Capitals and plinths in Persepolis were often in the form of animals.

230-231 As is documented, the magnificent Portal of the Nations was built by Xerxes I. It leads into the Apadana, the monumental room in which thousands of people could fit to attend official ceremonies.

231 top Persepolis was so rich that, as Herodotus recounted, when Alexander the Great destroyed the city in 330 BC, 10,000 mules and 5,000 camels were required to carry off its treasures.

231 bottom A symbol of Achaemenid power at the entrance to the Apadana, this mythological creature is a lamasu, a sphinx with the body of a bull, a human head, and a pointed beard.

232 top left When shown moving from place to place, as in this frieze on the Tripylon, Darius is always attended by slaves who carry a sunshade and a fly-swater. In portraits, he always expresses a sense of power and almost supernatural beauty.

232 top right Enthroned and with his feet on a stool, Darius welcomes his subjects in a hieratic pose. In reliefs, the king is always shown larger than the other figures.

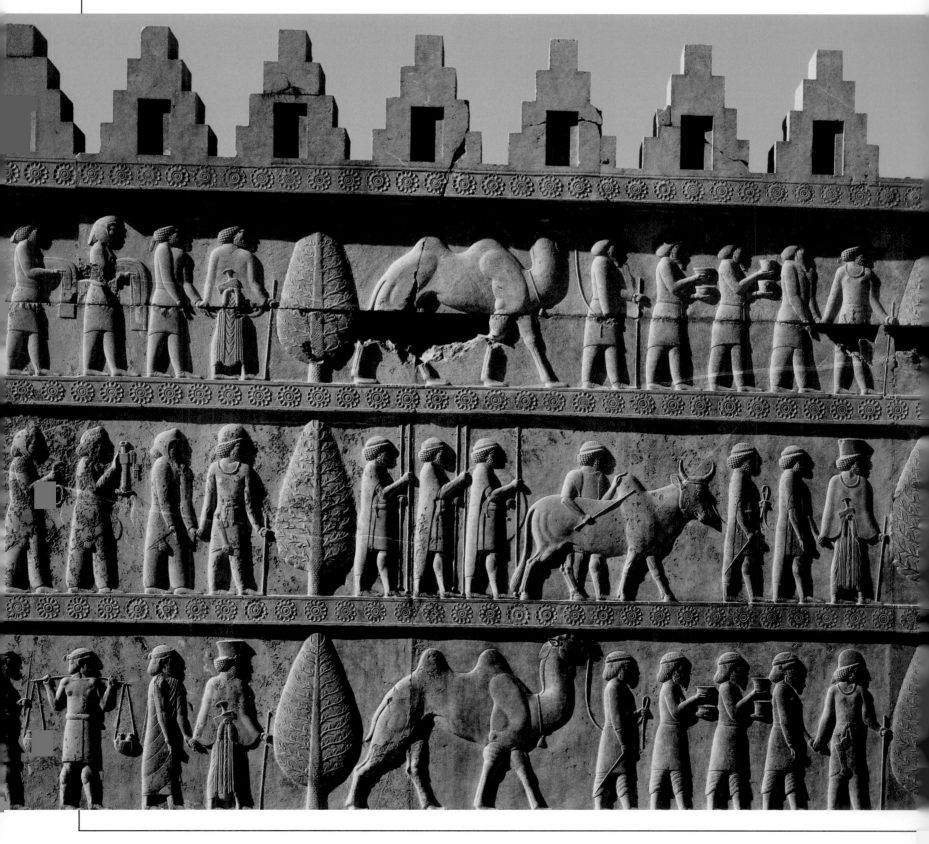

235 top The various peoples in the majestic procession can be identified by their clothing and the goods they bear as gifts. Here we see the Cilicians bringing Darius rams.

235 center top The representations of horses are particularly detailed and well-proportioned. As Xenophon wrote, the Persians were excellent horsemen and rode without the use of stirrups.

235 center bottom The Lydians carried their offerings to the king on a chariot. Each delegation was guided into the Achaemenid capital by a "gate officer."

235 bottom A royal guard in his parade uniform holds his lance with two hands and has his quiver slung over his back. This is a detail from a bas-relief on the east stairway of the Apadana.

236 top Two noblemen from the frieze on the east stairway of the Apadana. The king received strong support from the Persian aristocracy: he gave them important decision-making positions, like that of satrap.

236 bottom A procession of high dignitaries in one of the bas-reliefs on the Tripylon. The Achaemenid ruler usually dispensed precious gifts to them to reflect their prestige; the most important was the akinake, the ceremonial court sword.

237 top Beards and a moustaches were a sign of virility and social distinction for the Persians. Beardless figures depicted on the reliefs in Persepolis were often eunuchs, members of the extensive domestic staff in the royal palace.

237 bottom left The different styles of dress indicate the ethnic variety of the Achaemenid Empire. In this detail, a Persian can be recognized by his traditional pointed felt hat, called a bashlyk.

237 bottom right A detail of the left hand of Darius in one of the friezes. The flower he holds while receiving the nobility and peoples of subjected nations represents his benevolence towards those who approach him.

The Minaret of Jam
AFGHANISTAN

District of Shahrak, Ghur
Registration: 2002
Inscription on the World Heritage in Danger List: 2002
Criteria: C (ii) (iii) (iv)

KABUL

JAM

238-239 The narrow valley is dominated by the 213-foot-high minaret. An inscription says that it was completed in 1194 by Sultan Ghiyath ad-Din Muhammad. It is not known though whether it was part of a mosque or simply a "victory tower" to celebrate the Ghorid dynasty.

238 bottom This view shows off the delicate geometric and floral patterns on the minaret. In the upper part the monument has a band of turquoise majolica tiles.

The minaret of Jam stands in a narrow valley at an altitude of 6,230 feet at the meeting point of two rushing rivers, the Hari-rud and Jam-rud. Providing it with a worthy crown are the high and bare mountains of the region of Ghar in mid-western Afghanistan.

Unknown to the world for centuries, with the exception of rare shepherds and travelers, the monument was discovered by chance during the 1930s by a lone pilot who has remained anonymous. On his return to Kabul, he provided the coordinates of the minaret, but only in August 18, 1957 did an expedition led by Ahmed Ali Kohzad, the president of the Afghan Historical Society, and French archaeologist André Maricq succeed in reaching the remote valley. They had traveled for days on appalling roads but their efforts were rewarded. The minaret was one of the oldest and most superb examples of Islamic architecture in Central Asia.

Standing 213 feet tall, it is an elegant tower made of bricks arranged in elaborate geometric and floral patterns. Even its form is unique: octagonal in the bottom third, it becomes circular in the upper two thirds, and is topped by a domed balcony supported by six slender arches. The decoration in the upper section consists of a band of blue and turquoise tiles with an inscription of the name of the builder in Kufic characters. Invented in Kufa (in present-day Iraq) by the fourth caliph, a cousin of the Prophet, Kufic script is one of the earliest forms of Islamic writing and is distinguished by the angular letters and lack of diacritic marks. Inside the minaret, a double spiral stairway winds up to the balcony.

The inscription tells us that it was completed in 1194 for Sultan Ghiyath ad-Din Muhammad (1163–1203), who was a member of the Ghorid dynasty that reigned over the region from 1146 to 1214 and even conquered Delhi. In fact, the Qutb Minar, the tallest minaret in the world, erected in 1186 in the Indian city, is the "offspring" of the minaret of Jam, copying both its architecture and decoration. Yet, here ends the list of known facts about the structure, leaving one unsolved puzzle – one of many in Afghanistan's mysterious and tormented history: why was it built? Was the minaret of Jam part of a mosque of which there is no trace left today? Was it a "victory tower" to glorify the Ghorids? Or, was the valley the site of Firuzkoh, the legendary capital of the sultanate razed to the ground by the Mongols under Genghis Khan? The answers to some of these questions may be found in the ruins of a fort, a building that seems to have been a palace, and fragments of a defensive wall on the north bank of the Jam-rud. Moreover, in 1960, Italian archaeologist Andrea Bruno found traces near the minaret of an ancient bazaar and some historiated tablets – today in the archaeological museum in Kabul – that suggest there was once a Jewish cemetery on the site.

In 1974, UNESCO assigned Andrea Bruno the task of restoring the minaret, the stability of which was being undermined by the erosive action of the Ham-rud, the stronger flowing of the two rivers, which has gradually dug out the ground beneath the tower causing it to lean. Four years later, work began on the construction of an embankment formed by metal gabions anchored with stones in preparation for work on the tower's foundations. Then war stopped everything.

For this reason, when UNESCO inscribed the minaret of Jam on the list of

239

239 top The base of the octagonal minaret – an unusual shape in that era of towers with a circular form – shows the brick structure of the interior. The original entrance lies about 13 feet deep, buried under sediment.

239 bottom The stability of the minaret, which already leans noticeably, is threatened by the erosive action of the Ham-rud, one of the two rivers in the valley. Construction of a dam was begun but the war stopped all work on it.

World Heritage sites, it was also included on the Red List of endangered sites. When Bruno finally succeeded in reaching the valley after many years, he found the situation to have worsened: some of the decorated tiles had disappeared, stolen by thieves who trade in antiquities.

The Caves of Mogao

CHINA

DUNHUANG, PROVINCE OF GANSU
REGISTRATION: 1987
CRITERIA: C (I) (II) (III) (IV) (V) (VI)

240 *The 492 grottoes at Mogao were dug out of a cliff of crumbling rock roughly 15 miles from Dunhuang Oasis. Some of these have been protected by a reinforced-concrete barrier to prevent sand from entering.*

240-241 *The frescoes primarily illustrate episodes from the life of the Buddha. In this cave – number 285 – the Buddha in meditation pose is 14 feet high.*

241 top left *Protected by a seven-story pagoda, the largest of the 670 statues from the Tang era (113 feet tall) is of a serene-faced Buddha.*

241 top right *As in the other caves, the statues of modest size in Grotto 57 (the "Grotto of the Bodhisattva of the Red Lotus") were made from terracotta, then lined with stucco and painted in painstaking detail.*

In AD 366, a monk named Le Zun was passing near Dunhuang on one of the most important caravan routes of the Silk Road when he saw a flash of a golden light in which the faces of thousands of Buddhas appeared to him. He thus believed that this place – an oasis on the edge of the Gobi and Taklamakan deserts in western China, 1,200 miles from Beijng – had to be made into a Buddhist sacred place. He collected offerings from the inhabitants of the zone and began to dig the first niche in a soft sandstone wall at Mogao, about 15 miles south of Dunhuang. News quickly spread through the region, and for the next ten centuries, travelers, as an offering to wish the long journey that lay before them well, made their contribution to the exceptional inventory of Buddhist art that the grottoes of Mogao soon became.

Whether or not Le Zun ever really existed is unknown, but the fact remains that between the fourth and fourteenth centuries, in one of the most inhospitable regions of Asia, the art of the Middle Empire produced 492 grottoes, 2,000 sculptures, and 450,000 square feet of frescoes. Perhaps the most impressive work of art at Mogao is the enormous statue of the Buddha, standing 113 feet high and protected by a seven-story pagoda. Erected in 695 during the Tang dynasty, the statue has a gilded face and an expression of great serenity.

Yet, the most valuable aspect of Mogao is not in the works themselves but their unbroken record of the stylistic evolution of traditional Chinese art. The grottoes contain frescoes and sculptures from at least five dynasties: the Northern Wei and Western Wei, the Northern Zhou, the Sui (a short-lived transition dynasty), and the Tang, under whose rule China achieved a level of artistic perfection probably only equaled during the Ming dynasty.

The style of Mogao's mural and sculptural art – whose vivid colors have

MOGAO

BEIJNG

242 top This detail of the large painting in Grotto 217 shows the Buddha at the center of the Western Paradise of the Land of the Pure. Executed during the period of Tang art's greatest splendor, this fresco is a reflection of the architectural perfection achieved during the period.

miraculously survived the ages – reveal the meeting and fusion of Western culture and Chinese tradition, as well as the evolution of the customs and religiousness of the observance of Buddhism. In the works of the first few centuries, the figures and their clothing show the unmistakable influence of Persia and, above all, India, the country in which Buddhism originated. With the Western Wei, a synthesis of styles occurred: the faces grew rounder, the

noses thinner, the eyes longer, and the clothes began to be more oriental in cut. With the integration and harmonization of the Han with the central Asian peoples that lived in the Dunhuang region, the two styles merged during the Northern Zhou dynasty, eventually achieving the perfection of the Tang sculptures.

However, the greatest works of Mogao art have not been in China for a hundred years or so. Abandoned in the fifteenth

century, the grottoes were rediscovered at the end of the nineteenth century by the Taoist monk Wang Yuan, who came across a hollow in which ancient handwritten documents were preserved. Wisely, the monk decided to wall up access to the grotto to safeguard the works from looters and the dry desert air, which would quickly have ruined them. Nonetheless, word of the discovery reached Sir Aurel Stein, an English collector, who organized an expedition in

242 bottom The walls of the Mogao grottoes are covered with more than 500,000 square feet of frescoes. There are innumerable images of the Buddha and bodhisattva: over 4,500 have been counted of apsara (celestial dancers) alone in 270 grottoes.

242-243 Unlike other dynasties, portraits of dignitaries from the Tang era are frequent in the Mogao frescoes. Often the figures are large and occupy prominent positions. In some cases, it is the patron who is represented next to the Buddha.

243 top The ceilings of the grottoes are populated by mystical figures from a wide range of religions: bodhisattva, apsaras, and the asura king Vimalacitra (shown here) from Buddhism, Garuda, the king of the birds, and Vishnu from Hinduism.

243 bottom 56 feet wide and 22 deep, Grotto 158 (the Mahaparinirvana) is one of the most spectacular at Mogao. This detail on the west wall shows bodhisattva and disciples looking at the large statue of the Buddha reclining.

order to see the contents of what today is known as Grotto 17. Stein convinced Wang to hand over the documents in return for a modest donation towards the restoration of the grottoes, and he left Mogao with 24 chests of manuscripts painted on canvas and linen. He also managed to take possession of the Diamond Sutra, a xylograph from 868 that is the oldest known printed book. Today Stein's purchases can be seen in the British Museum in London.

244 top The wall paintings are frequently inspired by the Jataka, i.e. the stories of the 550 lives of the Buddha on the path to perfection and Enlightenment.

244-245 This detail from one of the frescoes in Grotto 217 shows the City of Illusions narrated in the Lotus Sutra. In this, followers of Buddhism are taught that only by practicing the discipline with assiduity and perseverance can immortality be achieved.

245 top Three gazelles flee in a detail from a hunting scene painted on the ceiling of Grotto 249, produced at the time of the Northern Wei dynasty, which dominated China between AD 386 and 634. The paintings in this cave illustrated the daily life of the nomadic peoples in northwestern China.

245 center A detail from the fresco in Grotto 419 illustrates the story of the generosity of Prince Sudana, a story told in the sacred text of the Visvantara Jataka. The cave was decorated during the Sui dynasty, which included some of the most devout Buddhist emperors in Chinese history.

245 bottom This wall painting is of a group of yaksha. In Buddhist mythology, yaksha are benevolent spirits whose responsibility it is to guard the treasures hidden underground and in the roots of trees.

The Tomb of the First Qin Emperor

CHINA

Lintong Plain, Province of Shaanxi
Registration: 1987
Criteria: C (i) (iii) (iv) (vi)

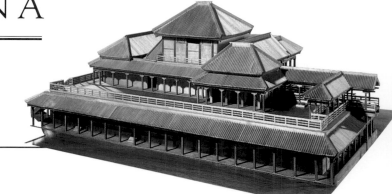

BEIJNG

XI'AN

246 top This model in Xi'an Museum was built according to the descriptions made in 249 BC by the court historian Sima Qian. It is a hypothetical reconstruction of the emperor's final dwelling place, though even today archaeologists have not discovered the burial chamber of Qin Shi Huangdi.

246-247 The roughly 8,000 statues that make up the Terracotta Army of the first emperor, Qin Shi Huangdi, are covered by a structure protecting them from the natural elements.

247 top Originally the soldiers bore weapons with wooden handles, but these have decomposed over the centuries. Other accessories, however, remain: bronze arrow heads, blades of daggers used in hand-to-hand combat, and signal bells.

247 center The significance of the statues is controversial. Some experts believe that they represent the real imperial guard, whereas others think they are mingqi ("surrogates") to avoid the sacrifice of human lives upon the death of the emperor.

247 bottom In addition to the statues, the mound was found to contain architectural fragments, tools, and a metal collar. The collar indicates that prisoners were used to build the mausoleum and confirms accounts from the third century BC. These refer to a total of some 700,000 slaves who worked for 36 years.

Aweek, journey time included: this was the duration estimated by the functionaries of Beijing for archaeologist Yuan Zhongyi's mission to Lutong, about 20 miles from the city of Xi'an. The young scholar had been given the task of confirming word that a terracotta statue had been found by a farmer while digging an irrigation canal on a shared farm in Yanzhai. It was 1974 and no one expected that the life-size statue of a warrior was but one tiny piece in the incredible mosaic that was the legendary tomb of Qin Shi Huangdi (259–210 BC), the first emperor of China.

Thirty years have passed and excavation of what is known across the world as the Tomb of the First Emperor is still ongoing. Yuan Zhongyi, now an archaeologist of world fame, is director of the site museum. His name will remain a part of the history of the People's Republic of China, linked to the most important archaeological discovery of the twentieth century in Asia.

The term "tomb" does not do justice to the monument. In 2002, an approximate map was finally drawn up of the underground city built in the form of a dragon covering about a hundred square miles of the plain, bordered to the north by the Lishan Mountains and to the south by the Wei River. For now, visitors can only enter three pits containing the roughly 8,000 statues of the terracotta army that were put in place to guard the emperor for eternity. Each of the statues is solid to the height of the belt and hollow in the trunk and head; they each weigh about 480 pounds and stand between five feet eight inches and six feet six inches

tall. There are foot-soldiers, cuirassiers, archers, crossbowmen, horsemen, senior officers of the imperial guard, horses, and war chariots, each armed with wooden and metal weapons, and each exceptionally realistic down to the smallest detail. Though many of the mineral colors with which they were painted have faded away, the facial features and individual characteristics of each and every statue that was forged are evident, down to their scars, harelips, and cut ears.

Though they are more than two thousand years old, they seem to be alive, in the same way that the emperor wanted

his city – a replica of his empire – to exist in the afterlife.

The mound in which Qin Shi Huangdi was buried was entirely lined with bronze and lay over a water-bearing stratum. It lies near a miniature copy of his palace, which in turn is included in a perimeter wall seven and a half miles long. In a series of buildings arranged around courtyards, archaeologists have found a sequence of rooms in which gold, precious stones, sophisticated objects, food, and exotic birds were stored. In addition, they contained the bodies of concubines, servants, monks, and

248-249 top This covered chariot was part of the grave goods found in Pit 2, the one containing the officers of the imperial guard. Besides the terracotta horses, the remains of about 400 real horses were found southwest of the mound, which were probably buried alive during the funeral of Qin Shi Huangdi.

248-249 bottom A team of four horses is harnessed to the calash of a high dignitary. They are shown with their muscles tensed, nostrils flaring, and mane flying. The craftsmen of ancient China reached the height of their skills when modeling horses.

gardeners who were buried alive with the emperor to cheer his journey after death. The "underground empire" also contained a vast graveyard, a scale model of Chang'an (the ancient name of Xi'an, the capital of the Qin Empire), a planetarium in which the constellations were reproduced in pearls, and mechanically operated streams of mercury representing the most important rivers in China.

Completion of this immense project took 36 years and the labor of 700,000 slaves who, according to the legend, were walled up alive so that they could not reveal the secret of the treasures hidden underground. Qin Shi Huangdi himself ordered the construction in 246 BC. At the time, he was just 13 years old and had only just taken the throne of his clan, the Qin. Despite his tender years, he was already obsessed by the fear of death, and had he not been tormented by this nightmare – which turned into an illness leading him to surround himself with wizards, soothsayers, mystics, alchemists, and charlatans – he would be remembered for

his undoubted capabilities as a warrior, politician, and administrator, on a par with great men like Augustus and Alexander the Great.

It can be said that Qin Shi Huangdi was the man who brought China into being. In 221 BC, after freeing himself from the clutches of a difficult tutor, the greedy Lu Buwei, he conquered the lords of seven rival clans and found himself ruling a vast territory inhabited by many different sorts of people. To protect the empire, he began the construction of the extraordinary defensive system known as the Great Wall. He abolished feudalism, organized the territory using a complex bureaucratic system, encouraged the development of agriculture with the construction of large irrigation canals, and standardized weights, measures, and the distance between wheels on carts so that roads could be planned. He introduced a single currency based on round coins with a square hole at the center (a form that was to remain in use in China until the twentieth century) and created a single system of ideograms so that a standard written and spoken language existed in every corner of the empire.

250

250 left *The statues display archaic traits and some errors of proportion (for instance, the arms are too short), but the realism of the details in the clothing, hairstyles, and, above all, the faces, which reveal the soldiers' regional origin, is quite astounding.*

250 right *The statues represent different types of both individuals and human. The individuality of the expression is accentuated by the multiplicity of the postures, like the one that characterizes the statue of the kneeling archer shown here (48 inches tall).*

On the other hand, to build his fabulous tomb, which he did at the expense of the state, he needed a large and constant inflow of money, with the result that the people were subjected to increasingly heavy taxes. Moreover, Qin Shi Huangdi, who considered himself a god, wanted to cancel from the collective memory the teachings of Confucius, the sage that the emperor, in his megalomania, considered a rival. He therefore ordered the burning of all books of the Confucian school with the exception of those dealing with divination, medicine, pharmacology, agriculture, and gardening.

As he grew older, he became more and more of a

cruel despot, as his obsession with finding the magical formula of eternal life absorbed him completely. Affected by a physical as well as mental illness, he died in 210 BC as soon as he set foot on Chinese soil on his return from a journey to Japan where he had been told he would find the potion of immortality.

The funeral procession that crossed much of the empire was majestic. When his body reached the tomb, the first emperor was buried with at least 1,000 people, whom he had ordered to be sacrificed with him. The "underground empire" was then entirely covered with earth. Since then, the plain has been used to grow wheat.

251 left Traces of paint in certain points indicates the colors used, which in turn helps to identify the military rank of the soldiers. The kneeling archer, seen here from behind, wore a green uniform, while some red is still visible on the links between the plaques on his armor.

251 right Despite the abundance of detail, statues like this one of an armored foot-soldier cannot be considered portraits. It is known that they were stamped from one of eight possible molds, but the features of the faces were modeled by hand.

Mount Emei and the Leshan Giant Buddha

CHINA

Province of Sichuan
Registration: 1996
Criteria: C (IV) (VI)

The Chinese call it *Da Fo*, "Great Buddha," and the Buddha of Leshan is indeed the largest statue of the holy figure in the world, except that it is not in fact the Buddha but Maitreya, one of his disciples, who will return to the world as a messiah. This solemn figure stands 233 feet tall against the hill of Lingyun at the meeting point of the Minjiang, Dadu, and Qingyi rivers. Its

head is 48 feet three inches long and 32 feet ten inches high, its hair is tied up in a spiral of 1,021 enormous curls, and its ears, a traditional iconographic element, are 23 feet long. On a single foot, 100 people could stand with room to spare.

Yet, its cyclopic dimensions are only one aspect of the statue's fascinating charm, as its history is as ancient as it is bizarre. The statue was begun in 713 during the first year of the reign of Emperor Tang Xuanzong, and it was completed in 803 under Dazong, another member of the Tang dynasty. Although the sovereigns financed the enterprise, the sage Haitong from the monastery of Lingyun argued for its construction. Haitong claimed that only the protection of an enormous Buddha would save the lives of the fishermen in local waters from the anger of a dragon that sank the boats by sucking them into powerful whirlpools. Assailed by robbers looking for the money allocated to the statue's construction, Haitong was blinded by one and died before the work was finished. Fortunately, it was then completed under the supervision of the monks Zhang Chou and Wei Gao, the most faithful of Haitong's disciples. Miraculously thereafter, the dragon ceased demanding a blood price from the local people. In fact, the waste materials from the giant statue were thrown into the confluence of the rivers, thus altering the bed and eliminating the whirlpools.

The Buddha of Leshan is surrounded by ancient symbols of the Buddhist faith. A monastery overlooks its head from a rocky spur, and the hill itself is dotted with 2,400 images of the Buddha dating back to the age of the Han dynasty. The eyes of the statue look toward Mount Emei, one of the five sacred mountains in China.

From the highest peak on the mountain, at a height of 10,095 feet, the dawn is an extraordinary sight. The light of the rising sun emerges from the mist and represents, according to tradition, the daily perpetuation of a miracle that allows pilgrims to witness the sacred halo radiated by the Buddha. The mountain is covered by a forest over a thousand years old, with picturesque trees that have been reproduced thousands of times on rice paper by Chinese artists. This enchanting landscape has been protected since the tenth century when the monastery of Wannian, founded in the fourth century at an altitude of 3,420 feet, was designated the custodian of Mount Emei's natural setting. Wannian features a magnificent bronze statue of the *bodhisattva* Puxian, the guardian deity of the mountain, seated on an elephant. It stands 29 feet high and weighs 62 tons. Of the many Buddhist sanctuaries in this corner of Sichuan, the monastery of Bauguo also deserves mention: standing at the base of the mountain, it holds a porcelain effigy of the Buddha eleven feet six inches tall.

252 top The temple of Wennai was built between 397 and 401. It contains a splendid bronze effigy of the bodhisattva Puxian, the guardian deity of Mount Emei, which dates back to 980, the fifth year of the reign of the Northern Song dynasty.

252 bottom and 253 As the ratio between the human figure and the foot of the statue (about 1:30) demonstrates, the Leshan Buddha is enormous, even the details. The nose is over 18

feet long, the eyes and mouth are over 10 feet wide, and the curls of hair on the Buddha's head number 1,021. Various paths and panoramic points allow the sculpture to be seen in its entirety.

BEIJING

MOUNT EMEI

The Longmen Grottoes
CHINA

LUOYANG, PROVINCE OF HENAN
REGISTRATION: 2000
CRITERIA: C (I) (II) (III)

254

Reading the number of grottoes at Longmen is like reading a list of Guinness world records. There are 2,345 of them; some just tiny niches, some large caves, which extend for almost a mile along the slopes of the mountains lining the Yi River. Together they contain more than 100,000 Buddhist images ranging in size from less than an inch to more than 55 feet, plus 43 pagodas and more than 3,600 stone tablets bearing inscriptions of priceless value relating to the history of ancient China.

Considered the richest collection of Chinese art from the period between the Northern Wei dynasty and the Tang dynasty, these images were sculpted over four centuries starting from AD 493 when the capital was moved from Datong to Luoyang. Lying on the Yi River, the city lies about seven miles from two mountains that face one another from either side of the river, creating a huge natural passage that the ancient Chinese called Yi Que, "the gate on the Yi River." When Luoyang became the capital, the name was changed to Longmen, "the gate of the dragon."

Among the thousands of Longmen grottoes, all of which have been dug out of the rock walls, the most impressive is probably the Feng Xian Si Temple, built between 672 and 675 during the Tang dynasty. When it was sculpted, it was closed over by a roof to protect from the elements the largest of the Longmen statues, a 56-foot-three-inch-high Buddha with two disciples and two *bodhisattvas* at its sides. According to tradition, the colossal statue demonstrates a perfect combination of moral integrity, elegance, and tranquility. In a more down-to-earth explanation, it is said that the features of the sculpture are those of the empress Wu Zetian, which is why it is also called by that name or the "Venus of the East."

No less interesting is the Gu Yang

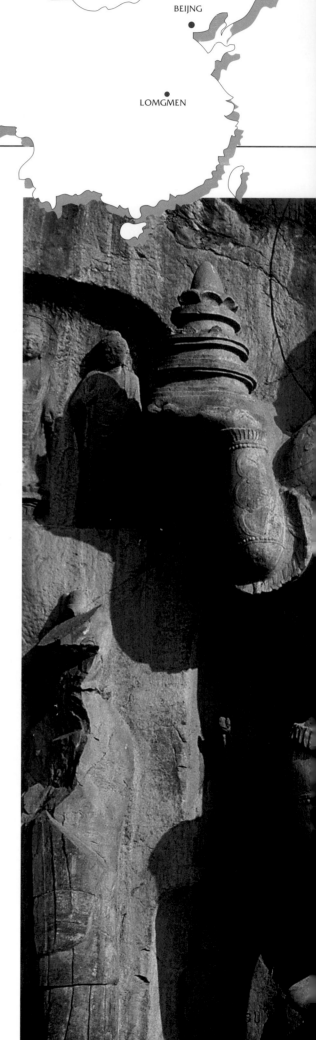

254 A view of the cliff, eroded by the Yi River, in which the 2,345 Longmen grottoes are located. They were created over a span of about 400 years starting in 493, at the time of the Northern Wei dynasty.

254-255 The king of the Heavens holds the Divine Pagoda in his hand and crushes a creature from the underworld. Next to him is Vajra, a demon with a ferocious appearance. These are two of the figures in the Feng Xian Si temple, decorated using iconography from the Tang era. The cave was built between 672 and 675.

255 top left The most extraordinary statue at Longmen is the colossal figure of the Vairocana Buddha in the cave known as the Feng Xian Si temple. Here we see the face, which was modeled on the features of the empress Wu Zetian.

255 top right Wearing a precious diadem, this is one of the large statues that ring the Vairocana Buddha in the Feng Xian Si temple.

Grotto, dug out between 495 and 575 and the first to be excavated in the sides of these mountains. It contains the highest representations of the art of the Northern Wei: a Buddha meditating on an altar with two lions at his feet, as well as other sculptures, paintings, and 19 of the 20 Longmen scripts.

Wan Fo Grotto, built in 690, is distinguished by the number of representations of the Buddha it contains. Called the "Grotto of the 10,000 Buddhas," the actual number of statues sculpted out of its north and south walls is over 15,000, while on the back wall 54 lotus flowers have been carved, with a *bodhisattva* on each one. Lian Hua Grotto

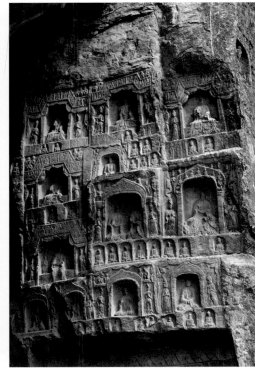

257

256 top Thousands of images of the Buddha adorn the north wall of Wan Fo Grotto (the "Grotto of the Ten Thousand Buddhas"). In fact, there are at least 15,000, with the smallest less than an inch tall.

256-257 Commissioned in 690 by emperor Gaozong and his consort Wu Zetian to invoke the goodwill of the Buddha on their children, the Wan Fo Grotto centers on the statue of the Buddha seated on a lotus flower.

257 top left Protection and charity are the qualities expressed by the hand gestures of this Buddha, represented respectively by the open palm and the back of the hand facing downwards. Two bodhisattvas flank the Enlightened One.

257 top right Aside from the site's exceptional artistic value, the sculptures in the Longmen Grottoes have provided scholars with valuable information on civil architecture, the economy, and dress in China during the Northern Wei, Tang, Sui, and Song dynasties.

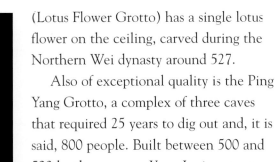

(Lotus Flower Grotto) has a single lotus flower on the ceiling, carved during the Northern Wei dynasty around 527.

Also of exceptional quality is the Ping Yang Grotto, a complex of three caves that required 25 years to dig out and, it is said, 800 people. Built between 500 and 523 by the emperor Yuan Lo in memory of the emperor Xiao Wen Di and his wife, the central cave measures 40 feet by 36 and is 30 feet high. Inside there are nine statues of the Buddha, the largest of which reaches 27 feet in height. On the ceiling, once again, there is a large lotus flower with ten servants. Unfortunately, the marvelous adoration scenes that decorated the walls were taken away in 1935 and are now displayed in an American museum.

Although they are generally in good condition, the Longmen Grottoes have suffered damage from natural causes like erosion as well as from vandalism, and the recent economic growth in the urban area of Luoyang has added the threat presented by acid rain and automobile fumes. However, the renewed awareness of the Chinese towards their artistic heritage has resulted in suggesting that the central and local governments consider taking radical measures such as moving all tourist facilities away from the area, transferring the nearby village of Longmen to another site, and rebuilding the access road to minimize vibrations and dust generated by motorized vehicles.

257 bottom The dimensions of the statues carved in the Longmen Grottoes vary substantially. The average, as in this case, is little larger than life size, but the tiniest are just an inch or so high and the largest over 50 feet tall.

The Yungang Grottoes
CHINA

DATONG, PROVINCE OF SHANXI
REGISTRATION: 2001
CRITERIA: C (I) (II) (III) (IV)

I

n the largest of the grottoes at Yungang, number 19, there is a statue over 52 feet high. Seated in the lotus position, the figure bears a serene expression and holds the palm of one hand out towards the observer in the traditional Buddhist gesture associated with peace and benevolence. At first glance, the figure might seem to represent the Buddha himself, but that is not the case. According to experts, he is the emperor Taiwu of the Northern Wei dynasty, though when he was in power, around AD 446, he was anything but benign towards Buddhists. Under the influence of his prime minister, Kou Qianzhi, he abandoned Buddhism for Taoism, terrifying his own family in the process. He destroyed the monasteries and obliged the monks to return to secular life, using force and committing all kinds of atrocities along the way.

It is said that his son, the heir to the throne, died of a broken heart. When, in 452, the emperor was assassinated, his nephew Wencheng ascended the throne, draining the state coffers in an attempt to restore Buddhism and rehabilitate, in some manner, the figure of Taiwu. The Yungang Grottoes, containing roughly 51,000 religious images carved in the sandstone, are the result of Wencheng's splendid efforts.

They are the earliest and most emphatic example of Buddhist rock art in China. Situated on the southern slopes of the hills of Wuzhou, not far from Datong, the capital of the Northern Wei dynasty, the grottoes were created in several phases between 460–465 and 494 when the imperial capital was moved to Luoyang in the modern province of Henan. Ancient registers recount that the work required more than 10,000

craftsmen, from sculptors to painters, to carve the figures and paint them in the bright colors that are still visible today.

The 53 grottoes form the monumental section of an archaeological site consisting of a thousand or so small rock temples and votive shrines. Experts have subdivided them into three groups, spread across the half mile of hillside. The five earliest grottoes (numbers 16 to 20) were carved under the supervision of the sage Tan Yao.

They are oval shaped and are those in which the sculptural style was most greatly influenced by the Gandhara art from India (Buddhism's land of origin), which in turn had been influenced stylistically and iconographically by Hellenistic art. In Yungang, the images of the Buddha and *bodhisattvas* are given Caucasian features (some even have a moustache) and the decorative elements

258 top With carefully sculpted facial features and typically Chinese ornamentation, this face of the Buddha was created in the most recent phase of construction at Yungang, when the Northern Wei attempted to make Buddhism comprehensible to their subjects.

258 bottom left The wall in which the grottoes have been dug seems almost like a honeycomb. The massive undertaking took over 10,000 sculptors and painters 30 years to complete.

258 bottom right With roughly 51,000 religious images in the 53 grottoes and a thousand or so shrines and small temples, Yungang is the oldest and most vigorous example of rock art in China.

259 left Grottoes 16, 17, 18, 19, and 20 (the last is shown in the picture) were carved in 460 and represent the original nucleus of Yungang. Each one contains a large effigy of the Buddha, identified with each of the emperors of the Northern Wei dynasty.

259 top right A double opening allows the colossal image of the Buddha in Grotto 18 to be admired. Though rather unrefined, the oldest statues are pervaded by an incomparable sense of power.

259 bottom right The Buddha identified with the emperor is seated in European fashion in one of the oldest caves. For the Northern Wei (Tartars who came to China from Central Asia in 386), the grottoes symbolized the divine nature of the dynasty.

258

BEIJNG

YUNGANG

260 top left Grottoes 9 and 10 are reached via a monumental portico with columns dug out of the rock. Inside there are elegant sculptures of a series of musicians with instruments.

260 top right The variety of the images of the Buddha is extraordinary: some have been given Caucasian features, and the decorations reflect the influence of Gandhara art.

include vine shoots, acanthus leaves, and tridents. Grotto 17 is particularly beautiful, in which the large figure of the Buddha Maitreya is surrounded by a multitude of miniature Buddhas, some barely an inch tall.

Among the other grottoes, the most visually impressive– some of which have entrances carved to resemble a wooden structure – are numbers five to thirteen. Number five contains a 56-foot-tall statue of the Buddha seated in the lotus position, and, on the south wall, a beautiful five-story pagoda carried on the back of an elephant. In grotto number six, there is a richly decorated column 49 feet tall, whereas the walls are covered with pictures telling the detailed story of the episodes in the life of the Buddha from the renunciation of his earthly goods to his reaching Nirvana. In grotto number nine, an image of Shiva is found, demonstrating the syncretism that existed between Buddhism and Hinduism.

Each of the grottoes was carved with architectural elements and figures such as *apsara* (celestial dancers), musicians, and high dignitaries in the Chinese court wearing richly embroidered clothes. These images have provided historians with important information about the customs and habits of ancient China.

260-261 Grotto 5 contains the largest statue in Yungang. At 56 feet tall, it portrays the Buddha seated cross-legged. The exactness of the proportions and the figure's overall harmony are remarkable, and very difficult to achieve in a sculpture so large.

261 top Grotto 13 is part of the Wuhua Group, the 5 most spectacular grottoes in Yungang. Number 13 contains the 43-foot tall statue of the seated Maitreya Buddha, with the figure of a vajrapani holding up his right hand.

261 bottom This is one of the many niches in Grotto 13, painted in bright colors that have survived the centuries. Some decorations, for which blue and turquoise were widely used, are Central Asian in style, the land of origin of the Northern Wei.

The Seokguram Grotto and Bulguksa Temple

SOUTH KOREA

PROVINCE OF GYEONGJU
REGISTRATION: 1995
CRITERIA: C (I) (IV)

Carved from a single block of granite, the main statue in Seokguram Grotto stands eleven feet six inches tall and represents Seokgamoni, the Buddha at the moment of his enlightenment. His face is an enigmatic combination of masculine strength and feminine beauty, his eyebrows are shaped like crescent moons, and his half-closed eyes signify he is in a state of deep meditation. His hair is curled in ringlets with a sort of bun (*usnisa*) on the top of his head, indicative of supreme wisdom. Seated on a platform shaped like a lotus flower, his hands face outwards in the gesture (*mudra*) that invites the earth to witness his enlightenment. He is dressed in elegantly draped garments with a cut suggesting a Korean interpretation of the Indian style of dress from the era of the Gupta dynasty. The Buddha is surrounded by an assembly, carved in the walls of the grotto, of three *bodhisattva*, ten disciples, and two Hindu gods; at his eye-level, there are ten niches each containing a miniature statue of Buddhist sages. The monument itself is carved with four statues of the Celestial Kings and two bas-reliefs portraying the guardians of the temple (Vajrapani) and eight other guardian divinities.

Despite its small size – the chamber's diameter of only about 23 feet makes it smaller than the same type of caves found in India and China –, Seokguram plays a role of primary importance in the Buddhist artistic heritage of the Classical period. The interior space has a tangible philosophic aesthetic, and, in regard to its technical construction, has no rival in the world. Unlike the Indian caves at Ajanta and the Chinese Longmen grottoes, which were all dug out of soft rock, Seokguram was assembled by hand, given that the hard granite of Mount T'oham, on which it stands, did not permit any other method. This extraordinary undertaking does not cease to amaze archaeologists, given the limited technical

SEOUL

SEOKGURAM
BULGUKSA

equipment that the Koreans had available to them in 742, the year in which construction was begun.

At that time, Buddhism had existed in Korea for 400 years, though it was only in the mid-seventh century that it became common on a national level when the Silla dynasty unified the various kingdoms on the peninsula. Seokguram Grotto, standing on the top of the mountain, with its large statue of the Buddha Seokguram facing the sea, was built to be a supernatural bastion that would protect the kingdom.

The legend in the *Samguk Yusa*, the *Histories of the Three Kingdoms*, written in the fourteenth century, says that Kim Dae-seong, the prime minister under the king Hyegong, built the cave to honor the memory of his parents in previous lives. The legend continues to recount that Kim Dae-seong organized construction of the temple of Bulguksa in 751 halfway up the side of Mount T'oham, dedicating it to his royal parents. The account is less precise on who designed and built the two monuments, but it is evident that Seokguram was intended to be a private chapel for the monarchs whereas Bulguksa – a vast complex of stone temples and pagodas – was for their subjects.

In the fourteenth century, the Korean rulers suppressed Buddhism in favor of Confucianism, and over time, Seokguram and Bulguksa were forgotten. Rediscovered in the early twentieth century, the two monuments have been restored. After an early botched attempt that undermined its stability, the grotto has been fitted with a dehumidification system and a protective glass window. The wooden pavilions in the temple complex have all been rebuilt.

In 1996, excavation of the Seokgamoni Pavilion (the largest monument at Bulguksa) led to the discovery of a collection of treasures that included the paper scroll of the *Dharani Sutra*, datable to between 706 and 751. The scroll is 20 feet four inches long and 2.6 inches wide and is believed to be the first printed document in the world.

263

263 Standing 11 feet 6 inches tall and carved from a single block of white granite, the statue of Seokgamoni (the Buddha at the moment of the Enlightenment) is the jewel of Seokguram Grotto.

262 left A sense of serenity permeates the room of the Daeungjeon, part of the temple of Bulguksa, in which a statue of the Sakyamuni Buddha is surrounded by his disciples.

262 right This granite panel of Seogkuram grotto displays the effigies of the guardian Devas. These were the celestial kings whose task it was to watch over the universe from the cardinal points of the compass.

262-263 The theological basis for the construction of the temple of Bulguksa (begun in 751) was the sacred text of the Avatamskara Sutra.

The Monuments of Ancient Nara

JAPAN

PREFECTURE OF NARA
REGISTRATION: 1998
CRITERIA: C (II) (III) (IV) (VI)

"The kings of the Shang dynasty brought prosperity to the kingdom after moving their capital five times. The kings of the Zhou dynasty ensured peace in the kingdom after moving their capital three times. Today our king, having listened to the soothsayers, has chosen to build his new capital in the Nara Valley, where it will stand protected on three sides by mountains, at the meeting of the points marked by the Black Turtle, Heavenly Dragon, White Tiger, and Red Bird. The list of building materials will be drawn up and approved before the start of the works. Building will begin following the autumn harvest."

So reads the text of the edict relating to the birth of the city of Heijô-kyô, a document made public on the fifteenth day of the second month of the first year of the Wadô era (March 11, 708) and recorded in the *Shôku-Nihongi*, the official chronicle of Japan in the eighth century.

Heijô-kyô, or Nara, as it was later called, was the capital of Japan from 710 to 784. During that period, Japan underwent profound changes, transforming itself into a state with a government, bureaucracy, and centralized legislative body based on the Chinese model. Furthermore, for little more than a century, Buddhism too had been in Japan after arriving from China.

Built on the model of Chang'an (present-day Xi'an), the capital of the Tang dynasty, Heijô-kyô was planned in keeping with the principles of Chinese geomancy. It was rectangular in plan, with a central axis – the Suzaku-Ôji –

that separated it into the Sakyô ("left city," to the east) and Ukyô ("right city," to the west).

Each of these two sections had a market and was divided into a grid by nine *jô* (streets running east-west) and four *bô* (streets running north-south). The imperial palace stood at the center of the north zone. The city districts south of the palace were the location of the houses of the court nobility, and the others were where the craftsmen and traders lived.

In a zone called Gekyô (outer city) close to the northeast side of Heijô-kyô, about fifty Buddhist temples were built that were part of the "six Nara schools" – *Jôijitsu, Sanron, Hossô, Kusha, Kegon,* and *Ritsu* – each of which was run by a Chinese monk.

These six schools were the powerhouse that spread Buddhism throughout Japan at the expense of the "indigenous" Shintoism. The most enthusiastic supporter of the new religion was the emperor Shômu (724–749), who ordered that a temple (*kokubunji*) and a monks' convent

264 top Originally built in the eighth century, Kasuga-ji is the most famous Shinto temple in Japan. Dedicated to the patron gods of the city, it was also the temple of the guardian spirits of the Fujiwara, the most powerful clan in Japan in the Nara and Heian epochs.

(*kokubunniji*) be built in every province. In addition, he had the Tôdai-ji (Great Eastern Temple) built in the capital, where all the monks were ordained.

Construction of the cyclopic Tôdai-ji was completed in 752. The main room (*Daibutsuden*) contained a bronze statue of the *Buddha Vairochana* (Buddha, Lord of the Universe) that stood 59 feet tall and weighed 450 tons. The room itself, 157 feet high, is the largest wooden building in the world.

The original temple and the statue were both destroyed in a fire and rebuilt on a smaller scale at the end of the sixteenth century. Still spectacular, the "new" Tôdai-ji is the heart of modern Nara, where there are many Buddhist

264 bottom *The bronze statue of the Vairocana Buddha dates back to the sixteenth century. It stands 52 feet tall in the main room of the Tôdai-ji. The original, which dated back to the eighth century, was even larger.*

264-265 *The Daibutsuden (Great Eastern Temple) is the main building in the Tôdai-ji. Constructed in 752 by emperor Shômu, it is the most important temple in Nara and stands in the center of the modern city.*

complexes from the Heijô-kyô era, such as the Kôfuku-ji, Gangô-ji, and the Kasuga-ji, the most famous Shinto temple in Japan. They are all made up of pavilions and pagodas, some seven stories high, and are painted vermilion, in wonderful contrast with the green of the conifer forest surrounding the city.

When Heijô-kyô was abandoned in 784, the imperial palace was left as a reminder of the city, while the rest was turned into rice paddies. Today, only the foundations remain of this building (though some sections have been rebuilt and are open to the public), but excavation of the area has turned up thousands of wooden tablets describing the life of the eighth-century Japanese court in every detail.

265 bottom left *One of the oldest temples in Japan, the Yakushi-ji was built in the seventh century by emperor Tammu so his wife would be cured by the Buddha. The main room (restored in the 1970s after a serious fire) contains three Buddhas known as the Yakushi Trinity, a masterpiece of Buddhist art in Japan.*

265 bottom right *At just 52 feet high, the Muro-ji is the smallest five-story pagoda in Japan. The 3,000 pink rhododendron plants that surround it have earned it the name "pagoda of the flowers."*

The Buddhist Monuments in the Hôryu-ji Area

JAPAN

IKARUGA, PREFECTURE OF NARA
REGISTRATION: 1993
CRITERIA: C (II) (IV) (VI)

An inscription on the halo of the Yakusi Nyorai Buddha (literally, "the Buddha who comes to heal") tells the story of the foundation of the Hôryu-ji, the Buddhist temple that is the oldest wooden building in the world. Here it is written that the emperor Yômei, suffering a serious sickness, had the temple built so he might pray there for his own cure. He did not achieve his goal, but as he laid on his deathbed the empress, his wife Suikô, and his son, Shôtoku, promised to carry out his wishes.

Construction of the temple was completed in AD 607. It constitutes the main pavilion (Kon-dô) in a complex of over 200 buildings covering an area of 46 acres. However, the first "piece" of the Hôryu-ji was as ephemeral as the old

TOKYO

HÔRYU-JI

266 bottom The bronze sculptural group represents the Sakyamuni Buddha – or Shaka Nyorai, the Historical Buddha, flanked by the two bodhisattva Monju Bosatsu and Fugen Bosatsu – and was built in 623 in memory of prince Shôtoku, who, a few years prior, had introduced Buddhism to Japan.

267 top Originally built in 607 and rebuilt after a terrible fire in 670, the main pavilion in the Hôryu-ji – or Kon-dô – is the oldest wooden building in the world. At the start of the twentieth century, it was completely dismantled and put back together again after a project lasting nearly 50 years was carried out to clean and strengthen it.

267 center The octagonal Yume-donô ('Pavilion of Dreams') is the main building in the East Enclosure. It was built in 739 on the site of prince Shôtoku's house which was destroyed, along with the temple, in the fire of 670.

267 bottom Naraen Kongô is the name of one of the two statues of Kongo Rikishi, the guardians of Buddhism that stand on either side of the Chumon (the central gate). This is one of the structures in the Hôryu-ji that best represent the architecture of the Asuka age.

emperor, for, according to the *Shôku-Nihongi*, the document describing the chronology of the Japanese empire, "a great flame swept the temple away" on the night of April 30, 670, though the statues inside were saved from the fire. Straightaway, the building was replaced by another, more grandiose structure, along with additional annexes.

Even at that time, the Hôryu-ji was of historical importance to the Japanese. When it was built, Buddhism had only been present in the land of the Rising Sun for fifty years, since Prince Shôtoku (574–622) had brought the new philosophy from China. Shôtoku himself became a legendary figure and a model to be followed by generations to come. He is remembered as one of the ablest politicians of all time in Japan, and the author, in 604, of the constitution with the 17 articles that contained the fundamental principles of the State.

Located in the city of Ikaruga, present-day Hôryu-ji consists of two complexes made from camphor wood, bearing proof of 1,400 years of Buddhism in Japan. Standing at the center of the Western Enclosure (*Sai-in Garan*), the *Kon-dô* contains not only the splendid statue of the Yakusi Nyorai Buddha but also a bronze image of the Amida Buddha – executed in honor of the empress Suikô – and the Triad of Shaka. Cast in 623 in memory of Prince Shôtoku, who died the year before, this bronze sculptural group still features fragments of the gold leaf with which it was lined. It depicts the Shaka Nyorai Buddha (Buddha of History) with two *bodhisattva*. Also of special interest is the wooden platform on which the statues stand. It is decorated with a frieze bearing images of the Shi Tennô, the four celestial sovereigns in the Buddhist tradition. Another impressive building in the complex is Japan's oldest pagoda (*Goju-nô-to*), which rises five stories with an almost feminine elegance and is adorned with demons and dragons.

In the Eastern Enclosure (*To-in Garan*), the Pavilion of Dreams (*Yume-donô*) was built in 739 by the monk Gyôshin Sozu on the site of the palace of Prince Shôtoku that had also been destroyed in the fire. An octagonal construction, it contains a gilded statue whose features seem to have been modeled on those of the prince. Long kept a secret by the monks, today the statue is displayed to the public for five days in spring and autumn. Next to it stands a statue of Gyôshin Sozu himself, who holds in his right hand a terracotta statuette of a monk with a worried look on his face. It represents Dosen Risshi, who instigated the first restoration work on Hôryu-ji in the ninth century.

Over the centuries, the delicate wooden structures have undergone a number of restoration operations. The most intensive was initiated by the shoguns Toyotomi and Tokugawa in the sixteenth and seventeenth centuries, but early last century, the *Kon-dô* was dismantled and reassembled during the process of cleaning and consolidation projects that lasted nearly fifty years.

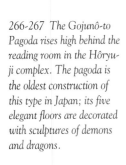

266-267 The Gojunô-to Pagoda rises high behind the reading room in the Hôryu-ji complex. The pagoda is the oldest construction of this type in Japan; its five elegant floors are decorated with sculptures of demons and dragons.

The Buddhist Monastery of Takht-i-Bahi and the Ruins of the City of Sahr-i-Bahlol

PAKISTAN

NORTH-WEST FRONTIER PROVINCE
REGISTRATION: 1980
CRITERIA: C (IV)

PESHAWAR
ISLAMABAD

268-269 The Takht-i-Bahi
monastic complex stands on
a rocky spur 500 feet high
overlooking the plain of
Peshawar.

268 bottom left A tunnel
led to the cells of the monks
and pilgrims. Originally,
the monastery had two
floors but today only the
first floor remains.

Peshawar is the capital of the North-West Frontier Province in Pakistan. It is a harsh terrain inhabited by proud Pashtun tribesmen and warlords, one of whose activities is arms-smuggling between Pakistan and the tormented country of Afghanistan. The only law in this region is brawn over brains.

Little more than two thousand years ago, the region was the setting for the flourishing of one of the greatest empires of the Indus civilization, the Kushan. Founded by descendants of the soldiers of Alexander the Great, who had been left to guard his conquests in the East, it reached its apogee in the second century AD when, thanks to a long period of peace, it took control of what was to become known as the Silk Road by acting as the intermediary for trade between China and Rome.

Right from the early days of the empire, the Kushan embraced Buddhism, and its wealth enabled the construction of cities, monasteries, and temples adorned with magnificent works of art. Known by the name Gandhara, Kushan's sculptural school was unique, and perhaps even paradoxical in the history of oriental art. The "Greek" origins of the empire, in addition to its position at the crossroads of various cultures, led its artists to interpret Buddhist iconography in a "Western" manner, representing the Buddha with a face similar to Apollo, surrounded by tritons, nymphs, centaurs, and vine sprays. Elements typical of Classical Greek and Roman art, they had neither precedent nor consequence in the Eastern world.

Very little remains of the cities of the Kushan Empire, but in the frontier region of Pakistan and Afghanistan stands the Takht-i-Bahi, the largest and best conserved Buddhist monastery in the Indus Valley.

Perched on a rocky spur 500 feet high where the Peshawar plain meets the heights of the Swat, the Takht-i-Bahi – the name means "Throne of the Origins" – was built at the start of the first century AD and remained active until the end of the seventh. Song Yun, a Chinese traveler in the second century, left behind a written record of the monastery and of Sahr-i-Bandol (a city that stood nearby) in which he described magnificent buildings defended by walls, and statues lined with gold leaf.

Of Sahr-i-Bahlol, over which a Pashtun village was later built, there remain only the ruins of a stupa (a dome-shaped Buddhist reliquary) and some stones with religious inscriptions in Kharoshthi, the language of the Kushan. What was must have been superb statuary in the Takht-i-Bahi was in great part either removed, destroyed in raids by Hindus and Muslims over the centuries, placed in safety by the British army who rediscovered the monastery in the second half of the nineteenth century, or conserved in the Peshawar Museum.

Nonetheless, the Takht-i-Bahi is an extraordinary place. Built in gray granite with green streaking, the same material that the statues were made from, the monastery has an entrance with two Corinthian columns that leads into the "Great Court of the Stupas." This large space encloses 38 votive stupas containing large statues. A few steps lead to the courtyard of the monastery lined by three buildings that once had two floors, though only the ground floor with the cells for monks and pilgrims has survived.

A passageway leads to the kitchens and refectory, and, at the top of a wide flight of stairs, there is another courtyard containing the base of another stupa that was probably about 30 feet in height. Around the courtyard are the audience room, a terrace, and chapels with their stucco vaults still intact. On the terrace, covered by a canopy, a few wonderful statues survive intact; the Buddha has the face of a Greek god.

268 bottom right At the
center of this courtyard is a
wide platform on which,
according to Song Yun, the
Chinese monk who visited
Takht-i-Bahi in the second
century, there was once a
stupa 33 feet high.

269 top One of the few
statues of the Buddha still
in situ. Kushan sculptors
invented the Gandhara
style in which Buddhist
iconography was interpreted
in a Hellenistic manner.

269 bottom This statue
probably lost its head to
Muslims who raided the
monastery on several
occasions. Nonetheless, the
Hellenistic style of the
statue is evident in the
softness of its draped robe.

Lumbini:
The Birthplace of the Buddha
NEPAL

PLAIN OF TERAI
REGISTRATION: 1997
CRITERIA: C (III) (VI)

In her tenth month of pregnancy, Queen Maya Devi started out on a journey between Kapilavastu, where she lived with her husband, the sovereign Suddhodana, to her parents' home in Devadaha. During the trip, she spotted a small lake surrounded by a lush garden and wished to stop for a swim. Her labor pains began as soon as she came out of the water, so she grabbed hold of the branch of a tree and gave birth to prince Siddhartha Gautama.

It was a morning in May 623 BC, the place was called Lumbini, and the prince in question was to become the Buddha, the Enlightened One. Pictures celebrating the birth typically show the mother lying on the ground in the shade of the tree gazing happily at her son. Siddhartha's head is already crowned by a halo and he stands on a lotus flower between the gods Brahma and Indra, who wash him with water and flower petals.

Mother and son returned to the palace at Kapilavastu, but Maya Devi died a week later, leaving her newborn son in the care of her sister Prajapati. Siddhartha spent 29 years of his life in the palace before renouncing earthly goods and setting out on the journey to enlightenment. In his wanderings, he returned once to his birthplace, on which occasion 500 subjects of the kingdom decided to follow him in the ascetic life, including his son Rahula, his half-brother Nanda, and Upali, the barber who was to become his most important disciple.

Referred to by the Buddha as one of

the five main places of pilgrimage for the faithful, Lumbini was visited in 249 BC by the Indian emperor Ashoka, the ruler who played a central role in the spread of the Buddhist faith in much of Asia. At Lumbini, Ashoka had a column erected bearing a commemorative inscription of the birth of the Buddha with the effigy of a horse placed on the top. Next to this, a

270 top In 249 BC the emperor Ashoka raised this column to commemorate the birth of the Buddha and mark the date of his own pilgrimage to Lumbini. The monument stands 20 feet tall, of which 10 are underground.

270 bottom The well that marks the exact spot where prince Siddhartha Gotama was born lies in the ruins of the temple of Maha Devi (the Great God). Siddhartha was the future Buddha and was born in 623 BC.

270-271 *Monks practicing the deambulation ritual around the Sacred Garden, where the remains of ancient monasteries and stupas lie.*

271 top *The Pushkarni is the small lake in which Maha Devi bathed before giving birth to Siddhartha. It has been ringed by a rectangular enclosure of brick steps. The water reflects the long-lived Bo tree sacred to the Buddha.*

LUMBINI

KATHMANDU

The rebirth of Lumbini began at the end of the nineteenth century. Though broken in several places, Ashoka's column still existed as proof of the sacred place, along with a few stupas, the garden, and the pool of water ringed by stepped walls. In addition, in the middle of the twentieth century, archaeologists discovered the remains of the royal palace of Kapilavastu about 12 miles away.

As excavations were under way, Lumbini began its return to being a place of pilgrimage for Buddhists from all over the world. In 1978, thanks to a large investment made by UNESCO, the famous Japanese architect Kenzo Tange was commissioned to design a "new Lumbini," a sort of international city of peace whose spiritual and archaeological center was to be represented by the sacred garden and Ashoka's column. The project included the construction of an auditorium, a museum, a library, a monastic enclave, and two building complexes with temples and accommodation for pilgrims, for followers of the Mahayana or Hinayana schools respectively. Due to disagreement between UNESCO and the Lumbini Development Trust (the non-governmental organization managing the project), to date only some of the buildings have been completed. On May 16, 2003, in the presence of Gyanendra, the king of Nepal, the new temple dedicated to Maya Devi was inaugurated, which contains the stone placed by Ashoka to indicate the exact place where the Buddha was born.

stupa (a dome-shaped reliquary temple) was built.

From the account written by the Chinese monk Hsuan Tang, who went to Lumbini in AD 636, it is known that only the foundations of the stupa remained at that time. Meanwhile, the garden and lake had been ringed by enclosures, a sort of temple dedicated to

Maya Devi had been built next to Ashoka's column, and, surrounding the site, a series of other stupas and monasteries had been constructed. Lumbini remained an active center of Buddhism until the fifteenth century, when the Muslim troops of the Moghuls destroyed the temples and the place fell into oblivion.

Khajuraho
INDIA

State of Madhya Pradesh
Registration: 1986
Criteria: C (I) (III)

A legend that is still heard today in Madhya Pradesh tells that the founder of the Chandella dynasty was the fruit of the union between a young and beautiful Brahmin woman and the god of the Moon. A soothsayer told the woman to give birth to the child in the woods of Khajuraho and predicted that her son would become a king by defeating a tiger with his bare hands, then go on to build an immense and wonderful empire.

Legends of this sort are fairly common and are generally instigated by the ancient rulers themselves to legitimate their divine origin. The dynasties of northern India claimed equally to be either *Chandra vamsha* or *Surya vamsha*, in other words clans descended from the Moon or Sun respectively. Ancient inscriptions found at Khajurano show that the Chandella were descended from Chandrateya, the son of Atri, a wise and "lunar" man. Although the name Atri was associated with a number of clan chiefs under the influence of the Gupta Empire from the sixth century on, it was only in the ninth century that the Chandella founded an independent kingdom. It flourished between 950 and 1050 and managed to maintain its supremacy until the thirteenth century when it was defeated by the troops of the sultan of Delhi. During the century of its greatest glory, the Chandella built 85 temples at Khajuraho of which 20 have survived till today. Carved out of sandstone, they were one of the highest expressions of Indian art of all time. The first to describe their extraordinary beauty was the Arab traveler Ibn Battuta around 1335, who

272 left One of the marvelous sculptures on Lakshmana temple, this female figure with a halo of naga (serpents) is a nagini, i.e. a nymph whose task it is to dispense spiritual and material gifts.

272-273 On the portico of the small Mahadev temple there is a superb statue of the shardula, a lion rampant fighting a warrior. Scholars believe the lion was the symbol of the Chandella dynasty that built Khajuraho.

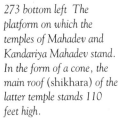

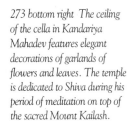

273 bottom left The platform on which the temples of Mahadev and Kandariya Mahadev stand. In the form of a cone, the main roof (shikhara) of the latter temple stands 110 feet high.

273 bottom right The ceiling of the cella in Kandariya Mahadev features elegant decorations of garlands of flowers and leaves. The temple is dedicated to Shiva during his period of meditation on top of the sacred Mount Kailash.

273 top left The cella in Kandariya Mahadev temple encloses a lingam, the phallic symbol of Shiva. The threshold of the monumental entrance (torana) is in the form of a lotus flower.

273 top right The Kandariya Mahadev (seen here, a detail from the decoration) is the most elaborate and majestic temple in the western group: the building is decorated with 870 statues.

reached a place he called Kajarra where he entered into philosophical conversation with longhaired Hindu wise men. Then nothing was written about Khajuraho for a further five hundred years until captain T. S. Burt of the British army, stationed in Bengal, rediscovered them. The first Westerner to provide a description and detailed map was another English officer, Sir Alexander Cunningham, in the second half of the nineteenth century. Cunningham was the one to divide the temples into a "western group" (in the best state of conservation) and two "eastern groups." These latter groups were subdivided into Hindu and Jain sections depending on the religion practiced.

Although different in size, the temples all have the same architectural plan, based on the Hindu conception of the universe, later slightly modified in the Jain version. Built on a platform (a symbol of the sea and earth inhabited by man), they represent the abode of the gods and rise over 100 feet into finely carved conical pinnacles called shikhara. On the external walls and on the shikhara of the two most spectacular temples – Kandariya Mahadev and Lakshman – there are more than 900 sculptures of divinities each at least three feet tall. A richly sculpted portal leads into the shrine of the god, which is unadorned and situated partly in shadow to symbolize the calm at the nucleus of

274 top left The entrance to Lakshmana temple. The temple is dedicated to Vishnu though its name refers to the brother of Rama, the hero of the epic poem the Ramayana and avatar (manifestation) of Vishnu. Built in 954, it is thought to be the oldest of the sanctuaries in the western group at Khajuraho.

274 top right A small temple stands at each of the four corners of the rectangular platform of Lakshmana temple. They consist of a portico, a shikhara, and a tall row of ornamental sculptures.

274-275 Gods, warriors, animals, and female figures form a marriage procession on the outer walls of Lakshmana temple. Note that each group rests on its own base.

275 top One of the erotic scenes that decorate the southeastern facade of Lakshmana temple. Sculptures like these caused Victorian-era British archaeologists to consider the art of Khajuraho obscene.

275 center The vestibule of the cella in Lakshmana temple. Apart from the capitals of the massive columns and the ceiling adorned with protective figures, the room is unusually bare.

275 bottom In this detail from the inner-wall decorations of the deambulatory in Lakshmana temple, young women are represented performing actions such as "in private" admiring themselves in the mirror, washing their bodies or hair, and rubbing themselves with ointments.

the universe. Each of the temples is dedicated to a specific god but – with the exception of the Varaha Mandap and Nandi Mandap, which respectively have majestic sculptures of a Varaha, the incarnation of Vishnu as a boar, and Nandi, the calf that was Shiva's mount– the attributions of the temples are not clear to those who are not well-versed in the vast Hindu pantheon.

When Khajuraho was rediscovered, straitlaced Queen Victoria ruled the British Empire, and though the skill with which the temples had been created was recognized, their decorations were found to be highly embarrassing. They were described as immoral, indecent, highly offensive, and even disgusting. The reason was the presence of erotic representations in which nothing was left to the imagination, placed in evident positions on the sides and rear of the temples.

Victorian academics vehemently debated the significance of the erotic portrayals. According to the most intransigent, Khajuraho was the symbol of a decadent phase of Indian history in which moral values had fallen so low that even in places of worship the most basic of instincts were celebrated. Others argued that a Tantric sect practicing esoteric rites had built the temples, and yet others believed that they represented a sort of "visual guide" to the *Kamasutra*, the ancient manual of Indian lovemaking.

However, they were all wrong. The more daring sculptures (by Western standards) were not carved with pornographic intent, but philosophic. One of the most well-known Hindu myths regards the marriage of Shiva, the multi-form and ruthless god that creates and destroys, to Parvati, the goddess of passion and sensuality. It is said that the union

between the two was the idea of Brahma and, to foster it, he sent Kamadev, the Hindu version of Cupid to fire his arrows of love at the ascetic Shiva, who lived on a mountain at the time. However, Shiva did not welcome the intrusion and opened his third eye, thereby reducing Kamadev to ashes. At that moment, the *lingam* (a sort of obelisk with a clear phallic symbolism) emerged from the mountain to affirm that only by renouncing earthly desires was it possible to gain eternal life.

276 Carved on the temple of Parshvanatha in the eastern group, this female figure is a surasundari, a nymph of supreme beauty who in Indian mythology was a messenger for the Shakti, the divine power.

277 center right The cella in Parshvanatha temple, takes its name from the statue of the god seated in meditation with a halo of serpents. The shiny black stone statue, however, was made in 1860, whereas the temple dates back to 950.

277 top A representation of the guardian deity Vishnu on Parshvanatha temple. The temple is adorned with sculptures of all the Hindu pantheon surrounded by a procession of nymphs and musicians.

277 center left Three couples embrace tenderly on the east wall of Parshvanatha temple. The mithuna, the representation of "being in a couple," is the symbol of the reunification of the cosmic principles of Spirit and Matter.

The myth has a happy ending, however: Shiva fell in love with Parvati and decided to marry her after all, their union being the cosmic event that, according to Hinduism, allowed the cycle of life and death of every human being to be perpetuated. The Chandella dynasty built the temples of Khajuraho as an earthly representation of the ceremony, called the Maha Shivatri, of the marriage of Shiva and Parvati.

Erotic figures aside, the marvelous buildings contain sculptures of figures and moments from the wedding procession, with lines of caparisoned elephants, musicians, carts adorned with garlands of flowers, and dozens of well-endowed, sensual female figures adorned with jewelry, portrayed as though the event had taken them by surprise as they went about their daily business. They flirtatiously look at themselves in the mirror, wash their hair, make up their eyes with kajal, rub ointments into one another's skin, or paint the soles of their feet with henna. They represent an endless tribute to female beauty that is reflected in the excited faces of the women of Khajuraho who each year, for an entire night, visit the temples to re-evoke the sacred union of Shiva and Parvati with hymns, music, and dancing.

277 bottom left Unlike the other temples at Khajuraho, which all stand on high platforms, Parshvanatha temple was built on the ground. This construction is one of the group of Jain temples.

277 bottom right Part of the southeastern group, Chaturbhuj temple is the only one with an entrance that faces east. Inside, there is a monolithic statue 9-foot-tall of Hari-Hara, an unusual combination of Shiva and Vishnu.

The Buddhist Monuments at Sanchi

INDIA

STATE OF MADHYA PRADESH
REGISTRATION: 1989
CRITERIA: C (I) (II) (III) (IV) (VI)

NEW DELHI

SANCHI

278 top Sacred animals in the Buddhist cosmogony, these elegantly carved elephants protected by parasols are at the top of the west torana of the Great Stupa.

At first sight, it seems like just a small hill rising 300 or so feet out of the immense Indian plain, yet the place has an ascetic solemnity that makes one forget its modest size. Sanchi is the site of the subcontinent's most ancient religious monuments that uninterruptedly reflect the spiritual and iconographic progress of Buddhism from the third century BC to the thirteenth century AD, when the religion in India returned to Hinduism.

There is no evidence that Prince Siddhartha stopped at Sanchi on his path to nirvana. Credit for the sanctuary goes to Ashoka, the king of the Mauryan dynasty whose empire spread across most of the subcontinent from 273 to 236 BC. Converted to Buddhism with his wife, born at Vidisha near Sanchi, he ordered the construction of various stupas (hemispherical monuments made from bricks and mortar to symbolize the sacred mountain joining Earth to Heaven) to hold relics of the Buddha, such as his hair, teeth, and shoulder bones.

The most majestic of Sanchi's stupas is 121 feet in diameter, stands 56 feet high, and is crowned by a *chattra* (umbrella) symbolizing the Three Jewels of Buddhism: the Buddha himself, the Dharma (doctrine), and the Sangha (community of monks). It stands on a platform around which pilgrims continue to practice the rite of perambulation. The stone railing around the stupa is pierced by four *torana* (gateways) carved with exquisite bas-reliefs of the life of the Buddha, his previous incarnations, and chronicles of

the deeds of Ashoka in his spreading of Buddhism throughout his empire. Two of the most interesting reliefs feature the Buddha impassive to the temptations offered him by the evil demon Mara, and of the legend of Prince Makakapi Jataka, who saved 80,000 monkeys by extending himself like a bridge across the Ganges so that they could escape the enemies pursuing them.

Statues of the Buddha meditating welcome the faithful to the platform. These were added in the first century BC during Gupta rule when taboos prohibiting the human image of the

278-279 The northern torana is the most elaborate and best preserved of the four entrances to the Great Stupa (also called Stupa 1). They were added to complete the monument in the first century BC during the Satvahana dynasty.

278 bottom left Detail from the second and third architrave on the northern torana of the Great Stupa. At the top there are sculptures of a lion and wood nymph.

278 bottom right This bas-relief of the Wheel of Law supported by bodhisattva is also from the north torana. The reliefs narrate episodes from the Vessantara Jataka, which tells the story of one of the incarnations of the Buddha before he achieved Enlightenment.

279 top As it appears today, the Great Stupa dates back to the second century BC, but it incorporates an older section attributed to Ashoka, the emperor of the Mauryan dynasty that spread Buddhism throughout the subcontinent.

279 bottom Carved in sandstone and corresponding to the west torana, this effigy of the Buddha meditating is, like the other three in the Great Stupa, an addition made to the monument in AD 450 by the Gupta dynasty.

280

280 top The gana, the paunchy dwarves that are traditionally associated with Shiva in Hindu tradition, support the architrave of Stupa 3's only torana.

280 center left In 1851, two valuable relics were found in Stupa 3: they were fragments of bone set with pearls, crystals, amethysts, and lapis lazuli, and belonged to two of the Buddha's foremost disciples. Today these objects are in the British Museum.

280 center right With a single torana, Stupa 2 stands on a medhi (platform) and is enclosed by a balustrade decorated with bas-relief medallions. It was probably built in the second century BC.

280 bottom left Temple 17 is a splendid example of Gupta architecture and the precursor of the classical Hindu style that was later developed at Khajuraho and in Orissa. The temple has a flat roof supported by four columns decorated with lions.

divine became less stringent, whereas in the bas-reliefs of Ashoka, the Buddha is shown as a bo tree (under which he achieved enlightenment), as a wheel of the Law (which represents his sermons), as a horse (to symbolize his abandonment of earthly riches), and as a line (an emblem of his path towards nirvana).

Next to the south-facing *torana*, Ashoka placed a stone obelisk on which a sort of guide to the places of pilgrimage was carved in Pali, the most ancient language in India. Dozens of other stupas were built around the Great Stupa, all smaller and in various states of conservation, as are the remains of the temples and monasteries that belong to various stages of the Buddhist faith in Indian history. Temple 18, from the seventh century, is surprising for its unmistakablly Greek appearance, proof of the cultural legacy left by Alexander the Great during his expedition to India.

The merging of the asceticism of Buddhism with the more melodramatic and theatrical set of Hindu cults is demonstrated by monasteries 45 and 47 on the south side of the hill. Here the elaborate high reliefs portraying the Buddha surrounded by the divinities of the Ganges and Yamuna rivers, sensual dancers, and even erotic scenes inaugurated a new spiritual and artistic era that was to reach its apogee in the temples of Khajuraho.

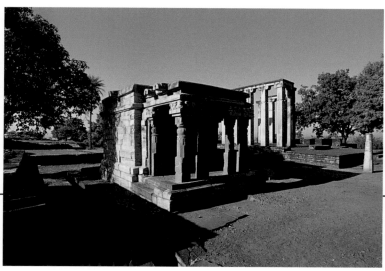

280 bottom right Vihara 45 is Sanchi's most majestic and best-conserved monastery. Note the temple at the center; this was built between the ninth and tenth centuries when Buddhism was slowly being supplanted in India by Hinduism.

281 top The elephant is one of the animals depicted in the medallions carved on the balustrade of Stupa 2. Pilgrims practiced the deambulatory ritual called pradakshinapatha around it in a counter-clockwise direction.

281 bottom Crowned by a richly decorated halo of floral motifs, this statue of the Buddha meditating is found in Vihara 45. The monastic complex also has statues of the Hindu river gods Ganga and Yamuna.

The Caves at Ajanta

INDIA

State of Maharashtra
Registration: 1983
Criteria: C (I) (II) (III) (VI)

NEW DELHI

AJANTA

282-283 The monumental chaitya (a Buddhist sanctuary with naves) in Cave 26 has some of Ajanta's most refined architectural and decorative features. At the back of the room there is a stupa with an effigy of the seated Buddha that, curiously, faces west.

282 bottom The richly decorated exterior of Cave 26. This is part of a group of five caves, some of which were never completed, dug in the seventh century at the southwest end of Ajanta's horseshoe-shaped cliff.

In the *Padmapani*, the Buddha is shown gracefully holding a blue lotus flower between the thumb and forefinger of his left hand. A heavy crown weighs down his head and his large almond-colored eyes are half-closed in an expression suggesting sublime peace. Around him, there is a festive group of musicians, lovers, monkeys, and peacocks. In the *Simhala*, though, the scene features cruel overtones, with a *bodhisattva* who saves a group of shipwrecked people from the cannibalism of a tribe of voluptuous and bloodthirsty she-devils.

These and many others are splendid illustrations of the *Jataka*, the sacred text recounting episodes from the life of the Buddha in the many incarnations he experienced on his path to enlightenment. Painted in the 30 caves at Ajanta, they are a series of works of extraordinary artistic and religious qualities. Moreover, they provide a vivid picture of the behavior and customs in India during the era of the Gupta dynasty.

Set in an attractive horse-shoe-shaped hill on a bend of the river Waghora in the Deccan Plain, the caves were home to a large community of monks from the second to sixth centuries, and provided shelter to travelers during the monsoon season. Some of the caves were temples (*chaitya*) and others monasteries (*vihara*). In the earliest of the caves, the iconography follows the dictates of the Hinayana school, in which the Buddha could only be represented through symbols, while in later caves the more libertarian Mahayana school is evident, in which each of the

Buddha's lives is described in figurative detail.

The scenes are very beautiful and feature large numbers of figures, and are at times cruel, serene, and sensual, and even have erotic undertones. They feature women, men, demons, creatures with human faces and birds' bodies (*yaksha*), musicians (*gandharva*), and heavenly dancers (*apsara*) in settings with flowers, trees, fruits, and animals. Many of the caves have architectural features and sculptures that merge perfectly with the paintings to create interiors of great beauty. Also remarkable is the iconographic

283 top left Detail of a high-relief in Cave 26. To the right of the Buddha, who sits in the lotus position, stands the bodhisattva Vajrapani. He holds a scepter (vajra) from which the Varayana school of Buddhism took its name.

283 top right A colossal Parinirvana statue in Cave 26 represents the Buddha lying on one side at the moment he passes from terrestrial life to nirvana. As it filters through the cave entrance, the light increases the transcendent effect of the effigy.

283 center This is the façade of Cave 19; it was carved in the second half of the fifth century at a time when the Mahayana school of Buddhism had reached its zenith.

283 bottom The chaitya in Cave 19 is the most spectacular in Ajanta. The columns are decorated with delicate images of bodhisattva and Buddha.

284 top Carved in the sixth century, Cave 2 is a monastery (vihara). Note the columns and ceiling, which are adorned with lotus flower medallions and a patterned barrel-vault. These were probably vestiges of the Hellenistic art brought to India by Alexander the Great.

284-285 Detail of the fresco in the portico of Cave 17 where episodes of the Buddha's previous incarnations are narrated. On the right, two individuals of royal birth embrace lovingly and share a last cup of wine before giving all their goods to the poor.

syncretism of the paintings, given that they were done largely by Hindu artists, particularly in the fourth and fifth centuries when Ajanta had a stable population of 200 monks.

The pictorial technique used was tempera *a secco*, in which the cave walls and ceilings were covered with a mixture of clay, cow dung, and vegetable fiber about three inches thick, and then with a thin coat of mud. Before the mud dried, the artist traced out the picture with a cinnabar stick. He then colored it in using natural pigments and lastly fixed it all with a layer of gluten.

Around 650, the caves at Ajanta were abandoned due to the decline in popularity of Buddhism relative to Hinduism and to the growing importance of the religious community at nearby Ellora. For centuries, the site remained forgotten, half-hidden by the vegetation. It was rediscovered by chance in 1819 by a group of British officers who had been led there by the traces of a tiger they were hunting. In contrast to this fortunate event, the

people who studied the masterpieces
were struck by misfortune: in 1866, the
English artist Robert Gill, who spent 26
years at Ajanta copying the paintings
onto paper, saw his work go up in flames
in a fire at Crystal Palace in London.
Ten years later, another blaze in the
Victoria and Albert Museum reduced
the efforts of his assistant to ashes. In
addition, the first, unrefined attempts
at restoration in 1920, sponsored by
the ruler of Ajanta, the nizam of
Hyderabad, produced more harm
than good.

Today the spell seems to have
ended, and conservation work by the
Archaeological Survey of India is
producing excellent results.

286 top One of the portraits on the walls of Cave 10. The frescoes in this chaitya were painted in the second century BC when the Hinayana school reigned supreme, according to whom the Buddha could only be represented symbolically.

286 center The barrel vault in Cave 10 has ribbing that frames the paintings of the Buddha meditating and lotus flowers. It was on these walls that British army officers wrote the date of their discovery of Ajanta.

286

286 bottom Cave 9 (first century BC) has a chaitya 45 feet long. Only a few fragments remain of the frescoes that once covered the walls; the stupa, topped by a reliquary in the form of an upside-down pyramid, is in good condition.

286-287 The principal sculpture in Cave 16, a vihara, also portrays an unusual (and not perfectly proportioned) Buddha sitting in Western style. The masterpiece in this vihara is a fresco called 'The Dying Princess'.

287 bottom Detail of a fresco in Cave 9; the brightly-colored images of the Buddha protected by jewel-laden parasols symbolize temporal and spiritual supremacy.

The Caves at Ellora

INDIA

State of Maharashtra

Registration: 1983

Criteria: C (II) (III) (VI)

288 The chaitya in Cave 10 has a life-size effigy of the Buddha seated in European style, and a ribbed ceiling rising from octagonal columns.

289 top left A feature of the superb, two-level facade of Cave 10 is the balustrade onto which a wide, three-part window opens.

289 top right Built in the sixth century, Cave 21 is the oldest Hindu cave at Ellora.

289 bottom left The elaborate, porticoed entrance to Cave 21 has a podium in front of the main entrance that supports Nandin, the white bull that Hindus consider Shiva's mount.

289 bottom right Also dedicated to Shiva, Cave 29 has an unusual cross-shaped plan; a square cella at the center has an entrance on each side. The portals have remarkable high-reliefs of guardian deities.

Dakshinapata was the name given by the Indians to the road that passes through the most important places of pilgrimage on the subcontinent. Traveled by merchant caravans, over the centuries it was adorned with huge numbers of monuments as symbols of the wealth of the rulers and the fervor of the pilgrims. Among these sights, the caves of Ellora stand out, enclosed in the basalt hill of Charanadari on the Deccan Plain close to the modern city of Aurangabad.

The term "cave" does not do them justice, nor does it pay tribute to the devout rulers of the Gupta dynasty who commissioned them, nor to the caves' exceptional cultural, religious, and artistic value. They are, in fact, a set of temples (vihara) and monasteries (chaitya) carved out of the rock and completed with a series of sculptures documenting the sequence, and overlaying, of the Buddhist, Hindu, and Jain cults in India.

Crossing the hill from south to north, the visitor first comes to the Buddhist and earliest caves (sixth and seventh centuries). There are 12 in all and the style in which they were produced mirrors the passage from the austere Hinayana school of Buddhism, which forbade the human representation of the divine, to that of the Mahayana. This school of thought expanded the religion and introduced the concept of bodhisattva worship, venerating the series of prince Siddhartha's various incarnations on his journey towards enlightenment. Also represented in the Buddhist caves is the mystic Vajrayana school, which arose when Buddhism began to rival Hinduism. The most magnificent of the Buddhist caves is number five, called the Maharwada; it has a main chamber over 65 yards long that was once used as a refectory. However, the most important sculptures are found in cave number six, which contains an effigy of Mahayamuri, a god of knowledge portrayed sitting on a peacock. This bird was later assimilated

to Sarasvati, a Hindu goddess of analogous powers. The transition from Buddhism to Hinduism is evident in cave number 12, called Tin Tala, an enormous vihara on three levels.

Nothing in the ascetic Buddhist caves, though, prepares the visitor for the extraordinary 17 caves that follow. Dug between the seventh and ninth centuries, they are mostly dedicated to Shiva, the most powerful and ambiguous of the gods that crowd the Hindu pantheon. Cave number 16 – its gray rock covered with white stucco to symbolize the perennial snow – is an astonishing reconstruction of Kailash, the mountain sacred to Indian mythology as the abode of the gods. Built on the orders of King Krishna I Rashtrakurta (756–773), the cave is the largest monolithic structure in the world. It took more than 100 years and 1,000 men to remove the 220,000 tons of rock, but its massive dimensions – double those of the Parthenon – are only one of the characteristics that make this construction unique. The carvers were

290 top left Nandin's sanctuary is one of the many temples in the spectacular Cave 16.

290 top right The porticoed room on the north side of the first floor of Cave 16 has massive columns adorned with friezes.

290-291 Cave 16, Ellora's masterpiece, was conceived by King Krishna I (756–773) as a model of the sacred Mount Kailash.

291 top Cave 12, known as Tin Tala (three floors), marks the passage from Buddhism to Hinduism at Ellora.

291 center top The effigies of five bodhisattvas and seven Buddhas decorate the top level of Cave 12, which was used for teaching and meditation.

291 center bottom The courtyard facing Cave 32 is dominated at its center by an elegant pavilion crowned by an elaborate pyramid structure inspired by the temples of south India.

291 bottom The tree spirit Yaksha Matanga (in the middle of the picture) graces the top level of Cave 32.

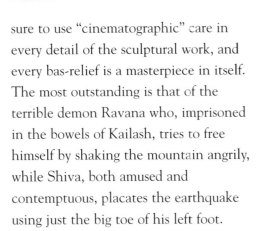

sure to use "cinematographic" care in every detail of the sculptural work, and every bas-relief is a masterpiece in itself. The most outstanding is that of the terrible demon Ravana who, imprisoned in the bowels of Kailash, tries to free himself by shaking the mountain angrily, while Shiva, both amused and contemptuous, placates the earthquake using just the big toe of his left foot.

The last four caves on the hill were excavated between the ninth and eleventh centuries when Jainism began to be more widely practiced in India. Although an attempt was made to compete with the Hindu caves, none could match their magnificence. However, their delicate decorations seem like lacework, their most conspicuous features being the sense of serenity that pervades them and their total absence of violent images. The Jain religion still professes a "fundamentalist" form of peace, and its monks are obliged to wear a bandage across their mouth so that no living creature can be disturbed by their presence, not even by their breath.

The Monuments of Hampi

INDIA

District of Bellary, Karnataka
Registration: 1986
Inscription on the World Heritage in Danger List: 1999
Criteria: C (I) (III) (IV)

292-293 Slightly off the beaten truck compared to the monumental complexes of Vithala and Hampi bazaar, the temple of Acyutaraya lies near Matanga Hill. Its sculptural decorations are of great beauty.

292 bottom A detail of the stucco-lined arches on the first floor of the Lotus Mahal. The lovely building was a present from king Krishna Deva Raya to his consort; its design included an efficient ventilation system.

NEW DELHI

HAMPI

In 1443, the Persian ambassador Abdu'r-Razzaq was visiting Hampi, the capital of Vijayanagar (City of Victory), and was so impressed he left behind a dazzling description of it. For the inhabitants of the magnificent city, he wrote, roses were indispensable to the daily meal. They were everywhere, and the petals were sold in large sacks at the bazaar. There, on the stall counters, it was possible to buy rubies, sapphires, pearls, and diamonds, the same stones that adorned the women at court.

The city was the heart of what was to be remembered as the last great Hindu empire of the subcontinent. It covered an area corresponding to the present-day states of Karnataka, Andhra Pradesh, and Maharashtra. It enjoyed a favored position in a hollow protected on three sides by mountains and, on the fourth, by the fast-flowing Tungabhadra River. The city was founded in 1336 by Hakka and Bukka, two Hindu brothers who had been forcefully converted to Islam by the sultans of Delhi and who then betrayed the new religion. The site was chose for reasons of both defense and religion, given that in the epic poem *Ramayana*, Kishkinda, the kingdom of the monkeys, was located there and that, according to legend, the first amorous encounter between Shiva and Parvati took place on the banks of the Tungabhadra.

The later rulers of Vijayanagar restored and beautified the Hindu temples in much of India and revived the art and literature that had been part stifled by the arrival of the Moghuls. However, in their capital they introduced an architectural style that took Islamic aspects and enriched them with an almost unconventional form of Hindu iconography.

Hampi is dotted with towers that were built to allow the members of court to observe from above the celebrations of the Dussehra, a religious festival whose fame extended beyond the borders of

India. The city also boasts wonderful works of architecture like the Pavilion of the King's Balance, in which the ruler used to sit on a plate while another was filled with an equal weight of grain and money to be given to the poor. The Queen's Bath is a pool ringed by galleries and fountains in the form of lotus flowers from which perfumed water flowed. Then, the Lotus Mahal was an exquisite pavilion reserved for the women at court, and, next to it, there were the magnificent elephant stables crowned by ten high domes.

293 top The walls of the city that was the capital of the Vijayanagar Empire are 19 miles long and in some parts are 33 feet high.

293 center The Queen's Bath is a square construction featuring an architectural design and decoration that reveal a strong Islamic influence. Note the elegant balconies overlooking the open-air pool. The building was for the exclusive use of the women at court.

293 bottom Built as a refuge from the hot summer weather, the Lotus Mahal is the most elegant pavilion in the zenana, the section of the royal city where the women lived in a gilded enclosure.

294 top A tall, smooth column is a feature of the small Jain temple known as the Ganigitti. In the east part of Hampi, it is one of the oldest in the city (late fourteenth century).

294 center left Carved in an S-shape from a single block of granite, the columns are the most surprising feature of Vithala temple. The building was dedicated to Vishnu, but legend has it that the god himself considered it too sumptuous and therefore impious.

294 center right A granite processional chariot, a rathi, stands on the east side of Vithala temple. The extraordinary sculpture includes a representation of garuda, the phoenix that symbol of Vishnu.

The bazaar is a colonnaded street that leads to the temple of Virupaksha, in which there is a courtyard supported by columns carved with strange sea creatures. However, it is in the temple of Vithala that the "living" architecture of Vijayanagar reached its peak. The building appears as a series of sinuous columns and towers carved with floral and zoomorphic motifs. Standing in front of it is an imaginative granite representation of the chariot of the gods, the wheels of which actually turn around an axle. This marvel was commissioned by Krishna Deva Raya, during whose reign (1509–1529) Vijayanagar achieved its greatest splendor. Shortly after him, in 1565, the Moghul army descended on the empire with fury. In six months, Hampi was stripped of its treasures, the court was exterminated, and the city was left in ruins. Set far away from the main tourist trails, Hampi is a magical place. Its temples are inhabited by communities of *sadhus*, the "holy men" of the Hindu religion, and the atmosphere is fascinating. Unfortunately, to remind visitors that they have not wandered into a fantasy world, two modern bridges overlook the city, which are used by an increasing number of motorized vehicles. UNESCO long opposed the construction of the bridges, but the government of Karnataka remained deaf to the organization's remonstrances, considering the modernization of the road network essential for economic development. For this reason, Hampi was inscribed on the list of World Heritages Sites in Danger in 1999.

294 bottom left Decorated with a continuous frieze of dancers, elephant fights, and figures of humans and assorted animals, the royal platform was built so members of the court could have a good view of the celebrations of the traditional Dussehra Festival.

294 bottom right The magnificent elephant stalls are a series of large rooms topped by domes. Note the colonnaded pavilion at the top: this is where the musicians played as the elephants left the stalls to take part in royal ceremonies.

295 Detail from one of the columns in Vithala temple. Note the superb anthropomorphic and zoomorphic high-reliefs.

The Monuments at Mahabalipuram

INDIA

State of Tamil Nadu
Registration: 1984
Criteria: C (i) (ii) (iii) (vi)

296 top and 297 bottom left The enormous bas-relief of the Krishna mandapa recounts the episode in which the god lifted Mount Govardhana with a single finger to protect his friends the shepherds. Here Krishna is shown milking a cow with one of the gopa, the companions of his youth.

296 bottom Mahishasuramardini Cave is, like the others, a mandapa, or rock temple. It is named after the splendid bas-relief that depicts the struggle between the goddess Durga and the buffalo-demon called Mahishasura.

From the earliest hours of the morning, the village of Mahabalipuram echoes with the tapping of hundreds of chiselers producing religious statues. Sculpture is the principal activity in this coastal zone of Tamil Nadu, a corner of ancient India just 32 miles from Chennai (Madras). The skills of the chiseler have been handed down from father to son for generations. King Narasimha Varman I set up a school of sculpture in Mahabalipuram in the seventh century. The dynasty he belonged to, the Pallava, governed much of southern India from the first to eighth centuries. Their capital was Kanchipuram, wheras the territory's port was located at Mahabalipuram. Narasimha Varman I wished to beautify the village so that as one left by boat, it would provide the traveler with a beautiful memory of the land just left. Today the village's monuments are considered the most refined examples of sculptural art in India.

On a rock, split by a crack, a bas-relief was carved measuring 98 by 39 feet. The scene is of an episode from the epic poem, the *Mahabharata*, in which the hero Arjuna performs penance in order to win Shiva's favor and obtain a magic weapon from the god. On the left side of the relief, Arjuna is shown standing on one leg watching the sun through a prism formed by his two hands. Next to him, Shiva appears, and, further down, a temple dedicated to Vishnu. The rest of the scene shows wise men meditating, animals, and, where the crack has been used to represent the Ganges River, pilgrims busy performing the rite of *Sandhya vandhana* in honor of the sacred river. The right side of the relief features

elephants and monkeys, and there is even an emaciated cat imitating the posture of Arjanta and surrounded by rats made brave by the cat's promise to do penitence. This is a story within a story, and reveals a sense of humor that is quite unusual in Indian art. At the time of Narasimha Varman I, a water tank over the relief allowed water to trickle down the crack of the Ganges to arouse the astonishment of the many pilgrims that visited the site.

Also of interest are the *mandapa*, the caves carved to function as temples. Adivaraha *mandapa* has several panels: in one, Vishnu is shown in his incarnation as the boar Varaha; in the one next to it, the same god rests on a bed of serpents;

296-297 This is one of the most unusual bas-reliefs in India: it represents the penitence of Arjuna, one of the key episodes in the epic poem the Mahabharata. It was carved in the seventh century and is commonly known as the "descent of the Ganges". The sacred river is represented by the wide crack in the rock.

297 top The bases of the columns at the entrance to the Varaha II mandapa are carved with horned lions. The portal to the cella is sculpted with two dvarapala (guardian deities).

NEW DELHI

MAHABALIPURAM

297 bottom right The bas-
reliefs in the Varaha II
mandapa tell the story of
Vishnu, the protector,
saving the Earth goddess

from the mud. Here the god
is lying down; he can be
recognized by the crown of
serpents (naga) that he
wears.

298 top The Dharmaraja and Bhima constitute the complex of Pancha Pandava ratha, named after the five heroes in the Mahabharata. Their architecture provided the basis for the successive Dravidian style that developed across all of southern India.

298 bottom Built at the start of the eighth century, this temple, thought to be the oldest stone temple in all India, represents the cosmic mountain and stands on the Mahabalipuram beach.

298-299 Four of the five ratha at Mahabalipuram. They are small monolithic buildings carved in imitation of temples but never used for worship. Note the life-size effigy of a bull representing Shiva's mount.

299 top According to experts, the elephant in front of the ratha of the twins Nakula and Sahadeva is the most realistic and accurate in all Indian art.

299 center The figures on the panels of the Dharmaraja ratha include Ardhanarishvara (Shiva and his consort Parvati in a single figure), Brahma, king Narasimha Varman I, and Hari Hara (a combination of Shiva and Vishnu).

299 bottom The entrance portico to the Bhima ratha the largest on the site. The construction remained uncompleted, probably as a result of the death of king Narasimha Varman I.

in another there are human figures, attributed to the Pallava king Simhavishnu (574–600) and his son Mahendra I (600–630). Mahabalipuram's most elegant sculpture is to be seen in the Mahishamardhani *mandapa*; it portrays the terrible goddess Durga defeating a demon with the head of a bull. In another cave, to which a columned entrance was added at a later date, the exploits of Krishna are illustrated.

Behind the village, there are five *rathas*. Although the name means "cart," these are early monolithic temples representing Arjuna, Bhima, Dharmaraja, Nakula, and Sahadeva – the five Pandava brothers, the heroes of the *Mahabharata* – and their shared wife Draupadi. The reliefs are of great beauty but were never finished, probably due to the death of Narasimha Varman I.

The superb "Temple of the Beach" overlooks the sea. Dedicated to Shiva and richly decorated, it represents the final phase of Pallava art, which influenced the subsequent art of the Chola dynasty. The temple was built in the seventh century, during the reign of Narasimha Varman II, and has been made even more suggestive by the erosion of the sculptures by the action of the waves over the centuries. A legend claims that there used to be a further six temples next to it. Following an underwater survey in 2002 by a British team in collaboration with the Archaeological Survey of India, blocks of stone and sculptures covered by thick sea vegetation were discovered about 760 yards from the shore – evidence that every legend contains a grain of truth.

The Sacred City of Anuradhapura

SRI LANKA

DISTRICT OF ANURADHAPURA
REGISTRATION: 1982
CRITERIA: C (II) (III) (VI)

The history of the origin of the kingdom of Sri Lanka is blurry around the edges with legend. The first inhabitants of the island arrived from northwest India in 483 BC. They were Hindu Aryans – and here the myth comes into play – led by Anuradha, a disciple of an individual of divine origin, King Vijaya. The *Mahavansa*, the oldest text relating to Singhalese history, attributes the foundation of Anuradhapura, the capital of the country, to his son Pandukabhaya.

Little or nothing is known of the next

two centuries. Then – and here the legend presents itself again – King Devanapiya Tissa (260–210 BC) was party to an extraordinary encounter: out on a hunt one day, he found himself confronted by a procession led by Mahinda, the son of India's great emperor Ashoka. Welcomed by Devanapiya Tissa with all honors, Mahindra came to the capital, bringing with him a new religion: Buddhism. The Ceylonese king and all his court converted immediately, thus Mahindra gave the city the sacred relic of the Buddha's collarbone to sanctify their conversion. Meanwhile, Mahindra's sister, Sanghamitta, planted a shoot taken from the Bodhi tree, under which Siddhartha Gautama had received enlightenment thus becoming the Buddha.

Referred to as the Sri Mahabodhi, the enormous tree (a *Ficus religiosa*) is the world's oldest historically certified tree. It stands at the center of ancient Anuradhapura in a special enclosure, protected by three tiers of metal fence, and is visited by thousands of pilgrims who hang traditional prayer flags on the tree and bathe it with milk. It is forbidden to pick the leaves, even those that have fallen.

Since the day of the miraculous encounter, Anuradhapura has been the religious center of the island. On a secular level, the city remained the capital until the tenth century (with a brief interruption between 477 and 495), when the court transferred to Polonnaruwa.

The *Mahavansa* and two foreign texts, the *Periplus of the Eritrean Sea*, written by a Greek sailor in the first century AD, and the travel diary of Fa Hien, a fifth-century

300 top Built in the third century BC by king Devanapiya Tissa to hold the sacred relic of the Buddha's shoulder-bone, the Thuparama Dagoba is the oldest Buddhist building in Sri Lanka. It is part of the sacred Mahavihara complex.

300 center Elegant frescoes and sculptures decorate the wahalhadas, small refined temples placed at the four points of the compass to protect the dagoba in Anuradhapura.

300 bottom The eighth-century Mandalagiri Vihara contains an effigy of the Buddha meditating surrounded by lotus columns with capitals decorated with bas-reliefs of makara, mythological creatures symbolizing the Ganges.

Chinese monk, furnish a description of ancient Anuradhapura. The city was laid out on a precise plan and boasted a sophisticated water provision system, majestic temples, hospitals, and separate residential districts for court dignitaries, merchants, and foreigners. Because the houses and civil monuments were built of wood, all that remains of ancient Anuradhapura is an immense stone religious complex, with the exception of a few pools that collected rainwater and the foundations of a royal palace.

The city was designed as a "model of the cosmos." The 1,600 columns in the Loha Pasadra, built by King Dutugemini (161–137 BC), attest to the splendor of a monastery that once housed a thousand monks. It was originally a nine-story building with a bronze roof and

300-301 *The Ruwanweli Dagoba has a platform decorated with a frieze of elephants. According to the Buddhist cosmogony, elephants hold up the universe. At the top there is a two-foot-tall rock crystal tall brought from Burma.*

301 *bottom Almost double the size of an Egyptian pyramid, the Jetavanarama Dagoba stands 396 feet high on Anadhapura plain. It is named after the sacred garden in which the Buddha achieved Enlightenment.*

decorations in gold and precious stones intended to make it resemble paradise. Its several *dagoba* (dome-shaped reliquary temples) have a profound Buddhist symbolism. They were designed by architects in the shape of an air bubble in milk, as fragile and pure as the ascetic life. The largest, the 400-foot Jetavanarama Dagoba (restored with the aid of UNESCO) dominates the city; the oldest, the Thuparama Dagoba, was built in the third century BC to contain the Buddha's collarbone; and the most elegant, the Ruwanwelisseya Dagoba, features walls decorated with a continuous frieze of elephants.

It might be argued that the Samadhi Buddha, a statue that portrays him in a serene and compassionate pose, represents Anuradhapura's undying spirit. Pilgrims readily swear that the face of the Buddha on this statue changes expression with the alteration in the angle of the sunlight. Carved in sandstone in the third century AD, it is the most venerated image in Sri Lanka.

Sigiriya
SRI LANKA

DISTRICT OF SIGIRIYA
REGISTRATION: 1982
CRITERIA: C (II) (III) (IV)

Their skin is amber-colored and their full breasts are barely covered by the thin fabric of their garments. They smile in a complicit manner and shoot glances filled with longing as they offer lotus flowers to the observer. Some of them dance, swaying their heads ringed by diadems and arms bound with bracelets.

Perhaps divine creatures – *apsara*, the celestial dancers of Buddhist and Hindu tradition – or perhaps handmaidens at court, the enchanting girls painted on the west wall of Sigiriya rock are an ode to love, and their astounding realism is a derivation of the long established artistic practice of the mimetic imitation of nature.

According to the *Sihigiri Vihara*, the ancient Singhalese book that contains a sort of "tourist guide" to Sigiriya, an artist (unfortunately anonymous) painted a magnificent procession of 500 girls on the rock. They were so beautiful that whoever looked upon them fell in love forever.

During the reign of King Kasyapa I, terracotta statuettes of the girls were made and donated to visitors as souvenirs. Today, more than 1,500 years later, only 22 girls remain from the procession, but they have not ceased to arouse admiration.

Sigiriya Fort, a magnificent princely city built on top of a sandstone monolith towering 660 feet above the dense tropical forest in the heart of Sri Lanka, looks like heaven on earth. However, the seat of the Singhalese kingdom between 477 and 495 was built as the result of a hideous crime: patricide. As recounted in the earliest text regarding Singhalese history, the *Mahavamsa*, Kasyapa I built it after killing his father, Dhatusena I, by hanging him upside down in a tomb while still alive, and then usurping the throne from his half-brother Mogallana.

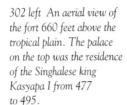

SIGIRIYA

COLOMBO

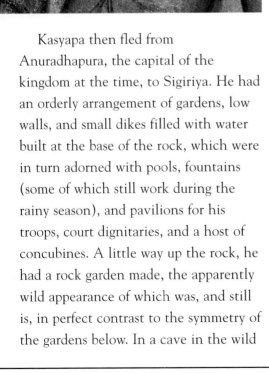

garden, Kasyapa had an audience room built with a 16-foot-long throne, various cisterns to collect rainwater, and a small theater where the first performances of music and poetry in the history of the island of Ceylon were held.

Around 1,500 graffiti with short verses and romantic poetry covered the Kat Bitha (Mirror Wall), a stuccoed wall rendered as shiny as a mirror that led to the entrance to Kasyapa I's palace. Here, a monumental gate was built in the shape of a lion using brick and wood lined with stucco, of which all that remain are the two paws and claws carved out of the rock. Entering through the lion's mouth, the visitor was obliged to climb an almost vertical flight of steps up the face of the rock where the procession of girls was painted. Today, only the foundations can still be seen, as the ancient stairway has been replaced by a safer metal one, but the view is still worth the climb.

Kasyapa I lived in the palace at Sigiriya for almost 18 years, the time necessary for Mogallana to organize a powerful army and march on the fort. To avoid being taken prisoner by his half-brother, Kasyapa killed himself, his end marking the end for Sigiriya as well. The capital returned to Anuradhapura, whereas, until the end of the fourteenth century, an ascetic community of monks occupied what had once been a place of earthly pleasures.

Kasyapa then fled from Anuradhapura, the capital of the kingdom at the time, to Sigiriya. He had an orderly arrangement of gardens, low walls, and small dikes filled with water built at the base of the rock, which were in turn adorned with pools, fountains (some of which still work during the rainy season), and pavilions for his troops, court dignitaries, and a host of concubines. A little way up the rock, he had a rock garden made, the apparently wild appearance of which was, and still is, in perfect contrast to the symmetry of the gardens below. In a cave in the wild

Polonnaruwa

SRI LANKA

DISTRICT OF POLONNARUWA
REGISTRATION: 1982
CRITERIA: C (I) (III) (VI)

POLONNARUWA

COLOMBO

304-305 One of the most interesting monuments in the city, the Vatadage is a round building built to house a small dagoba that contained relics of the Buddha. Though its wooden roof has disappeared, three of the four original statues of the meditating Buddha still sit inside at the four points of the compass.

304 bottom The face of the 23-foot tall statue in the Gal Vihara. It is still uncertain if the statue is of Ananda (the Buddha's favorite disciple) or the Buddha himself, portrayed during the second week after Enlightenment.

305 top The Nissank Latha Mandata is the small, elegant temple where king Nissankamalla usually went to listen to the monks chant the sacred text of the Pirith.

The Galpota, or "Book of Stone," is a granite mass in the shape of a palm leaf almost 30 feet long, a little over three feet wide, and weighing 25 tons. A procession of elephants dragged it the 59 miles from the quarry at Minithale to Polonnaruwa, the splendid capital of the island of Ceylon. The "Book" bears an inscription that tells of the deeds of King Nissankamalla I and provides instructions on good government left by the king to his successors.

Nissankamalla was in power from 1187 to 1196, nine years that marked the apogee of the Singhalese kingdom at Polonnaruwa. Unfortunately, his heirs did not follow his advice and the city declined as quickly as it was created. Perhaps this was simply its fate, in the same way that the Singhalese king Vijayabahu I decided to abandon Anuradhapura in 993 for Polonnaruwa as he fled from the army of the Chola kings of southern India that had landed on the island.

At that time, Polonnaruwa was not even a village. It was inhabited by a community of monks and comprised a temple and some lodgings where the royal family liked to retire in meditation. Even after the court had moved to the site, it remained small for some time as the succeeding sovereigns were more occupied with containing the Indian invasion than beautifying the place with monuments worthy of a capital.

Peace came in 1153 when Parakramabahu I ascended the throne. The over thirty years of his reign saw the flourishing of a marvelous city whose fame spread from the coasts of the subcontinent to Southeast Asia. The provision of irrigation water to the fields was guaranteed by the creation of a series of 165 reservoirs and 3,000 canals. This extraordinary engineering project had at its heart the Parakrama Samadra, a reservoir created just to the southwest of Polonnaruwa covering eight and a half square miles and bounded by a wall 40 feet high and eight miles long.

Polonnaruwa became a city of gardens enclosed within three concentric rings of walls, and Parakramabahu had a royal palace built that boasted a thousand rooms. Of the original seven stories, only three remain, built from brick and adorned with bas-reliefs (like the adjacent Audience Hall and royal baths). The four upper floors were made from wood and have consequently all been lost. The city's other constructions – temples, monasteries, and dagoba

305 center This statue of the Buddha meditating stands on a platform decorated with mythological motifs and is one of the four large granite statues in the Gal Vihara, the most outstanding complex in the ancient city.

305 bottom A pair of elephants protects a seated figure whose pointed cap is typical of Southeast Asia and a symbol of divine or royal dignity.

306-307 Two monks pay homage to the 45-foot-long statue of the Buddha in the Gil Vihara. He is shown lying in the position that represents nirvana. The softly draped body, half-

closed eyes, and half-smile are details that make the statue emanate a sense of sublime serenity.

306 bottom left The Kiri Vihara in the background

was also known as the Milk Dagoba because it was originally lined with white stucco, rises above the ruins of a temple in the dalada Maluwa, the complex containing the Vatadage.

306 bottom right Part of the large monastic complex of the Alahana Parivena, the Kiri Vihara is a large dagoba that, according to tradition, was given to the community by queen Subhadda, the wife of Parakramahu I.

307 top The temple of Hatadage is decorated with elegant bas-reliefs and sculptures. Its name means "built in 60 hours". As the ancient Singhalese divided the day into 60 units, the name signifies the temple was built in a single day.

307 bottom A view of the Lankatilaka, the brick temple that celebrates the glory of Polonnaruwa. Its walls, 55 feet high, are adorned with friezes of lions, trees, and houses in the kingdom, some of which are four stories high.

307

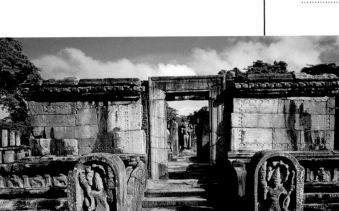

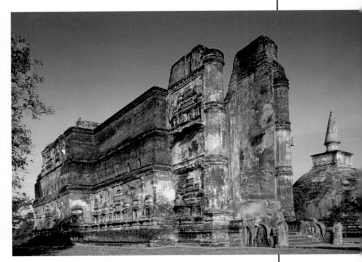

(dome-shaped reliquaries) – had the function of restoring Buddhism to Ceylon, which had been undermined by the advance of the Hinduism imported by the invaders. The most spectacular is the Gal Vihara, which consists of four colossal statues that were originally protected by brick structures. The first statue depicts the Buddha meditating, seated on a throne decorated with the effigies of two lions; the second portrays Buddha surrounded by his disciples; the third, 22 feet tall, is a standing Buddha; and the magnificent fourth statue is 46 feet long and shows the Buddha lying down in the position representing nirvana. A colossal image of the Buddha was also erected in Lankatilaka, a temple with 55-foot-high walls decorated with friezes celebrating the glory of Polonnaruwa.

Parakramabahu's constructions were widely embellished with statues and bas-reliefs, such as those decorating the "moonstones" that lie at the entrance to the temples. His successor, Nissankamalla, added the Nissanka Latha Mandapa, a building supported by columns in the form of lotus stamens in which monks chanted the songs from the sacred book of the Pirith. Most importantly, he built the Vatadage, an enormous dagoba containing one of the Buddha's teeth.

Nissankamalla's successors succeeded in preserving the sacred relic by taking it to Kandy, but nothing could prevent the new Indian offensive. In the thirteenth century, the Singhalese kingdom was broken up and the Chola occupied Polonnaruwa, building temples there in honor of Shiva and Vishnu.

Ayutthaya

THAILAND

PROVINCE OF PHRA NAKHON SI AYUTTHAYA

REGISTRATION: 1991

CRITERIA: C (III)

The enemy was attacking from the north, hidden in the hills behind Sukhothai. There were many of them and they were well armed. To the king, U Thon, any attempt at resistance seemed pointless, so one day in the year 1350, he took the painful decision to abandon the capital of Siam, which had been founded little more than a century earlier. He called on his military planners and ascetics for advice on where to build a new city. The first counseled him to head south into the plain, where future enemies could not arrive without being seen a long distance off. The second consulted the sacred texts and suggested looking for the *nam*, the water at the root of the Thai people's symbolism, where it flowed in a spiral.

With these instructions, the king sent his emissaries to reconnoiter. They returned having found an ancient Khmer settlement at the center of a complex river system created by the confluence of the Mae Nam Lopburi, the Pasak, and the Chao Phraya. U Thon went to the chosen site and removed the first spadeful of earth, revealing, as he did so, a snail – the spiral predicted by the ascetics. This was the origin of Ayutthaya, whose name means "the Invincible." It is derived from a Sanskrit word referring to Ayodhya, the abode of the god Rama in the Indian epic poem *Ramayana*.

Although the new capital – which it was to last until 1767 when it was destroyed by the Burmese army – never

308 bottom left A series of Buddhas in the meditation pose, now headless, line the brick walls of Wat Phra Mahathat, built in 1374.

308 bottom right Roots of a Ficus religiosa wind around the face of the Buddha from a statue destroyed centuries ago.

309 Wat Ratchaburana was built in the fifteenth century by Borom Rachathirat II, the seventh king of Ayutthaya, to commemorate his two elder brothers. They were both killed during a duel on elephant-back to win the succession to the throne following the death of their father, Intharacha I, in 1424.

308 top left Wat Ratchaburana was destroyed in a fire in 1967, but restorations have ensured that its towers can still be admired. The crypt in the central tower, recently opened to the public, still has fragments of frescoes.

308 top right Adorned with a yellow silk drape, this effigy of the Buddha stands at the foot of the prang, the Khmer-style brick tower now in ruins that stands in the middle of the splendid Wat Phra Mahathat.

310 Two chedi, reliquaries similar to stupas in the Buddhist world, flank the prang (central tower) in Wat Ratchaburana. Inside the chedi, like in the crypt of the prang, various objects of great value have been found that now make up the nucleus of the collection in the Chao Sam Phraya National Museum in Ayutthaya.

311 top left The architecture of the mondop, a large rectangular building in front of Wat Ratchaburana's central tower, was strongly influenced by Burma. The mondop was a pavilion that provided access to the temple.

311 top right Elegant and well-proportioned, the prang of the Wat Phra Ram rests on a stepped platform marked by chedi. Founded in 1369, the temple owes its current appearance to a fifteenth-century restoration and still has fragments of stucco decorations.

equaled the beauty of Sukhothai in the eyes of its rulers, European and Chinese visitors who were admitted to the court of Ayutthaya left behind enthusiastic accounts of its fabulous treasures. The "Ayutthaya period," during which the city boasted as many as one million inhabitants, coincided with the greatest splendor of the kingdom of Siam, which slowly extended its territory into what are now Laos, Cambodia, and Myanmar.

During the monsoon season, Ayutthaya seemed to float on water. The houses and palace were built on stilts and were all made from wood, as stone was only allowed to be used for religious buildings. The temples were constructed on earthworks that symbolized the vessel of redemption of which Buddhist mythology spoke. Consequently, only the temples remain of that marvelous city. The largest, Wat Phra Si Sanpet, was used by members of the royal family and contained a statue of the Buddha 50 feet tall covered with 550 pounds of gold leaf, but the Burmese invaders melted it down. The temple complex centers on a lotus-filled rectangular pool and is dominated by three

large chedi (bell-shaped reliquary monuments). At a slight distance stands the Wat Phra Mahathat with a tower in Khmer style (called a *prang*) supported by statues of the sacred bird Garuda. The tower is ringed with brick and stucco statues of the Buddha, around some of which tree branches have grown. Opposite, there are the ruins of Wat Ratburana with some chedi still bearing fragments of frescoes.

The ruins of statues, chedi, and monastery foundations dot the valley, half-buried by the vegetation. Fortunately, this natural covering helped to prevent theft by treasure hunters over the centuries. Thanks to the recognition of UNESCO, Thai authorities have launched a program of restoration work and have provided the site with a small army of security staff. Today Ayutthaya exists once more as a religious symbol, monks have returned to the site, and the statues of the Buddha are draped with orange silk.

311 bottom left Once full of treasures, the majestic Wat Phra Si Sanpet (built in 1491) is part of the palace complex of the rulers of Ayutthaya. It was used as a prayer hall by the members of the royal family.

311 bottom right This effigy of the Buddha covered in gold-leaf is in the collection of Ayutthaya Museum. The site's most famous statue is held in Viharn Phra Mongkol Bopit, next to Wat Phra Si Sanpet, and is an object of profound devotion by the Thai people.

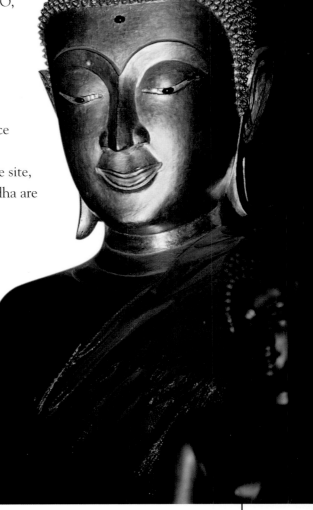

Angkor
CAMBODIA

PROVINCE OF SIEM REAP
REGISTRATION: 1992
INSCRIPTION ON THE WORLD HERITAGE IN DANGER LIST: 1992
CRITERIA: C (I) (III) (IV)

312

Zhou Ta-Quan arrived in Angkor in August 1296 as the legate of the Chinese emperor and remained for a year, noting down every secret of the Khmer Empire in his diary. "At the center of the kingdom stands a golden tower…," he wrote. "On the east side, there is a golden bridge guarded by two gold lions…[It is] an amazing sight…." The sovereign, who was treated like a demigod, lived surrounded by servants, wives, and concubines. The kingdom was governed by intricate ranks of ministers, generals, and priests under his command. The Khmer Empire had already begun its path of decline, but the account of Zhou

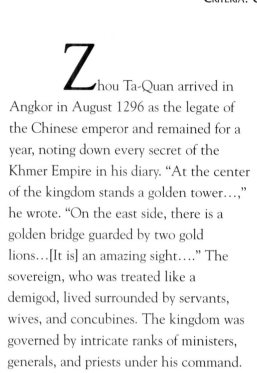

Ta-Quan – the only one to have survived of the civilization that dominated Southeast Asia from the ninth to fourteenth centuries – describes a world still flourishing, whose artistic sophistication had no equal in the Middle Ages.

The European discovery of Angkor is attributed to Henry Mouhot, who visited Indochina in the 1860s. "One of these temples" he claimed, in reference to Angkor Wat, "is more magnificent than any building left by the Greeks or Romans." Actually, Mouhot's *Voyage à Siam et dans le Cambodge* was published about ten years after the account written by the missionary Charles-Emile Bouillevaux, but that had gone unrecognized. Moreover, much earlier, Portuguese travelers had reached Angkor in the sixteenth century and described it as a city surrounded by walls. Even at the time of Mouhot's "discovery," Angkor Wat still accommodated a thousand or so monks.

Works of Khmer art were exhibited at the universal exhibition in Paris in 1878 with the result that Angkor soon became the destination of several French archaeological expeditions. These resulted in 1901 in the foundation of the Ecole Française d'Extrème Orient, the primary aim of which was to study the monuments of the Khmer Empire. Soon the first wealthy European tourists began to arrive, and the stones of Angkor became the highly sought-after prey of unscrupulous collectors. Among these treasure hunters was a young, enterprising French writer, André Malraux.

In 1924, Malraux sailed for the Far East in search of adventure. Given that he

312 top The central tower at Angkor Wat represents the most important of the five peaks on Mount Meru, the Hindu mountain of perfection, surrounded by continents and seas. At one time a gold statue of Vishnu, the god with whom the king identified, was held in the prang.

312 center Stretching more than 3,000 by 2,600 feet, the large perimeter wall at Angkor Wat has a gate on each side, but the main entrance, embellished by a portico 771 feet long and decorated with sculptures and carvings, stands on the west side.

312 bottom The third level of Angkor Wat has four courtyards surrounded by porticoes. Construction of the temple required laterite and sandstone from a quarry several miles away that was transported by raft down the Siem Reap river.

312-313 The temple is entered through the external wall down an avenue about 1,600 feet long flanked by balustrades in the form of naga, the sacred serpent of Indian mythology. Angkor Wat was built as the funerary temple of Suryavarman II, who ruled from 1112 to 1152.

ANGKOR

PNOM PENH

314 top Apart from the remarkable bas-reliefs on the perimeter walls, Angkor Wat boasts abundant statues and carvings of rare harmonious proportions, like these two dancers. Note the detail in their hairstyles, closely-fitting clothes, and the jewelry on their arms and necks.

314 bottom and 314-315 Three details from the battle of Kurukshetra on the south section of the east gallery at Angkor Wat. The battle is described in the Hindu epic, the Mahabharata. The armies of the Kaurava and Pandava arrive respectively from north and south and meet furiously in the middle of the panel; the combatants strike, twist, and cling to one another with exceptional plasticity in a scene of great beauty.

was rather short of money, when he arrived in Angkor he stole several sculptural blocks from the Banteay Srei (Temple of the Women) in order to sell them back in Paris. However, all did not go as planned: he was arrested under the accusation of smuggling antiquities and was only saved by the diplomatic activity of his wife, who rushed back to France in search of influential friends. Based on this experience, Malraux wrote his autobiographical novel *La Voie royale* (*The Royal Way*, 1930), which became his first literary success.

Historically, the Khmer's settlement of the area began in 802 when King

on a small island in the middle of a large reservoir.

Although its architecture is Angkor's most interesting feature, the Khmer capital's vast and complex hydraulic system merits a description. At the heart of the 147-square-mile site, two large reservoirs, the *baray*, lie on either side of the Angkor Thom citadel walls. Measuring five miles long by a mile and a half wide, the *baray* were fed by floodwater from the nearby Tonle Sap Lake, and it is believed that their waters were used to irrigate the fertile alluvial plain on which the city stood.

The center of attraction in Angkor is

Jayavarman II established his capital on Phnom Kulen, a hill 18 miles northeast of Angkor. Towards the end of the ninth century, the Khmer started construction of the large, permanent temples in the Roluos group: the Preah Ko, with six brick towers decorated with sculpted sandstone and stucco reliefs, the Bakong dedicated to Shiva, consisting of a pyramid flanked by eight towers and secondary sanctuaries, and the Lolei, built

Angkor Wat, the magnificent temple built by King Suryavarman II, who ruled from 1112 to 1152. Surrounded by a dike in the shape of a giant rectangle measuring 207 yards across, 1600 yards long, and 1400 yards wide, Angkor Wat is an immense temple-mountain three stories high made from sandstone and laterite (the two types of stone used by the Khmer). At the corners of the second and third floors as well as at the center of

the latter, towers were built topped by pointed domes. The wat is a classical Hindu temple, as demonstrated by the almost 900 yards of wonderful bas-reliefs decorating the perimeter of the central temple. Wandering through the corridors, a depiction gradually unravels of the battle of Kurukshetra between the armies of the Kaurava and Pandava kingdoms, taken from the Hindu epic poem the *Mahabharata* and scenes from the *Ramayana*. One wall commemorates the

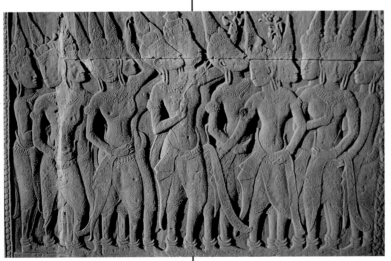

315 bottom Angkor Wat also has scenes of daily life, in particular on the corners of the portico. On the other hand, the large panels in the galleries are dedicated to war scenes, like the one between the army of Suryavarman II and the Cham, or represent mythological scenes from the Hindu tradition.

316 top Each of the 54 towers on the Bayon has enigmatic, smiling faces of the bodhisattva Avalokiteshvara at the cardinal points of the compass. These also represent the ruler contemplating his kingdom and watching over his subjects.

316 center The walls of the citadel of Ankkor Thom (seven and a half miles long and 26 feet high) were built by Jayavarman VII after the Cham sacked the Khmer capital. The five gates, 66 feet high, are adorned on the sides with elephant trunks carved in the stone.

deeds of Suryavarman II, portrayed on an elephant majestically cutting through the ranks of his army, and another illustrates a metaphor of the Hindu hell and paradise. Finally, there is a rendering of the "churning of the great sea of milk," in which 88 devils (the *asura*) and 92 gods (the *deva*) turn the sea to butter in order

to extract the elixir of immortality.

The triumph of Khmer architecture was achieved under Jayavarman VII, who reigned from 1181 to 1201. He was responsible for the construction of Angkor Thom (the citadel) and its 26-foot-high, seven-and-a-half-mile-long defensive wall. Within the walls there are many extraordinary buildings, such as the Bayon temple, in which Buddhism takes the place of Hinduism, with the spoils of the *bodhisattva* Alokitesvara featured above the 144 gigantic stone faces of the sovereign that gaze out in all directions. The walls of the Bayon are carved with fine bas-reliefs narrating the daily life at Angkor and the war conducted by Jayavarman against the Cham, the Khmer's traditional enemy.

The citadel contains many splendid temples, like the Baphuon, the Preah Palilay, the Tep Pranam, and above all, the Terrace of the Leprous King, a 23-foot-high platform decorated with five orders of superb sculptures that probably housed the crematorium of the Khmer sovereigns. Another outstanding construction is the Terrace of the Elephants, named after the pachyderm decorations on the walls, a long gallery that was used for reviewing the army.

Other temples worth mentioning out of the more than 100 in Angkor are the

Three-headed pachyderms on the Elephant Terrace stretch their trunks to the ground thus functioning as of a columns.

316-317 Built between 1181 and 1218 by Jayavarman VII, who was also responsible for many of Angkor's most memorable monuments, the Bayon was the first temple to mark the passage from Hinduism to Buddhism, and was, at the same time, one of the last mountain-temples at Angkor.

317 top Like Angkor Wat, the Bayon is decorated with superb bas-reliefs along all of its nearly 4,000 feet of perimeter walls, featuring more than 11,000 figures. Here we see the Cham army on the march.

317 bottom Until the 1920s, archaeologists studying Angkor believed that the Bayon was still a Hindu temple dedicated to Shiva. In 1928, Philippe Stern, curator at the Musée Guimet in Paris, and the epigraphist Georges Coedes revealed its Buddhist nature.

Ta Prohm, the walls of which are being crushed by the roots of enormous ceiba trees, the Preah Neak Pean, an unusual small temple on an islet in the middle of a large pool, and the Banteay Srei, the Temple of the Women that is considered the jewel of classical Khmer art for the delicacy of its sculptures and the sophistication of its engravings. Perhaps this was why it attracted the attention of an aesthete like Malraux.

Nevertheless, the times have not changed very much since the 1920s. In 1992, when Angkor was registered as a World Heritage site, UNESCO considered the Khmer capital to be one of the sites in danger. The United Nations had just intervened in the country after the war between Cambodia and Vietnam, and

armed bandits were still active in the area despite much of it having been laid with mines by the Khmer Rouge under Pol Pot.

Today, with the political situation stablized, art thieves are the main worry. Impossible to guard because of its vast size, the site is exposed to frequent thefts of priceless sculptures and fragments. The impoverished condition in which the Cambodian people live does not help to protect the art treasures. Although more than 7,000 statues have been stored away from the public and substituted with modern copies, every year examples of the art of the greatest civilization of Southeast Asia head for the West.

318 left Situated 12 or so miles northeast of Angkor Thom (the "pink temple" or "temple of the women") is Banteay Srei, a jewel of Khmer traditional art.

318-319 Banteay Srei is probably the Khmer temple in the best state of preservation despite being more than 1,000 years old. In this bas-relief of incomparable beauty, we see Indra, god of the sky and dispenser of the rain, on his three-headed elephant Erawan.

319 top Built at the end of the tenth century and dedicated to Shiva, Banteay Srei features a square layout with entrances on the east and west sides. Until a few years ago, it was practically impossible to enter, as the area had been heavily mined during the war between the Khmer Rouge and the Vietnamese army.

319 center Unlike the rest of the complex, the three central sanctuary-towers, adorned with male and female gods and carvings of great artistic value, probably date back to the end of the thirteenth century.

319 bottom It was in the library of the Musée Guimet in Paris that the twenty-year-old André Malraux read Henri Parmentier's description of the devata – the gods sculpted at the corners of the Banteay Srei, which inspired him to set out on his calamitous journey to Cambodia.

The Sanctuary of My Son
VIETNAM

DISTRICT OF DUY XUYEN, PROVINCE OF QUANG NAM
REGISTRATION: 1999
CRITERIA: C (II) (III)

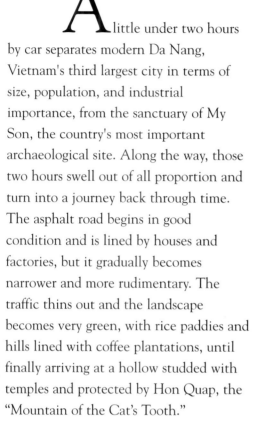

A little under two hours by car separates modern Da Nang, Vietnam's third largest city in terms of size, population, and industrial importance, from the sanctuary of My Son, the country's most important archaeological site. Along the way, those two hours swell out of all proportion and turn into a journey back through time. The asphalt road begins in good condition and is lined by houses and factories, but it gradually becomes narrower and more rudimentary. The traffic thins out and the landscape becomes very green, with rice paddies and hills lined with coffee plantations, until finally arriving at a hollow studded with temples and protected by Hon Quap, the "Mountain of the Cat's Tooth."

Today silence reigns over My Son, the place that was the religious and intellectual capital of the Cham dynasty from the late-fourth to mid-thirteenth centuries. Its temples may not have been as magnificent or sophisticated as those in Angkor (Cambodia), Pagan (Myanmar), or Borobodur (Indonesia), but they represent important architectural evidence regarding the longest-lasting kingdom in Southeast Asia.

Divided into two clans – the *Narikel Vamsa* (Coconut Clan) and the *Kramuk Vamsa* (Betel-nut Clan), which respectively governed the central and southern regions of Vietnam – the Cham appeared around the year 200 and held onto power until 1692, when they were overthrown by the Hué warlords. Right from the start, they remained independent of Chinese culture but maintained close contact with the Khmer in Cambodia and the rulers of Java. From this island, they borrowed, and then altered, many customs and beliefs, which Java had in turn absorbed from India. The Cham organized the kingdom into a caste system, adopted the Sanskrit alphabet, embraced Hinduism, and legitimized their power by claiming descent from a common origin with Shiva. My Son was dedicated to this god and represented the spiritual counterpart of Shimapura (today known as Tra Kieu), the political and administrative capital of the kingdom.

The buildings at My Son are divided into ten religious complexes identified by letters of the alphabet marked by the French archaeologists who first studied them. Each is characterized by buildings

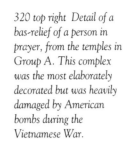

320 top right Detail of a bas-relief of a person in prayer, from the temples in Group A. This complex was the most elaborately decorated but was heavily damaged by American bombs during the Vietnamese War.

320-321 A view of Group C, built in the eighth century. An effigy of Shiva was worshipped in the main sanctuary (kalan), which is referred to as C1 and decorated externally with bas-reliefs.

320 left Few of the superb sculptures in the temples of My Son have remained in situ. However, a museum for the surviving buildings is being built inside Building D1.

321 top Made from brick and sandstone blocks, the temples of My Son are similar in structure to those at Angkor in Cambodia.

associated with the cults of the gods.

Although both the architecture and iconography of the temples is apparently borrowed directly from Indian, Javanese, and Khmer monuments, the Cham were technical innovators. Following a fire that destroyed the wooden temples at the start of the sixth century, they rebuilt them using brick and sandstone bound by a resin extracted from an indigenous plant. It is thought that they built each monument, covered it with a coat of the special binder, and then "baked" it before moving on to the decorative stage.

At the height of the Cham's splendor, there were 68 temples at My Son, but due to attacks and frequent floods, only 25 were still intact by the twentieth century. During the Vietnam War, bombs dropped by the American B52s destroyed a further five, including Complex A, the most important on the site. In 2003, the Vietnamese government launched a project for the study, restoration, and improvement of the drainage system in the surrounding land.

in the shape of square or oblong towers – the symbol of the sacred mountain of Shiva – similar to boats. Each set of buildings consists of an entrance, a main temple (called a *kalan*, which contains a *lingam*, the phallic obelisk that represents Shiva), a building to accommodate pilgrims, a storeroom for ritual objects and sacred texts, and a series of small temples dedicated to other gods in the Hindu pantheon that face the cardinal points of the compass. The buildings were decorated with statues (now in the museum in Da Nang) and bas-reliefs of divinities, celestial musicians, plants, and animals

The Temple Complex of Prambanan

INDONESIA

PROVINCE OF YOGJAKARTA, JAVA
REGISTRATION: 1991
CRITERIA: C (I) (IV)

A member of the vast Hindu pantheon, Durga is a goddess with a terrifying face and many arms who in India is worshiped with fear because of her irascibility and vindictiveness. In Java, however, her cult was associated with more tranquil characteristics and today, many centuries after Hinduism was replaced by Islam on the island, the effigy of the goddess – the most sophisticated in the temple complex of Prambanan – receives floral offerings from women invoking Durga's protection in matters of the heart.

The reason for the statue's special significance is linked to a legend according to which it portrays a princess in the guise of the terrible goddess. The princess, whose name was Loro Jonggrang, supposedly attempted to avoid marrying a king whom she did not love by promising she would marry him only if he succeeded in building a temple with a thousand statues in a single night. The legend goes that the king asked the help of supernatural powers, and when the princess saw the work almost completed, she lit a fire to simulate the light of dawn. But the king saw through the trick, and in revenge, he turned the princess into a statue that, ironically, was the thousandth piece to complete the Prambanan.

It hardly matters now whether the statue represents a princess or Durga. The features of the figure were softened by the skill of an ninth-century sculptor engaged by Rakai Pikatan, the king of the Sanjaya dynasty to who is attributed the construction of the Prambatan. The fact is that the legend survived in spite of the majestic temple complex being lost from memory after the volcanic eruption of Merapi covered the site with ash. In 1733, it was this legend, handed down orally by the women, that prompted Dutch explorers to track down the monuments.

Not until more than a century after the discovery, however, did the British clear the ash off what appeared to be heaps of stones and then begin their reconstruction. Today, enclosed within a brick wall three feet high, only the nucleus of the complex has been restored. It is composed of three main temples, three secondary ones, plus eight more, four of which form the gates at the center of each side of the wall and the other four at the corners. It is supposed, however, that Prambanan originally had an additional 224, which stood inside an external enclosure.

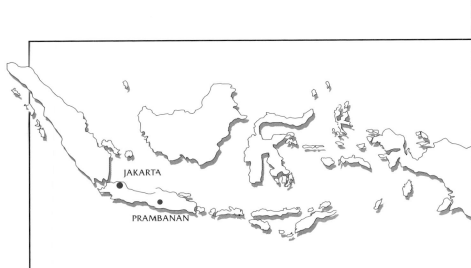

322 top right This high-relief of Shiva (recognizable from his symbol, the trident, on the right) adorns the small temple dedicated to the bull Nandin.

322 center Ganesh – the elephant god associated with knowledge, and with good luck – is depicted in the chamber west of the Candi Shiva Mahadeva.

322 bottom Candi Shiva Mahadeva is the most important temple in the complex and the most extraordinary example of Hindu art in Indonesia.

322-323 It has taken 35 years to restore the main temples at Prambanan. It is estimated that the complex had 224 sacred buildings, destroyed in the 16th century.

323 top A flight of stairs embellished with zoomorphic figures leads into the gallery surrounding the Candi Shiva Mahadeva. Opposite stands the temple of Nandin, Shiva's mount.

Though it is still only in a partial state, Prambanan is a majestic complex. The temple of Shiva – the object of particular devotion on Java – stands 155 feet tall in the center of the enclosure. Inside, four rooms contain respectively a statue of Shiva in his incarnation as the Destroyer, as Agastya (one of his many other incarnations), as Durga, and as Ganesh. On either side of the temple there are smaller twin temples dedicated to Brahma (the Creator) and Vishnu (the Protector) with their own statues. Facing these, the three secondary temples contain a statue of a cow (Shiva's steed), the swan associated with Brahma, and the phoenix – the Garuda, which is now the symbol of Indonesia – associated with Vishnu. All the temples are decorated with bas-reliefs of scenes from the *Ramayana*.

Prambanan lies a few miles from Borobudur, the magnificent Buddhist temple with which it shares both a more or less common age and fate.

Experts agree that their proximity to one another represents a close connection, probably resulting from a series of marriages between members of two dynasties, the Hindu Sanjaya and the Buddhist Sailendra. This expedient succeeded in the peaceful division of the island of Java and meant that the two great religions from India were able to coexist, albeit for a brief period.

324 top Several of the bas-reliefs are decorated with figures of great originality in the religious and iconographic tradition of Indian origin such as these graceful female figures engaged in the Balinese dance, the Kecak.

324 center Two lovers embrace tenderly in this relief in the temple dedicated to Shiva. Construction of Prambanan complex in the ninth century is attributed to Rakai Pikatan, a ruler of the Sanjaya dynasty.

324 bottom left Like in the panels in the adjacent temple dedicated to Brahma, these in the gallery of Candi Shiva Mahadeva feature episodes from the epic poem Ramayana. Which recounts the adventures of Vishnu in his incarnation as Prince Rama.

325 bottom right A remarkable similarity links the reliefs of Prambanan to those of Borobudur, attesting to relations between the Hindu dynasty of the Sanjaya and the Buddhist dynasty of the Sailendra. The two constructed the two religious sites respectively.

324-325 One of many, this image of Shiva on the temple dedicated to the god is particularly refined and detailed in the features of the face, the jewelry, and hairstyle.

326 top Seen from above it is clear that Borobudur was designed to imitate a mandala, the "sacred design" that Buddhists, Hindus, and Jainists consider a map of the Tantric course towards purification.

326-327 This spectacular view reveals the grandeur of the temple built in the eighth century by Samargunta, a ruler of the Sailendra dynasty that governed Java from the sixth to tenth centuries.

JAKARTA

BOROBUDUR

The Temple of Borobudur

INDONESIA

PROVINCE OF YOGJAKARTA, JAVA
REGISTRATION: 1991
CRITERIA: C (I) (II) (IV)

*327 top and bottom
Numerous statues of the
Buddha stand on Borobudur's
upper terrace (top); the last
series of bas-reliefs (below)
before reaching the terrace
tells the story of the final
phases of the Buddha's path
to Enlightenment.*

The name of Sir Thomas Stamford Raffles, the versatile and charismatic English colonial administrator, has always been linked to the natural world and history of Southeast Asia. In his honor, the largest flower in the world was named *Rafflesia*, which he discovered while exploring the forests of Malaysia. He was also responsible for the discovery of one of the most interesting and mysterious Buddhist monuments in the world.

The people of Java had always told fabulous tales about the temple of Borobudur – the name of which is an abbreviation of *Bhumisan Brabadura* (the Ineffable Mountain of Accumulated Virtues) – but when in 1814 Sir Thomas arrived in the valley that he had been told was the site of the fantastic monument, he found nothing but rocks scattered around the forest, half-buried by layers of volcanic ash. It took six weeks and the work of 200 men to clear away the debris and vegetation but, in the end, they found blocks of black granite, many of which were decorated with sophisticated bas-reliefs and sculptures. These were then numbered and catalogued, which left only for them to be reassembled in the correct order. The work begun by Raffles was completed successfully more than 150 years later thanks to UNESCO.

Today the temple of Borobudur stands majestically in the valley in all its ancient splendor. It is known that it was commissioned in the eighth century by Samaragunta, the king of the Sailendra dynasty that governed the island of Java from the sixth to tenth centuries. The Sailendra were a branch of the Indian Chandella dynasty (famous for having built the temples at Khajuraho) that had left the subcontinent after having converted to the Buddhist faith. It is therefore known that the construction techniques and iconography used were "Indian." What remains uncertain is the reason the temple was built, and what the meanings of the mass of symbols and esoteric messages inside the building were.

Borobudur is a sort of pyramid in the shape of the lotus, the flower that was sacred to the Buddha. It has six stepped, four-sided stories on which a further three circular levels stand, and these are crowned by a central stupa. The platform on which the monument stands is decorated with 160 bas-relief panels featuring scenes of the human world, which is governed by desires; the five successive stories bear 1,300 panels recounting the lives of the Buddha and 43 *bodhisattva*, with episodes narrated in the sacred text of the *Jataka*. The circular terraces above have no reliefs but are adorned with small stupas with square or diamond-shaped openings in which the statues of 92 Vajrasattva or Dhyani Buddhas are set. Each of these statues has its hands in a gesture (*mudra*) that indicates one of the five directions: the east, represented by the *mudra* that calls Earth to witness the Buddha's enlightenment; the south, denoted by the gesture of blessing; the west, with the *mudra* signifying meditation; the north, in which the hands indicate liberation

from all fear; and lastly, the center, in which the *mudra* represents the teaching of truth. The stupa that sits imposingly above symbolizes the Buddha, Enlightenment, and Infinity.

When looking at the overall layout of the Borobudur, it is clear that it was built as a *mandala*, or "sacred pattern," considered by the Buddhist, Hindu, and Jainist religions (three of the major faiths in India) a map of the Tantric path to purification. In consequence, beyond the magnificence of the monument and the refinement of its reliefs and sculptures, the temple is first and foremost a philosophical work, through which the rulers of the Sailendra dynasty wished to assert themselves, recognizing that it is only through rightful actions that man can aspire to eternal life.

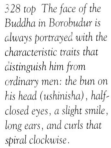

328 bottom *The detail refers to an episode in the Jataka, the sacred text that recounts the lives of the Buddha before he reached Enlightenment. The clockwise course followed by pilgrims towards the top of the Borobudur covers just over three miles. As the pilgrims study the bas-reliefs, they gradually obtain purification.*

329 top *Drummers follow a wedding procession in this detail of a relief from the middle terraces at Borobudur. It shows the world of humans still governed by the senses and the struggle between Good and Evil.*

329 bottom *Like the other bas-reliefs on the monument (which cover a total of 88,600 square feet), this panel of a group of musicians was originally painted in bright colors.*

328 top *The face of the Buddha in Borobudur is always portrayed with the characteristic traits that distinguish him from ordinary men: the bun on his head (ushinisha), half-closed eyes, a slight smile, long ears, and curls that spiral clockwise.*

328-329 *Extraordinary reliefs like the one shown, with graceful female figures among vegetation, have provided basic information on the architecture, daily life, art of war, moral values, clothing, dance, and commerce in Java in the eighth century.*

List of the Sites

The Americas

According to the *Saga of the Greenlanders*, in the year 1001 Leif Erikson – the son of the legendary Erik the Red – and his companions set foot on a blessed land. The streams were filled with salmon, and forests stretched in all directions as far as the eye could see. Nevertheless, it was not until 1960 that proof of the existence of a Viking settlement was found at L'Anse aux Meadows, a village at the tip of the Great Northern Peninsula on the island of Newfoundland. However, those first pioneers did not succeed in colonizing the new continent, so for Europeans the discovery of America continues to have occurred on October 12, 1492, when the caravels led by Christopher Columbus reached the coast of San Salvador.

In fact, *Homo sapiens* reached the Americas at least 30,000 years earlier across the 900-mile-long land bridge that crossed the Bering Strait between Siberia and Alaska. That along with a further two migrations led to the establishment of highly diversified peoples across most of the continent, at least according to the most accredited theories. However, recent finds at the Brazilian site of Serra da Capivara dating back to almost 50,000 years ago have revolutionized theories regarding the timeline of the population of the Americas.

With the exception of Serra da Capivara and the more recently discovered Cueva de las Manos in Argentina, the places of archaeological interest on the continent under the aegis of UNESCO are dominated by pre-Columbian civilizations, which flourished from Mexico to Peru between the start of the Christian era and the fifteenth century. The Aztecs, Mayas, and Incas all left traces of their passing, describing the evolution of complex and well-organized societies that developed systems of religious beliefs, produced high-quality forms of art, and even achieved significant results in the study of astronomy. The magnificent cities built by these peoples include the Mayan Tikal, Chichén-Itzá, and Palenque, the Aztec Teotihuacan, and the more modest but nonetheless beautiful ceremonial center of Machu Picchu built by the Incas. In addition, Latin America boasts an enigmatic heritage left behind by the very ancient civilization of Tiwanaku, the culture of Chavín de Huántar, and the peoples who created the colossal images known as the Nazca lines.

Much less has remained of the peoples that inhabited North America. Almost all the tribes of the North American Indians were semi-nomadic, living in daily contact with nature in temporary dwellings made from perishable materials. Any knowledge of their culture is the product of what has been preserved in the oral traditions of the few groups to have survived the arrival of the Europeans, with the exception of two sites: the *pueblos* of the Mesa Verde and in Chaco Culture National Historic Park, built between the ninth and twelfth centuries.

Mesa Verde
UNITED STATES

COLORADO
REGISTRATION: 1978
CRITERIA: C (III)

Professor J. S. Newberry was the first to talk about the Mesa Verde. It was 1859 and the geologist was drafting his report on an expedition carried out for the United States. He described a vast plateau that reached an altitude of 8,500 feet in southeast Colorado. He was referring to the Mesa Verde, or "Green Table" in Spanish.

It took 15 years before a photographer from the U.S. Geological Survey, W. H. Jackson, discovered the first rock shelter hidden by the walls of the natural wonder. That particular zone of Colorado seemed to be of interest to the mining industry and a few prospecting engineers accompanied Jackson into Mancos Canyon, where he

showed them what had unquestionably been a cliff dwelling, which, since then, has been called the Two-Story Cliff House. From this moment on, the area started to arouse much curiosity. A year later, another explorer sent by the government discovered the Sixteen Windows House, and shortly thereafter, the Balcony House.

On December 18th, 1888, while searching for cattle that had got separated from the herd, Richard Wetherill and his brother-in-law Charles Mason reached what today is called Sun Point, where they found a number of shelters, one of which was the Cliff Palace. A masterpiece of pre-Columbian architecture, Cliff Palace is built from rudimentary sandstone bricks and mud in the lee of the cliff and is one of more than 200 dwellings. There are also 23 religious constructions (called *kiva*), bedrooms, and storerooms for the harvest. According to specialists in the Mesa Verde Archaeological Project, who excavated the site from 1959 to 1972, Cliff Palace was built around the end of the twelfth century and could accommodate between 200 and 250 people.

The indigenous people, the Anasazi (Navajo for "the ancient ones'") settled here in the sixth century, living in the ravines or low shelters built on the plateau near the cliff face. They cultivated corn and beans on the flat top of the Mesa Verde (declared a national park in 1906) and hunted wild turkey. Their community numbered some thousands of inhabitants and was well protected from intruders because of the difficult approach to their territory. Only in the

eleventh century did they begin to construct stone buildings with several floors, referred to as *pueblos*, a term also used to indicate the people to distinguish them from the native peoples who lived in teepees. A little over a hundred years later, for reasons unknown, they abandoned the Mesa Verde to build new *pueblos* further south in the region of the Rio Grande.

MESA VERDE

WASHINGTON

332 top Characterized by elegant geometric designs, this terracotta vase was made by the indigenous people of the Acoma pueblo in New Mexico. They were one of the many tribes that considered the Anasazi their ancestors.

332 center A view from the top of Cliff Palace, the largest and most impressive of the Mesa Verde constructions. The people that lived in the area were the Anasazi, from which at least 23 indigenous tribes inhabiting Colorado, Arizona and New Mexico descended.

332 bottom In the photo the Spruce Tree House, takes its name from the huge Douglas fir that once stood in front of it. Built between 1200 and 1276, it has 140 rooms and nine kiwas, or ceremonial chambers.

332-333 Situated at the eastern end of Navajo Canyon, Square Tower House could accommodate 80 people. The focal element of this settlement is the three-story tower made of adobe, which has survived to the present day in excellent condition.

Around 3,900 sites of archaeological interest have been identified on the Mesa Verde, more than 600 of which are dwellings beneath overhanging rocks. Besides those mentioned, the most outstanding are the Long House (the second largest) and Spruce Tree House (the third largest), which was named by its discoverers in 1888 after the large Douglas fir cut down by another of the first explorers of the site. Step House is also remarkable because it is one of the few points in which evidence has been found of two successive occupations of the same site. A first basic shelter was built in the seventh century, whereas the grotto in which it was constructed was also occupied by a *pueblo* in the early thirteenth century. Recently, authorities have decided not to use the term Anasazi any longer to describe the peoples that inhabited the Mesa Verde and to refer to them instead with the more generic term "ancient peoples of the *pueblo*," the reason being that in addition to the Navajo, another 23 tribes claim to be descendants of the constructors of the Mesa Verde structures. These include the Ute, the Hopi of Arizona, and all the peoples whose ancestors lived in similar *pueblos* in New Mexico. None of these, though, reached the magnificent caliber of those built in the Mesa Verde.

Teotihuacan

MEXICO

District of México

Registration: 1987

Criteria: C (i) (ii) (iii) (iv) (vi)

334 bottom Built at the end of the Teotihuacan I period (third century BC to first century AD), the Pyramid of the Moon faces onto the square of the same name. This elegant construction is composed of four sloping floors and a monumental flight of steps.

334-335 A bird's-eye view of the ceremonial center of Teotihuacan with the Pyramid of the Moon in the foreground. Note the straight line of the Calle de Los Muertos (Street of the Dead), the city's main street, which is about half a mile long.

335 top left The Quetzalpapálotl Palace (Palace of the Quetzal Butterfly) stands to the left of the Plaza of the Moon and is the only example of an ancient covered building in Mexico.

While busy excavating the city of Teotihuacan, the Japanese archaeologist Saburo Sugiyama stumbled across an extraordinary grave in October 1999. In an underground *cella* near the Pyramid of the Moon, he found the skeleton of an adult male surrounded by roughly 150 burial offerings, including jade and obsidian figurines and tools, pyrite mirrors, sea shells, and the remains of eight eagles and two jaguars, which had probably been buried alive. Given the opulence of the grave furnishings, Sugiyama concluded that it was the grave of a ruler, the first of this sort of the 1,200 graves that had until then been discovered in the city.

Even though today the remains of a king have been uncovered, experts are still only able to make conjectures on the birth, development, and demise of Teotihuacan. It is thought that this, the largest and most important city in Mesoamerica, was founded in the third century B.C. by the union of a number of small agricultural communities. It grew rapidly between the first and seventh centuries A.D., boasting about 200,000 inhabitants during its period of greatest splendor. Then, in A.D. 750, it ceased to exist, perhaps destroyed by invaders from the city of Cacaxtla, perhaps by an epidemic, or maybe it was simply abandoned due to the fast erosion of the surrounding land. Forgotten for six centuries, the Aztecs rediscovered it, and, fascinated by the magnificence of its ruins, called it "the place where men became gods," which in the *náhua* language is translated as Teotihuacan.

Around 2,000 buildings remain on the city's 57 square miles. The monumental area runs along the Calle de los Muertos (Avenue of the Dead), a wide raised street (really a series of city squares joined by flights of steps) lined by low, wide buildings designed to exaggerate the visual impact of the pyramids of the Sun and Moon, the principal religious buildings.

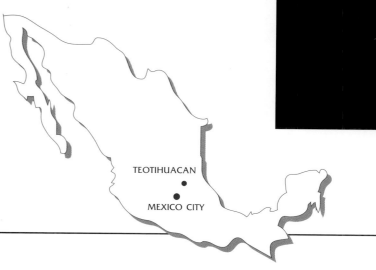

TEOTIHUACAN

MEXICO CITY

335 top right Probably inhabited by the sovereign or a member of the city elite, Quetzalpapálotl Palace gets its name from the inlaid decorations of sacred serpents and stylized butterflies on the columns in the patio, onto which the rooms face.

335 bottom Detail from the frescoes in the Temple of the Jaguar. The cat is shown with a feathered headdress blowing into a shell from which curls are exuded. These probably symbolize music or prayers to the god Tlaloc.

336 top and bottom Heads of long-fanged serpents wearing necklaces of feathers decorates the Temple of Quetzacoatl. These decorations were to become common in many Aztec and Mayan sites throughout Mexico.

336 center Found beneath a later pyramid, the Temple of Quetzacoatl is formed by four tiers decorated with the heads of feathered serpents and almost abstract masks of the god Tlaloc, recognizable by his prominent eyes.

The avenue is cut at right angles by streets leading to the residential districts, and also by the San Juan, the river that flows through the city center, which was canalized so as not to disturb the perfect symmetry of the city's layout.

At one end of the Calle de los Muertos stands the Ciudadela (Citadel), Teotihuacan's administrative center. It is a sunken plaza onto which the Temple of Quetzacoatl faces (so-named for its sculpted reliefs featuring the head of the sacred Feathered Serpent) and the buildings that were probably the houses of the priests. At the other end of the avenue stands the Pyramid of the Moon and, on the left, the Palace of Quetzalpapalotl, which is richly decorated with reliefs and frescoes of birds and butterflies and was probably the ruler's residence.

The most extraordinary monument in Teotihuacan is the Pyramid of the Sun, which stands halfway down the avenue. A square construction 235 yards long on each side, it stands 207 feet high; it has been estimated that it took over two and a half million tons of stone to build it, which were transported to the spot without the aid of either the wheel or beasts of burden. At the center of the Pyramid of the Sun, a cloverleaf-shaped cave is Teotihuacan's *sancta sanctorum*. It was also, it is thought, the reason why the city was built on this site, given that in the religion of Mesoamerica caves were thought to be where the gods and the people's ancestors were born, as well as the gateway to the world beyond the grave.

Nevertheless, this too is purely conjecture. Even the pyramid, as it can be admired today, is a reconstruction that is not entirely faithful to the original. Just like the on-and-off unscrupulous search for treasures supposedly hidden within it, in 1908, archaeologist Leopoldo Batres did not have any qualms about dismantling the structure. Unfortunately, his questionable methods have left his successors greatly perplexed.

336-337 Dated to around 100 AD, the Pyramid of the Sun is the most spectacular building at Teotihuacan. The two-and-a-half million tons of stone and earth needed to build it were transported to the site without the use of the wheel or beasts of burden.

337 bottom left The Pyramid of the Sun has five steeply inclined terraces. Inside, there is a grotto in the form of a cloverleaf that was probably formed by an underwater spring. It has been associated with the cult of the god Tlaloc.

337 bottom right The Citadel is an immense plaza surrounded by stepped platforms with a magnificent altar at the center. It was built to be the administrative center of the city.

Monte Alban

MEXICO

STATE OF OAXACA
REGISTRATION: 1987
CRITERIA: C (I) (II) (III) (IV)

The inhabitants of Oaxaca – one of the Mexican states with the highest percentage of indigenous people – claim to be descendants of the "people of the clouds." The name is a romantic one but it finds its justification in the fact that the Zapotecs, the ancient people that dominated the region for over a millennium, built their city on the top of a 4,450-foot mountain known at the time of the Spanish conquest as Monte Alban.

So far, nothing would seem out of the ordinary if it were not for the platform measuring 810 yards by 270 on which the city stood, which was leveled manually. In 500 B.C., a project of such

The city's name has, however, remained unknown. A few hieroglyphs mention a place called *Dauyacach*, the "Mountain of the Sacred Stones," while the Mixtecs, who occupied it from around A.D. 750 on, called it *Yucucui*, the "Green Mountain." The historical, architectural, and social development of the city has been divided into five phases. In the first phase (500–200 B.C.), Monte Alban was the capital of a state incorporating the settlements in the valley below. In the second phase (200 B.C.– A.D. 300), it took on the monumental appearance that it still has today and was embroiled in military campaigns and trading

338 left A view of the North Platform, believed by archaeologists to be the most important ceremonial complex in the city. It is thought that the buildings on the leveled section of the mountain top were frequented only by the priests and nobles in the theocratic Zapotec society.

338 right A detail of Building IV. The Zapotecs took their inspiration for the ceremonial center from Teotihuacan, the city to which they were closely linked and in which they had even founded their own neighborhood.

scope could only have been carried out with an enormous labor force. Also, as there were no springs on the mountain, the men themselves were obliged to provide the water, which they did by carrying filled goatskins from a long way down the valley. The water was then conserved in huge terracotta urns. The folly of building a city in such an inconvenient location can only justified by the will of the Zapotecs to demonstrate their dominion over nature.

with the nearby peoples.

During the third phase (300–750), the city's population came to number 30,000 and existed in close contact with Teotihuacan, the most important city in Mesoamerica. During the fourth and fifth phases (750–1520), the Zapotecs abandoned the city, probably as a result of the fall of Teotihuacan, and it was progressively occupied by the Mixtecs, who used it as a burial site.

338-339 A mystery surrounds the function of Building J, built in the third century AD. Shifted 45 degrees from the north, it is built in the shape of an arrow. Its off-center orientation compared to the strict north-south layout of the city suggests that it was linked to astronomical observation.

339 top The remains of the double row of six massive columns inside the complex referred to as the North Platform. are particularly interesting because of the fact that columns were very rare in the architecture of the earliest Mesoamerican cultures.

339 bottom left An aerial view of the city of Monte Alban at 4,600 feet above sea level. Rather than for its individual buildings, the site arouses admiration for the fact that before construction began the Zapotecs leveled the mountain top to create a platform measuring 2,460 by 820 feet.

339 bottom right Like the other pyramids at Monte Alban, Building M was built using the talud-tablero technique, which involved oblique walls alternating with vertical ones framed by slabs and originally lined with painted stuccoes.

To visitors today, Monte Alban is more striking for the dramatic nature of its buildings as a whole rather than for individual constructions. Despite recent restoration projects, it takes some effort to imagine it as it must have been in its prime, covered with brightly colored stucco. The great plaza is bordered by the ball court (it seems that in the Zapotec culture this game was not followed by ritual sacrifice) and various buildings that were mostly ceremonial in nature. The North Platform, which is reached up a flight of steps, was the site of the main religious complex. At the center of the plaza were found a temple (connected to others by a secret maze of passageways that allowed the priests to make unexpected and miraculous appearances)

341 top left and right The stelae of Monte Alban are carved with human figures, glyphs and pictograms, names and numbers, jaguars, (the feline symbol of the Zapotec royal family), and Cocijo (the rain god).

341 bottom This famous mask (ca. 100 AD) made from 25 pieces of jade with inserts of mother-of-pearl represents a bat, the symbol of the god of the night and death.

340-341 An aerial view of the North Platform from the Hundido Patio. The patio is a sunken court with an altar at its center, a type of religious building that only existed in the Zapotec culture.

340 bottom The ball-court at Monte Alban features no evidence of scoring but At the center there is a stone in the middle on which the ball was placed at the start of the match.

and a building that has been called the observatory though no evidence exists of Zapotec knowledge of astronomy. However, the most interesting construction is the one the Spaniards named Los Danzantes. The reason for the name lies in the stelae lined up along the gallery: they are decorated with bas-reliefs of human figures in contorted poses or with their limbs cut off. According to certain experts, these images are the symbols of the cities dominated by the Zapotecs; others believe them to be a sort of "visual" medical treatise, supported by the fact that there is a birthing scene among the representations.

Further down from the esplanade, there are some of the tombs used by the Mixtecs. They have been found to contain many objects of great value such as a marvelous jade funerary mask and a gold pendant depicting Mictllanteuhtli, the god of death. Today these can be seen in the museum of Oaxaca, in the lovely baroque city that shares the inscription as a World Heritage site with Monte Alban.

Palenque
MEXICO

STATE OF CHIAPAS
REGISTRATION: 1987
CRITERIA: C (I) (II) (III) (IV)

342 left A steep flight of steps leads to the burial chamber in the Temple of the Inscriptions where the slab covering Pakal's sarcophagus was discovered.

342 right This extraordinary mosaic jade mask covered the face of Pakal (615–683), the lord of Palenque.

342-343 Thick tropical forest surrounds the lovely archaeological site of Palenque. The elegance of the architecture, the beauty of the landscape, the mist parted by shafts of sunlight, and the presence of water confer a mystical quality on this ancient Mayan city.

343 top Standing 82 feet tall, with eight sloping levels and a majestic flight of steps, the Temple of the Inscriptions is named for its ornate hieroglyphics telling the story of Palenque.

In the suffocating heat, with the torrential rain and clouds of insects, the effort of digging, at times just with hands protected by gloves, for hours each day, for months on end, is great. Then there are the snakes, the most dangerous of which was called *nawiaka* by the descendants of the Maya, whose bite would kill you within an hour. However, all this was forgotten, at least according to the accounts written by the Mexican archaeologist Alberto Ruz, when a triangular door was found at the end of a narrow stairway that opened into a chamber that had remained secret for centuries. It was shrouded by a thin mist and seemed like a cave lined with ice, with stalagmites and stalactites shining like crystals. Once his eyes had grown accustomed to the dark, Ruz found the finely-carved stone cover of a sarcophagus on the floor…

It may seem like a scene from the film *Raiders of the Lost Ark*, but this was really the way that, in 1952, after four years of digging, Ruz discovered the first pyramidal tomb in the Americas, the eternal abode of Pakal, the legendary ruler of Palenque. Today the exquisitely beautiful objects that made up his grave furnishings – including a priceless jade mask – can be seen in the Mexico City Museum, but the magnificent tombstone is still in the underground chamber at the heart of the Temple of the Inscriptions, the most spectacular pyramid in Palenque.

The name Palenque was given to the archaeological site long after the ancient Maya had vanished, perhaps based on the name of a village at the edge of the ruins, Bahlam Kin. The Maya, however, called it *Lakam Ha*, or "Great Water," which perfectly describes its setting. Situated in the valley of the Río Usumacinta, the area with the highest rainfall in all of Mexico, Palenque lies in a dense forest featuring many waterfalls. It was this abundance of water and the fertility of the soil that allowed the city to develop and become rich. Although the history of the city covers the entire Classic Period from A.D. 300 to 900, the ruins seen today only date back to the period of the city's greatest splendor, which occurred in the seventh century during the reigns of Pakal and his son Chan-Bahlum.

Having ascended the throne at the age of 12 and died at almost 80, Pakal was a sort of Charlemagne of Mesoamerica. A man of great political and administrative skills, he encouraged the city's architectural and artistic development.

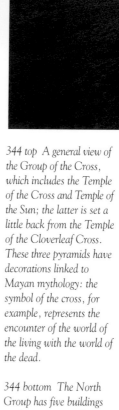

Besides the Temple of the Inscriptions – a steep pyramid 82 feet high divided into eight levels with a shrine on the top finely decorated with figures from Mayan mythology – the royal palace is in an excellent state of conservation. This is a set of residential and administrative buildings almost entirely covered with elaborate bas-reliefs. Also of great interest are the Temple of the Sun and Temple of the Cross, both of which are almost buried beneath liana vines. In pyramidal form, they have a sandstone shrine at the top adorned with reliefs of religious rituals and, on the inside, fragments of fine frescoes.

In Temple XIII, which stands a short distance from the Temple of the Inscriptions, a tomb similar to Pakal's was found a few years ago. It contained a series of jade and obsidian objects and trays that would have held food and drink for the journey to Xibalba, the Mayan world beyond the grave.

There were also the skeletons of a man and two women, one old and the other still an adolescent. The archaeologists tend to think that this is the tomb of Pakal's heir, Chan-Bahlum. Confirmation of the presumed family relationship between the two rulers awaits the publication of results of complicated laboratory tests that are currently attempting to reconstruct the DNA of the deceased.

344 top A general view of the Group of the Cross, which includes the Temple of the Cross and Temple of the Sun; the latter is set a little back from the Temple of the Cloverleaf Cross. These three pyramids have decorations linked to Mayan mythology: the symbol of the cross, for example, represents the encounter of the world of the living with the world of the dead.

344 bottom The North Group has five buildings used for ceremonial purposes built on a stepped terrace. One of these has a curious pagoda style of roof, and they all feature fragments of stucco decorations.

344-345 The sunset bathes the top of the Palacio with light. This set of administrative and residential buildings is the focus of Palenque. The purpose of the central tower is still debated: it was probably either a watchtower or an astronomical observatory.

345 bottom left The interior of the Temple of the Sun has panels of bas-reliefs that celebrate the power of Chan-Bahlum. The son and heir of Pakal, he took the throne in 684 and reigned for 18 years. He is credited with the construction of the temples in the Group of the Cross.

345 bottom right Superb reliefs of large figures, portraying elegantly dressed courtiers wearing feathered headdresses decorate the panels that line the base of the Palacio.

Uxmal

MEXICO

STATE OF THE YUCATÁN
REGISTRATION: 1996
CRITERIA: (I) (II) (III)

346 A series of masks of Chaac, the rain god, overlook one of the doors in the Nunnery Quadrangle. Images of this god are seen everywhere in the site: the Governor's Palace alone has 230, but it seems that there were originally 4,370.

347 top The most extraordinary pyramid in Mexico (the Pyramid of the Magician) is elliptical and stands 100 feet high with a temple on top. According to a legend it was built by a dwarf in a single night.

Published in 1843, *Incidents of Travel in Yucatán* was praised by George Byron as "the best travel book ever written." The author, the American John Lloyd Stephens, had spent two years on the sun-baked Caribbean peninsula feverishly noting down everything that he saw. The ruins of the Maya civilization had literally bewitched him, and the ancient city of Uxmal had impressed him more than any other. He compared it in magnificence to the Thebes of the Egyptians and stayed on the site for some time, camping inside the building the Spaniards had named the Palacio del Gobernador (Governor's Palace).

In truth, the king Chan-Chak-K'ak nal Ahaw – the first king to reside in the palace – was much more than a simple governor. According to the Mayan chronicles, he was descended directly from the gods. His portrait was carved on the main door of the palace and shows him seated on a throne, watched over by two serpents, and wearing the plumes of the sacred bird, the Quetzal, on his head.

The building has 20 rooms and measures 330 yards long, 39 wide, and 28 feet high. It stands on a platform composed of 500,000 tons of stone of which two-thirds are carved with decorations symbolizing the divinity of royal power. Of these, 230 show the face of Chac, the rain god, each of which is composed of 19 blocks of finely chiseled stone. Constructed between 900 and 915, the palace is the most outstanding monument in Uxmal. Archaeologists are unanimously agreed that the entire city is the most refined example of Mayan architecture, though Chichén Itzá is larger.

Uxmal was a flourishing center from the eighth to fourteenth centuries, and numbered 25,000 inhabitants. In the ancient language of the Maya, its name means "thrice born," even though the buildings of the city – built in Puuc style – were completed in the tenth century and there is no evidence of different building phases. The only

347 bottom left From the top of the Governor's Palace, the plain of Uxmal can be seen with the House of Turtles, the Nunnery Quadrangle, and the Pyramid of the Magician.

347 bottom right Originally part of a complex similar to the Nunnery Quadrangle, only the vast facade topped by an undulating crest of the building known as El Palomar remains.

MEXICO CITY   UXMAL

348 top An altar representing a jaguar stands in front of the Governor's Palace. Despite the name given to it by the Spanish, this extraordinary complex, built roughly 1,000 years ago, was the residence of the rulers of Uxmal.

348 bottom left The east building in the Nunnery Quadrangle (the building resembling a convent) features doors crowned with stylized geometrical motifs of Mayan huts.

348 bottom right The House of Turtles is dedicated to the animal linked to the myth of Creation. The Mayans identified the constellation of Orion with the creature's shell, out of which they believed the gods of corn-the cornerstone of the Mesoamerican diet-had been made to emerge by Chaac.

monument rebuilt five times is the Pyramid of the Magician, according to a tradition (though common to all pyramids in the Mayan world) that a temple should be built over an existing one at the end of every 52-year "cosmic cycle." Unlike the other Mayan pyramids, that of the Magician has an elliptical plan. The temple on the top has a richly decorated façade with an entrance that represents the open mouth of the god Chac.

Opposite the pyramid stands another masterpiece: the Cuadrángulo de las Monjas (Nunnery Quadrangle), a name suggested to the Spanish by the

place where those chosen as human sacrifices spent their last months. This hypothesis is backed up by the fact that next to the "Nunnery" lies the ball court, a traditional ceremonial event that culminated in the sacrifice of the losing team.

Other buildings in Uxmal worthy of note are the Pyramid of the Old Woman, perhaps the oldest of the city's monuments, the Grupo del Cementerio (Cemetery Group), with a series of altars carved with terrifying human skulls, and the Casa de las Tortugas (House of Turtles), dedicated to the animal linked to the Mayan creation myth. The

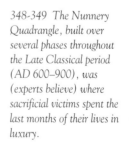

construction's appearance. Its 78 rooms, distributed between the four separate buildings of which it is composed, open onto a courtyard, just like in a convent. The courtyard also richly and uninterruptedly decorated with motifs of stylized flowers, zoomorphic figures, and images of the god Chac. It was probably the center of administrative power in Uxmal or, according to some experts, the

building has a stone façade carved to look as though it were formed by a closed row of narrow columns. In some way, the House of Turtles represents the thread uniting the ancient Maya to their modern descendants. There is a surprising similarity between its architecture and the humble bamboo huts seen today in the countryside of the Yucatán.

348-349 The Nunnery Quadrangle, built over several phases throughout the Late Classical period (AD 600–900), was (experts believe) where sacrificial victims spent the last months of their lives in luxury.

349 top An inscription in the ball-court has allowed this building to be dated to 649. Experts think the ball was made from rubber, but the Popol Vuh says that on special occasions one made from stone was used, which was made smooth by a layer of powdered bone.

Chichén Itzá

MEXICO

STATE OF THE YUCATÁN

REGISTRATION: 1988

CRITERIA: C (I) (II) (III)

The Toltecs and Aztecs called it Quetzalcoatl, but to the Maya it was Kukulcán. The "serpent with the feathers of the quetzal bird" (the translation of the name) was the protector of the priests and sovereigns, and the master of knowledge and the winds. In the Mayan pantheon, populated by bloodthirsty divinities, Quetzalcoatl-Kukulcán only asked the faithful for sacrifices of snakes, birds, and butterflies, and it was thought that one day he would return to make the earth his paradise. It was on this understanding that the Aztec king, Montezuma II, welcomed Hernán Cortéz, believing him to be that god.

In the ninth century, long before the arrival of the Spanish, the divine Toltec king Quetzalcoatl conquered the wealthiest Mayan city in the Yucatán. This, at least, is what one of the legends referring to Chichén Itzá recounts. Founded in the fifth century, it flourished throughout the Classic Period, then, around 850, it was taken by the Toltecs – or according to some experts – by the Itzá, a people related to the Toltecs. This hypothesis is supported by the city's name, which means "rim of the well of the Itzá." Be that as it may, what is exceptional about Chichén Itzá is its perfect fusion between the cultures of the Maya and Toltecs seen in its architecture, sculpture, and painting, and also in what we know of its customs. This blend survived until 1400, when the city was mysteriously abandoned.

As it appears today, the site is divided into two parts. The more ancient, Chichén Viejo, consists of buildings

350 top The skulls on the platform of the Tzompantli served to intimidate anyone who dared attack the city. The place was dedicated to military glory, and it was here that the decapitated heads of enemies were displayed.

350-351 El Castillo (or the Pyramid of Kukulkán) seen from the platform of the Temple of the Warriors. Note the sculpture of the feathered serpent on the base of the temple's flight of steps.

mainly from the Classic Period. The other section, Chichén Nuevo, consists of monumental constructions. The 180-foot-high pyramid standing on the plain was dedicated to the god Quetzalcoatl-Kukulcán. Named El Castillo (The Castle) by the Spaniards, each side is composed of a steep flight of 91 steps. If added to the entrance platform, they total 365 and therefore represent a sort of calendar. El Caracol, a shell-shaped building that functioned as a sort of observatory, is also evidence of the astronomic knowledge of the inhabitants. Another indication is given by the snakeheads carved in the stone at

351 top The temple at the top of El Castillo, stands 180 feet tall. This monumental pyramid features many symbols from Mayan cosmogony. Its nine terraces represent the nine levels of the Underworld.

351 center The interior of the Temple of the Jaguars. In the foreground, there is the enigmatic effigy of Chaak Mool; in the background, a red ceremonial throne in the form of a jaguar, probably reserved for the sovereign.

351 bottom The columns of the so-called Market (even though there is no evidence of commercial activity) are part of the large Toltec plaza. Originally, the columns were covered by a straw roof.

352 top The Temple of the Warriors and the Group of the Thousand Columns were built between 900 and 1200 and together formed the heart of Toltec Chichén Itzá. Once lined with brightly painted stucco, the columns represent armed warriors.

352-353 The entrance to the upper shrine in the Temple of the Warriors, guarded by Chaak Mool. Offerings were placed on the idol's stomach as it was thought that it would relay the requests of the devotees to the gods.

353 top left A view of the Temple of the Jaguars and the ball-court. Although it is almost certain that the competition's cruel ceremony originated in Teotihuacan, it was at Chichén Itzá that the most highly decorated and impressive court was built.

353 top right The holy of holies on the top of the Temple of the Warriors. The entrance was flanked by superb carvings of the head of the feathered serpent.

the start of El Castillo's main flight of steps, which at sunset project their shadows as far as the top of the temple to create the sinuous pattern symbolizing the god.

The pyramid of Quetzalcoatl-Kukulcán encloses a temple that contains a stone throne, set with pieces of jade, in the form of a jaguar. This cat was the symbol of the Toltec warrior class, and its representations can also be seen in the Temple of the Warriors, the Temple of the Thousand Columns (both of which stand in the Great Toltec Plaza), and the Temple of the Jaguars. All these buildings are decorated with detailed bas-reliefs of warriors, priests, masks of the rain god Chac, eagles, feathered serpents, and sculptures of jaguars feeding on human hearts.

Chichén Itzá features the largest and most elaborate ball court in Mesoamerica. Just under 100 yards long, it is bounded by walls decorated with bas-reliefs that represent one of the most extraordinary examples of Mayan art. One shows the decapitation of a player in the presence of his fellow players. The stone rings in the form of a serpent, through which the players had to pass the ball, are still found at either end of the court. Little is known of the game, and it is still debated whether it was the losers or the captain of the winning team to be beheaded at the end of the match. In any case, it is clear that the game was the most important moment in the religious rituals. In the *Popul Vuh*, the creation myth of the Maya, the divine heroes challenge the demons at the ball game. On that occasion, the future of an entire people was at stake.

353 center Curls perhaps representing fire or the invocation of the gods emerge from the mouth of a skull. This is one of the many bas-relief figures on the walls of the ball-court.

353 bottom A detail from the enormous bas relief around the ball-court. It shows moments from a game and the subsequent sacrifice. The horror of the players and the sacredness of the game are rendered with powerful expression.

354 top The upper part of the Observatory, also known as El Caracol due to its shell-like shape. The deep interest of the Mayans in astronomy resulted in their codification of a calendar that established the agricultural cycles and marked the social and economic events of the city.

354-355 The Nunnery lies in the southern and oldest section of Chichén Itzá. The architecture and decorations (including masks of the rain god Chac and other symbolic figures) make it a masterpiece of Puuc style.

355 top Erected between 1100 and 1300 in pure Toltec style, this platform was used to honor the god Kukulkán. It was named after Venus, an important planet in the astronomic knowledge and mysticism of the Mayans.

355 bottom Massive heads of the feathered serpent bound the Platform of the Eagles and Jaguars. This was probably built in homage to the warriors that formed the military elite in Chichén Itzá.

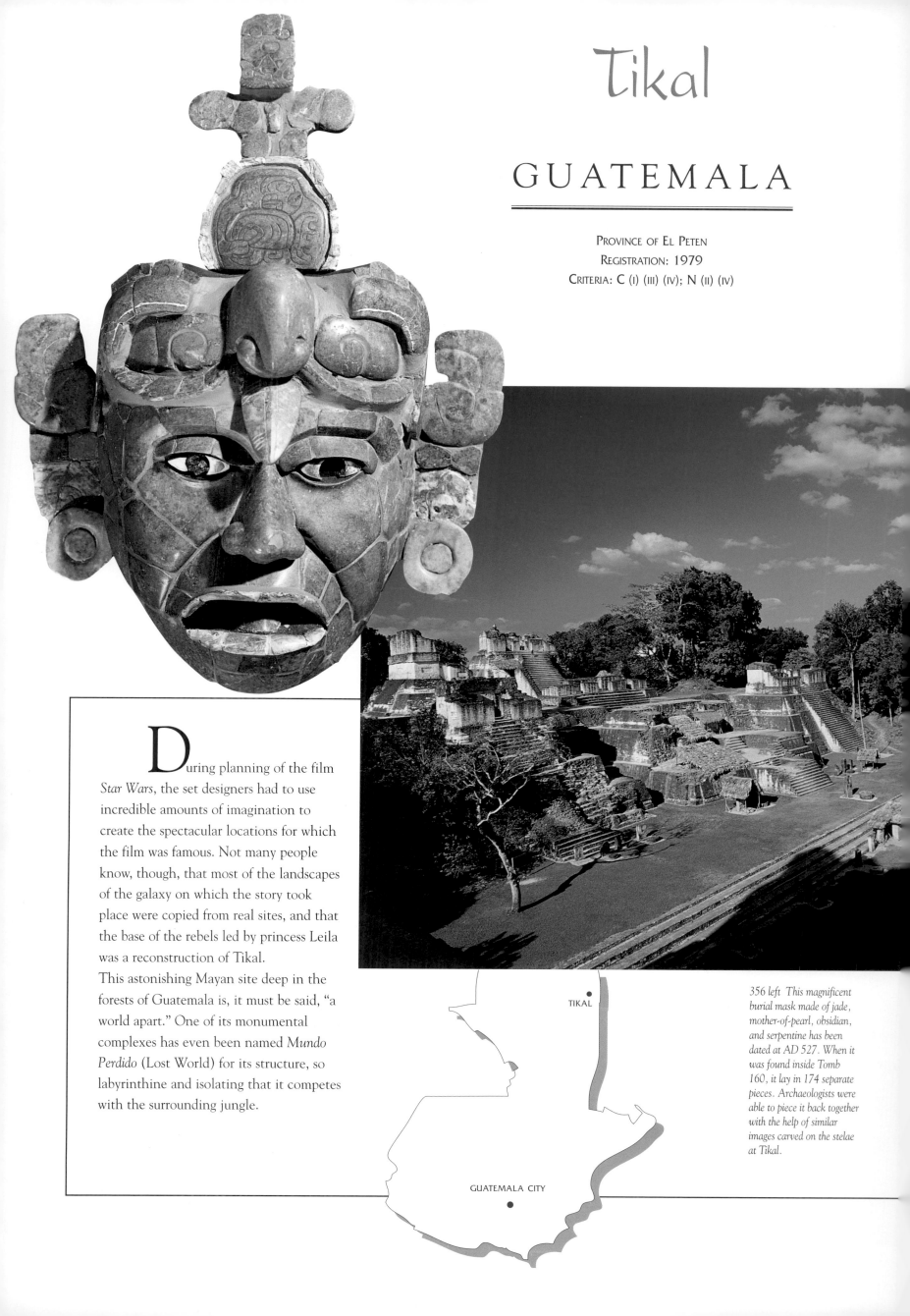

Tikal

GUATEMALA

Province of El Peten
Registration: 1979
Criteria: C (i) (iii) (iv); N (ii) (iv)

During planning of the film *Star Wars*, the set designers had to use incredible amounts of imagination to create the spectacular locations for which the film was famous. Not many people know, though, that most of the landscapes of the galaxy on which the story took place were copied from real sites, and that the base of the rebels led by princess Leila was a reconstruction of Tikal.

This astonishing Mayan site deep in the forests of Guatemala is, it must be said, "a world apart." One of its monumental complexes has even been named *Mundo Perdido* (Lost World) for its structure, so labyrinthine and isolating that it competes with the surrounding jungle.

TIKAL

GUATEMALA CITY

356 left This magnificent burial mask made of jade, mother-of-pearl, obsidian, and serpentine has been dated at AD 527. When it was found inside Tomb 160, it lay in 174 separate pieces. Archaeologists were able to piece it back together with the help of similar images carved on the stelae at Tikal.

357 center Temple IV emerges from the Guatemalan vegetation. This pyramid (200 feet high) was the tallest building in the Americas until the construction of the first skyscrapers at the end of the nineteenth century.

357 bottom One of the pyramids in the Mundo Perdido group, which was erected in various phases over a long period. New buildings were actually constructed over existing ones. The earliest ones date back to 400 BC.

At one time, the many sandstone pyramids of the ancient city (which represent the mountains where corn, a food sacred to the Maya, originated) were covered with stucco painted in dazzling colors featuring scenes of religious rituals or even entirely red. For example, the stelae in the Great Plaza were red, the ones carved with the portraits of 26 of the kings that ruled Tikal. The colors, which have been washed away by centuries of rain, were identical to the plumage of the parrots, toucans, and hummingbirds that today nest in the cracks of the temples.

Now protected in a 3,900-acre national park, Tikal was one of the most important cities in Mesoamerica. It was founded in the sixth century B.C. on a high ground abundant in edible fruits, high quality wood like *zapote*, good for building, and flint, which ancient peoples used to make weapons and tools. Tikal was already an important city when, in A.D. 230, Yax-Moch-Xoc took the throne and founded a dynasty that was to reign on and off until the tenth century when the city was mysteriously abandoned. During its long period of glory, Tikal numbered up to 100,000 inhabitants, traded with cities as distant as Teotihuacan in Mexico, and extended its dominion as far as the present-day state of Belize. There are roughly 3,000 palaces, pyramids, ball courts, and even thermal baths providing evidence of the architectural and artistic skills and originality of its builders.

The most amazing of the religious buildings in the city dates back to the eighth century. It is known as Temple I, or the Temple of the Great Jaguar. It was built in honor of Ah Cacau (682–734), the twenty-sixth lord of Tikal. It is a pyramid 144 feet tall with a shrine at the top that once featured an architrave carved with a representation of the 13 kingdoms in the Mayan paradise. The grave of the sovereign was discovered inside the monument and, with it, grave furnishings made from jade, gold, pearls, bone engraved with patterns and

356-357 A view of the Great Plaza, Tikal's monumental heart. The building on the left is the Central Acropolis, a labyrinthine building that may have been the residence of the royal family. To the right stands the 125-foot high Temple II, or Temple of the Masks.

357 top The Tikal archaeological site is situated in the middle of the Maya Biosphere Reserve, an area of primary tropical forest with mahogany, ceiba, and sapodilla trees up to 165 feet tall. In the background, Temple I, rises behind and to the left of Temple V.

358 top Today held in the site museum, this remarkable terracotta idol is part of the set of grave goods found in what the inscriptions on the sarcophagus have identified as the tomb of Huh Chaan Mah K'ina (king Curved Nose), one of the sovereigns of the city.

358 center Scholars believe that Temple II (left) was probably built by king Ah Cacau in honor of his wife, even if no burial chamber was found inside to prove it.

358 bottom left The Group Q complex was built by Yax Ain II, the third lord of Tikal. Standing on the open area before it are several stelae adorned with bas-reliefs. They were once painted red, as in all the most important monuments in the city.

358 bottom right This finely painted terracotta incense-burner from the grave goods of Huh Chaan Mah K'ina dates back to the sixth century.

358-359 The burial place of Ah Cacau, Temple I, faces onto the Great Plaza. The Central Acropolis, in the background, is composed of a series of ceremonial terraces and rooms decorated with paintings portraying gods and the main events in the history of Tikal.

359 top left The North Acropolis was the burial place of the lords of Tikal for more than five centuries, until AD 550.

However, beneath the surface structures, there are traces of an earlier settlement dating back to 800 BC.

359 top right The various pyramids in the set of buildings referred to as the Mundo Perdido Complex were built in alignment with the position of the sun. The largest is called the Great Pyramid and stands around 100 feet high.

358

hieroglyphs, and parsnip thorns used for ritual blood-letting.

Also of great interest are the squares onto which the pyramid and chamber temples face, and the set of buildings known as the Acropolis. It is still uncertain whether this was a complex of royal residences or an administrative or ceremonial center. It is composed of a hundred or so rooms arranged in an apparently haphazard manner due to the Mayan custom of building over pre-existing structures. The most ancient parts of the Acropolis date to around 400 B.C., whereas the enormous terracing overlooking the complex, richly decorated with masks of jaguars, feathered serpents, and other animals sacred to the Maya, is from the era of Ah Cacau, the leader who was most influential in giving the city its monumental appearance.

The name of this sovereign in translation is, amusingly enough, "King Chocolate." However, it is also true that the Maya actually invented the world's favorite sweet. Furthermore, they were also the first to chew the extract of the *chicle* tree, the forerunner of today's chewing gum.

The Archaeological Park of Quiriguá
GUATEMALA

Department of Izabal
Registration: 1981
Criteria: C (i) (ii) (iv)

Situated in the fertile valley of Río Motagua, on a site that has been inhabited since the second century B.C., Quiriguá was a Mayan city of medium importance that existed on trade and depended politically on its powerful neighbor Copán. However, in A.D. 737, its ambitious ruler Sky Cauac (723–784) decided to put an end to the city's uncomfortable state of subjugation and

360 top The steps of the Acropolis, the center of power at Quiriguá. The city was at the height of its splendor during the reign of Sky Cauac (723–784), but then its luck dwindled until, in the mid-ninth century, it ceased to exist, perhaps as a result of an earthquake or the impoverishment of the soil due to over-population.

360 bottom Full of fascinating sculptures and monuments, the Acropolis at Quiriguá was built in several phases. In the last, king Sky Cauac embellished his palace and had a ball-court built, a feature found in all Mayan religious centers.

oversee himself the transport of jade and obsidian that was quarried in the surrounding mountains and sold at great profit to Mayan cities on the coast. Having armed his troops, he went to Copán, took its king Eighteen Jog (Eighteen Rabbits) prisoner, and had him decapitated. Having become independent, Quiriguá enjoyed great prosperity, and Sky Cauac founded a dynasty that continued with his son Sky Xul and grandson Imx Dog, whose reign was usurped by Jade Sky in 810. Quiriguá survived until the mid-ninth century, when it was abandoned, probably following a violent earthquake.

Our knowledge of Quiriguá's golden period is made possible by the dark sandstone stelae that Sky Cauac and his successors began to erect in 754 at five-year intervals (referred to as *hotun*). The stelae are engraved on their sides and back with hieroglyphs recording the political and military events that occurred during the relevant period. Characteristic elements in both the Quiriguá and Copán civilizations, the stelae acted as a sort of proclamation poster for the kings. The front of the stones was adorned with religious symbols and surrounded by images of the gods and sacred animals, an iconography served to denote the legitimization of the king's divine power.

Apart from their historical content, the stelae at Quiriguá are admirable for their size and the precision with which they were carved. The largest is Stele E, a monolith weighing over 60 tons and standing 35 feet high, three of which are underground, and it is decorated with magnificent bas-reliefs up to 26 feet high. On the other hand, some of the highly sophisticated carvings on Stele D have been reproduced on the Guatemalan coin worth ten *centavos*.

To slow the erosive action of the copious rainfall, the nine stelae have been protected with canopies and stand in order like sentinels guarding what was once the city's Great Plaza. This square measures 110 by 87 yards in size and has at its center a rock mass referred to as Zoomorph G. This was probably Sky Cauac's funerary monument, as its bas- and high reliefs show the king with the features of a jaguar with the head of Eighteen Rabbits in his jaws. The north end of the plaza, where the Acropolis stands, is dotted with other stones bearing zoomorphic images (some of the most disconcerting in the Mayan world). The Acropolis is now a ruin but it is still a very elegant complex of buildings that once enclosed the palaces of Sky Cauac and Jade Sky, and even contained a series of baths (*temascales*). Next to the Acropolis lies the ball court, bounded by a wall decorated with images of Kinich Ahau, the Mayan sun god.

The ancient city of Quiriguá remained almost forgotten in the forest until 1841 when, after days of exhausting march, the American John Lloyd Stephens and Englishman Frederick Catherwood arrived there. A lover of the Mayan culture, Stephens attempted to buy the area on which the ruins stood from a peasant so that he could remove the stelae and ship them back to New York. However, the owner asked an exorbitant sum and the deal came to nothing. In 1910, the American United Fruit Company succeeded in purchasing the land and proceeded to cut down the forest in order to plant banana trees. It also financed excavation of the site by archaeologists from Pennsylvania State University. Returned to Guatemala in the 1970s, today Quiriguá is a national park.

361 left The image of king Sky Cauac wearing an elaborate diadem of feathers is carved on Stele J. The inscription on the back says it was erected on April 10, 756, and recounts the beheading of the king 18 Rabbits, the sovereign of Copán, on May 1, 738.

361 right Like the other stelae – all masterpieces of Mayan sculptural art – Stele F stands beneath a straw canopy to protect it from the rain. The stelae were erected by Sky Cauac at intervals of five years.

QUIRIGUÁ

GUATEMALA CITY

The Mayan Site of Copán
HONDURAS

HONDURAS
REGISTRATION: 1980
CRITERIA: C (IV) (VI)

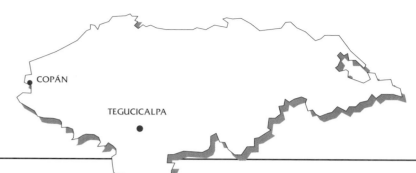

On March 8, 1576, Don Diego García de Palacio, a member of the royal tribunal in Guatemala, sent a letter to the king of Spain, Philip II, to inform him of the discovery of marvelous ruins located in present-day Honduras that the local people called Copán. The name may be derived from the Nahuatl word *copántl*, meaning "bridge."

However, Palacio's news created no stir, and the outside world remained oblivious to the city until 1839 when John Lloyd Stephens, an American diplomat, and his British traveling companion Frederick Catherwood began exploration of the site. A few years later, Stephens published *Incidents of Travel in the Yucatán*, in which the ruins of Copán were described, further enhanced by Catherwood's excellent illustrations.

Systematic study of the city by some of the greatest experts on pre-Columbian civilizations has made it possible to greatly increase understanding of the Mayan civilization. Unlike Tikal, Palenque, and other of the major cities in the huge Mayan Empire, Copán is distinguished more by its huge quantity of art

than by its architecture. The number of sculptures and stelae on the site is impressive: 4,509 buildings have been counted, 3,450 of which lie within an area of just nine square miles around the nucleus of the site. With five main areas of archaeological interest, this central archaeological group covers an area of 100 acres and is an open expanse created using more than one million cubic yards of earth.

First there is the acropolis, which is divided into two large spaces: the west and east plazas. The area features two temples (Temples 11 and 16) and an altar. Temple 11 represented the gateway to the

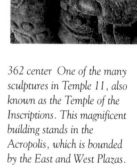

362 top right Stele M (seen here a detail) was sculpted between 709 and 755. The Stairway of the Hieroglyphics in the background is carved with the dynastic history of the site.

362 center One of the many sculptures in Temple 11, also known as the Temple of the Inscriptions. This magnificent building stands in the Acropolis, which is bounded by the East and West Plazas.

362 bottom left A view of the steps in the East Plaza in the Acropolis. Here, archaeologists have found the remains of 15 jaguars and various parrots, which were probably sacrificed for the glory of the deified sovereigns of Copán.

362 bottom right One of the most spectacular sculptural groups in the Acropolis is Altar Q. It stands in the East Plaza and is carved with the faces of the wealthy city's 16 rulers.

363 A detail of Stele F at the west end of the Great Plaza. Some traces of red, created with the use of cinnabar, still remain on the figures. Originally all the stelae were painted.

364 top left This mask is part of the sculptural decoration in Temple 11. It is of a bacab, one of the figures in Mayan mythology who supported the sky at the four corners of the universe.

364 bottom left Stele B was dedicated to 18 Rabbits, the thirteenth ruler of Copán, who was captured in battle by the king of Quiriguá and beheaded. 18 Rabbits' ascent to the throne is commemorated on Stele B.

364 right Erected in 731 to celebrate the king 18 Rabbits, Stele A is decorated with a succession of figures in elaborate costumes. Some wear a headdress in the form of a lily, which was the symbol of water and of the deification of the sovereign. The ruler was believed to be able to invoke the rain for the religious ceremonies.

365 top left Carved in 730, Stele H is dedicated to a female figure whose name is unknown. She was probably the queen or one of the princesses of the family of 18 Rabbits.

365 top right Stele F is one of the most elegant sculptures in Copán. The superb quality of this and the other stelae – whose shapes resemble tree trunks, the Mayan symbol of religious and temporal power – have led to the Great Plaza being nicknamed the "forest of the kings".

365 bottom left Two serpents form the extraordinary full-relief sculpture of Altar G1. An inscription dates the altar at the year 800.

365 bottom right Standing next to Stele D to the north of the Great Plaza, this altar is carved with the mask of Chaac, the Mayan rain god.

beyond, whereas Temple 16, which was built over the ruins of an earlier building, lies between the two plazas. The altar was dedicated to the rulers of Copán and bears their portraits. Then, there are the tunnels that run for a total of over two miles beneath the acropolis and date back to the earliest phases of the population of the area. In fact, Copán was built during the Classical Period and flourished between the third and ninth centuries A.D. However, an even earlier settlement of farmers in the area, who enjoyed the advantageous position of those fertile lands along the banks of the Río Copán, dates back to the first millennium B.C.

Another point of interest is the large plaza on the north side of the city, an immense, open grassy area dotted with stelae and altars. The stelae and the first buildings in the city were used as reference points for astronomic observation. Nevertheless, the most spectacular sites in Copán are undoubtedly the ball court – Central America's second largest – and the hieroglyph-covered stairway. Lying at the foot of the acropolis, the stairway has 63 steps and is decorated with 2,500 glyphs that have long attracted the attention of specialists. The longest text from the Mayan civilization to have ever survived, it tells the story of the royal dynasty of Copán. Unfortunately, it remains an unsolvable puzzle because part of the stairway has collapsed, making the complete message undecipherable.

Around the fifth century, the society inhabiting Copán had reached its greatest level of development. The city was governed by a king, the most important citizens lived in brick houses, and the manufacture of tools and pottery had reached a high degree of technical quality. By the start of the seventh century, further progress had been made and the city reached the height of its splendor in its architecture and sculpture, perhaps becoming the most important city in the Mayan Empire. Shortly afterwards, however, Copán was suddenly abandoned. The last glyph was carved in the year 800, and then its ruler, priests, and citizens left, walking away from the highest artistic expression ever achieved by the Mayan civilization.

Chavín de Huántar

PERU

DEPARTMENT OF ANCASH
REGISTRATION: 1985
CRITERIA: C (III)

CHAVÍN DE HUÁNTAR
LIMA

Timoteo Espinoza was laboriously breaking up the soil in his field when the point of his hoe got jammed in an enormous rock. By digging all around it with the help of other farmers, he discovered it was over seven feet long and had the enormous head of a cat sculpted on it. Years later, in 1873, Timoteo invited a *gringo* passing through Lima to lunch who, as he brushed his hand on the lower surface of the kitchen table, discovered it was carved with reliefs. Proudly the farmer stood the stone up to show it to the visitor. Today the "Raimondi stele" (named after the *gringo*, Antonio Raimondi, who spent his life exploring Peru on behalf of Lima

University) can be admired in the National Museum of Anthropology and Archaeology in the Peruvian capital. It is an emblematic article of what is called the "Chavín culture."

Now no more than a small village on the Callejòn de Conchucos, the narrow valley running along the east side of the Cordillera Blanca, between 1500 and 300 B.C. Chavín de Huántar – situated at an altitude of 10,300 feet, halfway between the Amazon forest and the coastal plains – was the site of a flourishing civilization that influenced all the successive cultures in Peru, including that of the Incas. A rather populous farming city, Chavín controlled the trade routes that led from the coast to the interior and those that cut across the cordillera from north to south.

It is probable that the Old Temple, the center of religious power and authority, was built between 1200 and 1000 B.C. It is a U-shaped platform open to the east with a courtyard in the middle. Its most important section was a maze of rooms and underground passageways that were used as storerooms, for the practice of religious rites, and that may even have been lived in by small groups of people who looked after the temple. Right at the center of the Old Temple, at the junction between two narrow tunnels, the statue of Lanzón was found, a figure with a human body and cat's face. According to the beliefs of the period, the priests were able to transform themselves into jaguars by swallowing hallucinogenic substances. A number of mortars, pestles, tools, and perforated seashells used to make musical instruments have been found, all of which were associated with religious ceremonies.

The New Temple shared a functional

continuity with the Old Temple, having the same passageways and used to perform the same rituals. Though it was larger – it is referred to as *el Castillo* by the locals –, its architecture is not noteworthy, being simply a vast rectangular block with two wings that both point to the east. Lying in front of the New Temple, down three steps, is the Plaza Hundida, an area of about 280 square yards with a rectangular platform on each side. This was where pilgrims gathered who, it is presumed, traveled to Chavín to practice religious rites. The plaza was also the place

366 top El Castillo with its highly decorated walls 33 feet high, make it the most majestic and spectacular monument in the ancient city, hidden in the Peruvian Cordillera Blanca.

366 center An enormous bas-relief panel on the west wall of El Castillo. The art of Chavín, with its high level of abstraction and clearly defined, stylized animal and human figures, fascinated Pablo Picasso.

366 bottom A male god, half human and half feline, is portrayed in the bas-relief on the Black and White Portal of El Castillo. The cults in the Chavín culture had a great influence on the other peoples of Mesoamerica.

366-367 Plaza Hundia lies at the foot of El Castillo and was the city's ceremonial center. It covers 2,690 square feet and is lined on all sides by a rectangular platform.

367 top Known as the Cabeza Clavos, this mask is repeated almost obsessively in Chavín architecture. It represents one of the guardian deities of the temples and combines the features of a bird with those of a feline.

367 center The Galeria de la Doble Mensula is one of the corridors, which, with stairs and passageways, forms the multilevel maze beneath the New Temple, the building renamed El Castillo for the magnificence of its architecture.

367 bottom At the end of a narrow passage under the Old Temple stands the Piedra del Lanzón, the white granite stele dedicated to the part-human, part-feline supreme god of Chavín.

where the Tello obelisk was found, named after the archaeologist who first studied the site. It is a masterpiece of figurative art in granite, which can also be seen in the museum in Lima.

The iconography of Chavín has suggested to archaeologists that three gods formed the ancient city's pantheon: the Moon, represented by a fish, the Sun, painted in the form of a falcon, and a Creator god, the jaguar. Each god was linked to a distinct level in Chavín's cosmogony: the fish to the ground beneath the Earth's surface, the eagle to the celestial forces, and the jaguar to earthly power. However it may have been, the art of Chavín – buried in 1945 by a landslide and damaged once more by a violent earthquake in 1970 – is typified by an extraordinary level of abstraction, in which the figures of animals and humans are stylized with clean, well-defined lines. Speaking of the city, Pablo Picasso remarked, "Of all the ancient cultures that I admire, Chavín is the one that surprises me most. To tell the truth, it has been the inspiration for much of my work."

Chan Chan

PERU

La Libertad Department, Province of Trujillo,
District of Huanchaco
Registration: 1986
Inscription on the list of
World Heritage Sites in Danger: 1986
Criteria: (i) (iii)

CHAN CHAN

LIMA

368-369 *The grandeur
of the site can be
appreciated from an aerial
view. Chan Chan covers
an area of roughly eight
square miles in the Moche*

*Valley, which separates the
Andes from the Pacific
Ocean.*

369 top *The elaborate
wall of one of the citadels*

*in Chan Chan. In 1450,
when the Chimu kingdom
was at the height of its
power and wealth, the city
had about 60,000
inhabitants.*

The myth that Chan Chan was founded by the creator of the Sun and the Moon, a dragon traditionally represented as a rainbow, the symbol of life and cosmic energy, is still taught in the schools of Trujillo. Though it is known that this extraordinary adobe city (the largest in the world according to the *Guinness Book of Records*) was the capital of the Chimu, the origin of the people is uncertain. They flourished between 1100, when they supplanted the Moche civilization, and 1470, and were the most advanced civilization in terms of technology and scientific progress in Peru. Some experts even believe that the Chimu were Maya colonists who had traveled from Mexico.

Be that as it may, the Chimu had a very complex and stratified political and social organization. They were skilful engineers able to design sophisticated irrigation systems and had a deep knowledge of metallurgy. Artistically, it seems they were not great aesthetes, preferring a utilitarian approach. Consequently, the objects they produced – including black ceramics, woven fabrics, and objects made from gold – were primarily functional. Chan Chan also seems to have been a functional capital that governed a kingdom reaching from the Gulf of Guayaquil in the north to the border with present-day Chile in the south.

Built in various phases, Chan Chan covered an area of about seven square miles and, at the start of the fifteenth century, numbered 60,000 inhabitants. Within its long perimeter wall there were at least ten citadels, each one built on a trapezoidal plan protected by walls up to 33 feet high and 13 feet thick, with roads up to 25 feet wide separating the citadels from one another. The buildings were made from adobe (unfired bricks made from a mixture of straw and earth) and then covered with mud.

369 center The Tschudi citadel (seen here, the north entrance), still in good condition. Built by slaves, the perimeter walls were up to 33 feet high and served to protect the citadel from the damp Pacific winds.

369 bottom The Chimu were a practical people who did not indulge in aesthetics, yet their adobe buildings, like the one shown in the photo, on the edge of Tschudi's central plaza, were decorated with geometric and zoomorphic motifs.

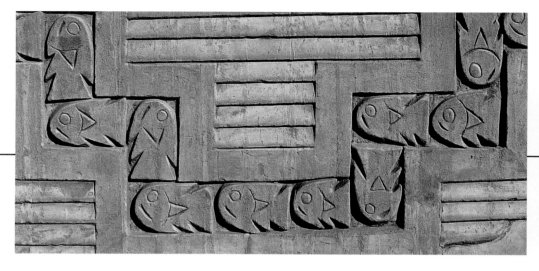

The walls seem to have been brightly colored or, in the most important buildings, lined with gold leaf. Another myth claims that the Chimu rulers had gardens with plants and animals made of this precious metal.

The citadel in the best state of conservation, and the one that has received the greatest restoration work, is the Tschudi Citadel, named after the Viennese traveler who was the first to study it in the mid-nineteenth century. Like its nine "twins," it has a ceremonial court lined by a myriad of rooms used for civil and religious purposes and connected by corridors. This leads to a second courtyard running alongside what was once an enormous pool for collecting water. After this, there are barracks for soldiers, the royal tombs, and the houses of the dignitaries. Besides the labyrinthine layout of the city, the friezes decorating a large part of the walls really grab one's attention. Though stylized, it is possible to recognize the waves of the sea, fish, and coypu,

demonstrating that the Chimu were prevalently a maritime civilization.

The origin of the people remains shrouded in mystery but its end is well documented. Between 1465 and 1470, having decided not to resist, the Chimu yielded to the advance of the Incas led by Tupac Yupanqui. This decision saved Chan Chan from raids and plundering, and the city remained empty but intact until the arrival of the Spanish. The Europeans, however, looted it of all its fabulous treasures. Reduced to an adobe shell, it remained in that state for centuries, slowly crumbling away as it lay exposed to the elements.

Despite the efforts of the Peruvian government and UNESCO, which has inscribed the site on the World Heritage in Danger List, the deterioration of Chan Chan is considerable and restoration efforts proceed slower than the action of the weather. Then there is another danger: the *huaqueros*, or grave robbers, who search for gold missed by Pizarro's troops.

370 top A detail of a
decoration on a wall in
Tschudi Square, features
stylized fish, indicating that
the Chimu civilization was
prevalently a maritime
people.

370-371 top The Huaca
of the Dragon, also known
as Huaca Arco Iris, is the
site's most spectacular set of
buildings. Its extraordinary
decorations portray reptiles,
humans, dragons and
rainbows, symbols of
fertility.

370-371 bottom
The aquatic coypu was
frequently used in
decorations on the Tschudi
citadel. To create them, the
adobe bricks were covered
with a thin, smooth coat of
mud that was then
"incised".

Machu Picchu

PERU

PROVINCE OF URUBAMBA,
CUZCO DEPARTMENT
REGISTRATION: 1983
CRITERIA: C (I) (III); N (II) (III)

A fire in the summer of 1988 raged through the forest surrounding Machu Picchu, destroying 10,000 acres of vegetation and risking the survival of many indigenous animal species as it licked at the edges of the ruins. Considered the worst ecological disaster in the history of Peru, it aggravated the already precarious situation of the eco-system in the magnificent Urubamba Valley, threatened by growing pressure from the development of tourism in the area and by the lack of funds and control from the Peruvian government.

It may seem an exaggeration to consider the archaeological site of Machu Picchu a fundamental element of the ecosystem, yet the beauty of the ruins rising above the rainforest are part and parcel of the landscape. Indeed, it was the presence of these mountains, the water of the Urubamba River, and the animals that determined the foundation of this fabulous city. The Inca people believed that the Pacha Mama (Earth Mother) was a creature with supernatural powers, and Machu Picchu was for them the sacred place where the world had originated.

Constructed between 1460 and 1470 under the leadership of the king, Pachacuti Inca Yupanqui, the ceremonial center of Machu Picchu was inhabited by about 1,200 people. Of these, the majority were women who had been chosen to be vestals of the Sun god (as demonstrated by the discovery of 175 mummies, 80 percent of which were female). The remaining 20 percent were priests and children.

The archaeological area consists of 200 buildings, most of which were either houses or warehouses, which were built on blocks of granite to "embrace" the rocks and exploit the morphology of the terrain. The doorways were trapezoid in shape and the roofs made from straw. The two-story houses were built in groups of ten around square courtyards and joined by narrow streets and raised passages. The areas set aside for domestic animals and the terraces on which the Incas grew corn and potatoes lay along the borders of the site.

The most important religious buildings were built around wide

372 View of one of the residential complexes at Machu Picchu. These comprised groups of ten two-story, straw-roofed stone houses set around courtyards and joined by narrow streets and raised passages.

372-373 A superb view of Machu Picchu, dominated to the north by the cone-shaped mountain called Huayna Picchu. Set in a natural cave on the side of this mountain the Temple of the Moon, and clinging to the mountain wall, is still a sacred place for the indios who live in the Urubamba Valley.

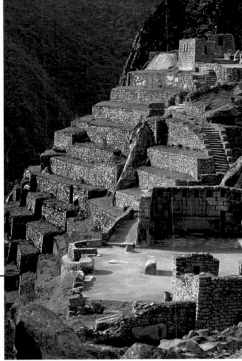

373 top left Built of perfectly squared and interlocked stones, the monumental trapezoid gates are a typical feature of Machu Picchu. This is what is referred to as a "double gate", which indicates the entrance to a sacred place.

373 top right With great skill, the Inca people dug the mountain into a series of terraces to be able to cultivate corn and potatoes to feed the community. The agricultural and residential areas of the ancient city cover 50 acres, double that of the ceremonial area.

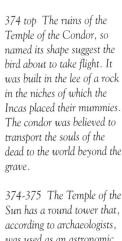

374 top The ruins of the Temple of the Condor, so named its shape suggest the bird about to take flight. It was built in the lee of a rock in the niches of which the Incas placed their mummies. The condor was believed to transport the souls of the dead to the world beyond the grave.

374-375 The Temple of the Sun has a round tower that, according to archaeologists, was used as an astronomic observatory. On December 21, the winter solstice, the sun rises in line with the building's central window.

ceremonial plazas: these were the Temple of the Sun, a circular construction like a tower with fine bas-reliefs, the Temple of the Three Windows, the so-called Principal Temple, and the Royal Temple. Though this last building was really used for worship and no tombs have been found inside it, it takes its name from its sunken position, and it is thought that it represented the "spiritual" access to the heart of the mountain. The Intihuatana is a fascinating carved monolith in front of which the priests made sacrifices in honor of the sun on

with bas-reliefs and features a massive stone throne set in the middle. Even today, the local inhabitants bring offerings of corn, tobacco, and coca leaves to the temple for the god of the mountain.

When the Spaniards led by Pizarro arrived in Cuzco in 1532, they utterly destroyed the Inca Empire, but never learned of the existence of Machu Picchu. Five years earlier, an epidemic of bubonic plague had caused the death of 50 percent of the Inca population, and the sacred mountain had consequently been abandoned. For

375 Machu Picchu was constructed between 1460 and 1470 by king Pachacuti Inca Yupanqui and was inhabited by 1,200 people. Its agricultural terraces are seen to the right of the central building known as the "prison."

the day of the winter solstice (summer for those south of the equator). The Temple of the Moon stands on Huayna Picchu, the splendid cone-shaped mountain that looks down on the site. Set in a natural cave in which five niches were dug out, it is decorated

centuries, only the few inhabitants of the Urubamba Valley knew of the site's existence, until July 24t, 1911, when the American archaeologist Hiram Bingham rediscovered it. In the meantime, it had been completely absorbed into the forest.

Cuzco

PERU

Department of Cuzco
Registration: 1983
Criteria: C (iii) (iv)

According to the Inca myth, Manco Capac and his sister Mama Ocllo, divine figures that emerged from the depths of Lake Titicaca near the islands of the Sun and Moon, founded the city of Cuzco in 1200. The pair searched for a site on which to build a capital, the most splendid the world had ever known, and, it is said, the location was chosen when Manco Capac drove his golden staff into the ground, whereupon it was swallowed up miraculously by the Earth. The first stone of the new city was placed in that exact spot. For this reason, the city was named Cuzco, or Qosq'o in Quechua, meaning "the navel of the universe."

In fact, evidence has been found that proves the existence of a much earlier settlement than that of the Inca myth. The site had already been inhabited by the eighth century by a farming people, the Killki, who had developed remarkable skills in working the hard volcanic stone, andesite. However, it took more than two centuries before Cuzco became the magnificent and powerful capital in the legend. In 1438, Pachacuti – the eighth descendant of the dynasty that originated with Manco Capac – began to expand the Inca Empire. He was responsible for the

construction of the ambitious and monumental city that had until then been nothing but a village. He channeled the Saphi and Tullumayo rivers and built Cuzco in the strip between them.

The new city was laid out in the shape of a puma, an animal sacred to the Incas. The Sacsayhuaman, the main religious center and, when necessary, its fortified citadel, represented the puma's head. The Pumacchupan, the point where the two rivers were freed from

376-377 The oldest and most famous Inca wall in Cuzco is the one that lines the narrow Calle Loreto in the city center. Before the Spanish incorporated it into the construction of a convent, it was part of the Acllahuasi, the residence of the "chosen women".

376 bottom At one time the Coricancha was lined with gold leaf. Today little remains of the building as the Spanish built the Iglesia de Santo Domingo over its walls.

their artificial bed, formed the tail. The Coricancha (temple of the Sun) were the loins, and the Huancapata, the ceremonial plaza (which more or less traced the same perimeter as the later Spanish Plaza de Armas), symbolized the animal's heart. From the plaza, roads fanned out to every corner of the empire. As a final touch, Pachacuti molded the surrounding slopes of the valley with terraces to encourage agriculture.

Over the following century, Cuzco and its wealth grew exponentially, and when Francisco Pizarro arrived there on November 8, 1535, he was enchanted by the city. The walls of the courtyard of the Coricancha were lined with gold leaf and a garden in the middle featured corn plants made from silver and gold and set with precious stones. Taking advantage of a dynastic feud that at that time plagued the Inca Empire, Pizarro

shrewdly succeeded in taking possession of the city's treasures and leaving 88 settlers from among his officers who were, on paper at least, subject to the new puppet ruler, Manco Inca. This pretence continued for three years until Manco Inca organized an army to chase the Spaniards out. Though it almost worked, his plan failed and he was obliged to flee to the remote city of Vilcabamba in the forest. Free to act as they liked, the Spaniards looted the city's monuments and, using the local

gold, built dazzling Baroque churches that today make Cuzco one of the loveliest cities in Latin America.

The Iglesia de Santo Domingo stands scornfully above the Corichanca. Only a cyclopic dry wall made of andesite blocks, each weighing about 160 tons, remains of the temple of the Sun. Of the Sacsayhuaman, the only part to survive is a tiny section of what was once a complex of altars, temples, and fortifications. The ruins of its nonetheless still magnificent ramparts are represented by a zigzag wall imitating the jaws of the puma.

What the Spanish were unable to do, however, was uproot the ancestral Inca culture. It re-emerged in the unique style (called *mestizo*) of the colonial paintings and the faces of the people of Cuzco, 90 percent of whom are of Andean descent.

377 top The main entrance to the Sacsayhuaman, built with perfectly smoothed blocks. Most of the buildings in the complex – which could accommodate 5,000 soldiers – were destroyed by Pizarro's troops after they put down the rebellion led by Manco Capac.

377 center This courtyard was originally used for ritual sacrifices and today is one of the few sections of the Coricancha that can be visited. The monumental

building held the mummified bodies of the Inca rulers. It had different chambers for the cult of the various gods and an astronomic observatory.

377 bottom The triple order of walls of the Sacsayhuaman, the set of buildings that was both a religious center and, when necessary, a fortified citadel. The zigzag form of the walls suggests the teeth of a puma, an animal that was sacred to the Incas.

LIMA

CUZCO

The Lines and Geoglyphs of Nazca and the Pampas of Jumana

PERU

Province of Urubamba, Department of Cuzco
Registration: 1994
Criteria: C (i) (iii) (iv)

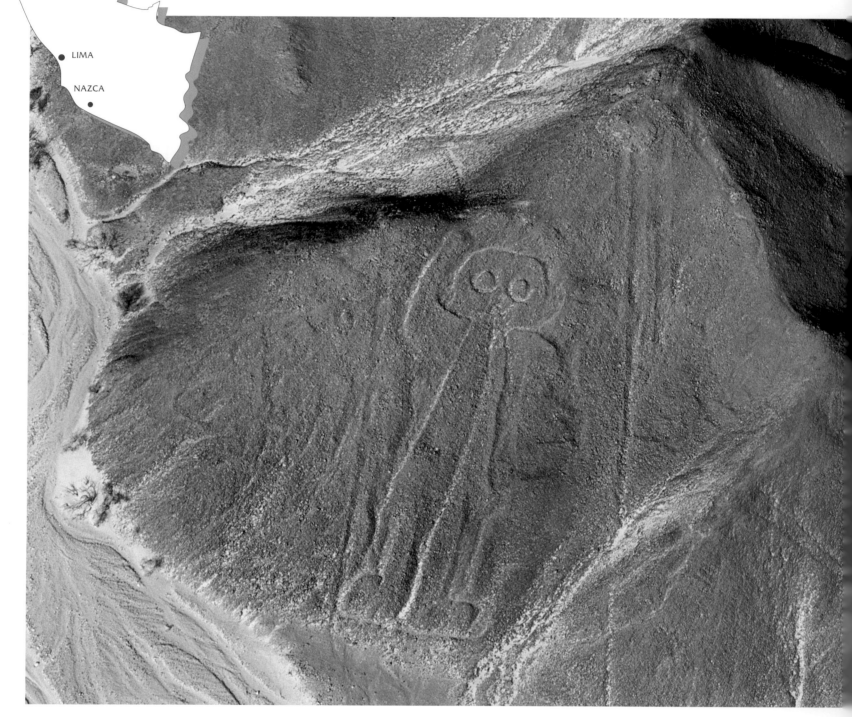

LIMA

NAZCA

378-379 This curious human figure is known as "The Astronaut" and was often considered "proof" of the theory (always refuted outright by the entire scientific community) that the geoglyphs at Nazca were created by extraterrestrial beings.

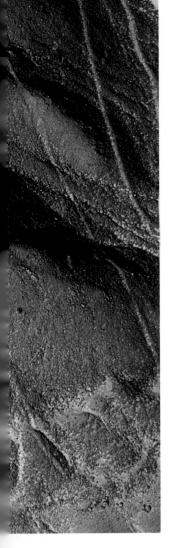

The ruins of irrigation systems built by local peoples in ancient history can be found along the coastal deserts of Peru. In 1941, Paul Kosok, an expert on pre-Columbian Latin America, was studying them in the Rio Nazca valley – one of the tributaries of the Rio Grande – when he came across what seemed to be a huge stylized bird on the ground, over 100 feet in length. It appeared that the design was deliberately traced out so that it would be visible from above.

Having enquired among his colleagues at Lima University, Kosok learned that there were several figures of that sort and that three years prior a Peruvian scholar had published an article in which he hypothesized that they were ceremonial images created by an unknown pre-Columbian civilization. Until that time, their presence had been pretty much ignored, with the exception of the occasional note made by Spanish chroniclers around 1600 and sketches drawn by archaeologist Julio Tello in 1926.

After an aerial reconnaissance mission in which he managed to identify a number of figures, Kosok left Peru with the idea that they were ancient viewing lines linked to astronomic observation, explaining his theory to the German astronomer and mathematician Maria Reiche who lived in Lima. Since that time, Reiche devoted forty years to the study of the Nazca lines, contributing to the discovery of their age and designers as well as a plausible explanation for their existence.

Half a century later, thirty or so images have been identified on the Colorada pampas, or the pampas of Jumana, the highlands covering more than 185 square miles that overlook the Rio Nazca valley. Some feature human or animal characteristics, whereas others are stylized plants. There are also famous images of birds, a monkey, a spider, and a killer whale, but there are also geometric patterns, in particular trapezoids and rectangles over a mile long, that apparently lack any immediate significance. The technique used to execute them is very simple: all that was done was remove the brownish stones covering the desert surface of the pampas, thus leaving the paler ones below to show through. Despite the simplicity of the method, the skill

used was masterful and the execution must have required enormous effort as there is no evidence that beasts of burden were used, and therefore one assumes that the work done was all manual.

A variety of hypotheses have been put forward over the years as to their meaning, including even outrageous ideas involving alien visitors, inspired by the vague similarity of the geoglyphs to airport runways and of the incredibly advanced technologies developed by ancient civilizations, but the Nazca figures are anything but a mystery. The lines on the Jumana pampas, and the many others along the Peruvian coast to the north, though less spectacular, had their origin in what is referred to as the "Nazca civilization," a pre-Columbian civilization that flourished between the second century B.C. and sixth century

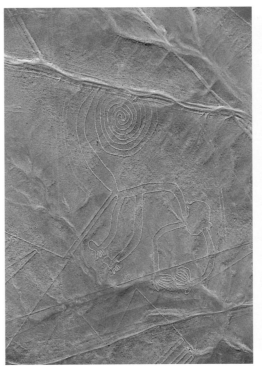

A.D. This fact has been proven by pottery found in the more clement areas in the region where those responsible for the figures probably lived, and from fragments also found in the area of the Rio Nazca. Some of the finds are decorated with motifs bearing a remarkable similarity to some of the figures. The untiring work of Maria Reiche has confirmed that the geometric figures played a role in marking the important events in the calendar, such as the solstices and the cycle of the seasons. Owing to the unusually arid climate on the Jumana pampas and the absence of wind erosion of the soil, the Nazca lines have survived in perfect condition to the present day.

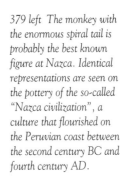

379

The Political and Spiritual Center of the Tiwanaku Culture

BOLIVIA

PROVINCE OF INGAVI, LA PAZ DISTRICT
REGISTRATION: 2000
CRITERIA: C (III) (IV)

The Gate of the Sun, the monumental entrance to the city of Tiwanaku, was carved out of a single block of andesite weighing 100 tons. The upper part is decorated with a bas-relief of 48 winged figures in three rows, of which 32 have human faces and 16 the heads of condors, elephants, and imaginary creatures. At the center, there is a god from whose face radiate the sun's rays in every direction. His cheeks are lined with tears as a symbol of the rain, and he holds two stylized objects in his hands, symbols of thunder and lightning. For the Aymara Indians, the dominant ethnic group on the shores of Lake Titicaca, the figure represents Viracocha, the god who emerged from the lake at the beginning of time to create the sun, sky, stars, rain, and human beings. He then wandered the earth as a beggar, teaching man the rudiments of civilization, before disappearing into the immense Pacific Ocean.

The Aymara are convinced that Tiwanaku is the "bellybutton of the universe," the place where their ancestors were born thousands and thousands of years ago. However, all legends apart, archaeologists have not yet succeeded in agreeing on the era the most mysterious pre-Inca civilization arose. Some say it was 10,000 years ago, as a port on the lakeside, giving as proof the unbroken line of white and yellowish deposits on the rocks near the site that they claim indicates the level of Titicaca at that time. Others prefer a date of around 2000–1600 B.C.; and others, basing their conjectures on material evidence, claim that Tiwanaku was founded in 400 B.C. on the banks of the Tiwanaku River that flows into the lake nine miles

downstream. However, scholars do agree on the theory that the Tiwanaku civilization reached its height between A.D. 500 and 900, and that the city fell into a state of abandon by 1100, when the Incas arrived. It is thought that during the period of its maximum splendor the city covered almost six square miles and was the capital of a community of 30,000 to 40,000 inhabitants. However, due to a lack of funds, excavation work has focused principally on what must have been the political, administrative, and ceremonial center of the city.

The Kalasasaya stands close to the Gate of the Sun; it is a sacred enclosure bounded by obelisks decorated with bas-reliefs. Further on, there is the Akapana, the "sacred mountain of Tiwanaku," a pyramid around 50 feet tall with a square base measuring 125 yards per side. The pyramid is made of andesite blocks weighing at least 100 tons and, most probably, encloses an underground temple. The immediate area has T-shaped ceremonial terraces where objects have been found made of obsidian, copper, and silver, plus the remains of sacrificed llamas and ceramic figures that may have represented members of the

LA PAZ
TIWANAKU

380 top One of the monolithic "totems" that mark the perimeter of the Kalasasaya. Like this one, some represent human figures with Caucasian, Negroid, Asiatic, or Semitic features.

380 center Carved from an andesite monolith weighing 100 tons, the gate of the Sun forms the entrance to Tiwanaku.

380 bottom Between AD 500 and 900, Tiwanaku

reached its apogee. The sacred enclosure of the Kalasasaya stands close to the gate of the Sun. We know nothing of the ceremonies carried out there.

380-381 and 381 bottom The walls of the so-called

"sunken court" feature mysterious sculpded human faces and delimit an area of 9,680 square feet at the center of which the people of Tiwanaku placed a series of sandstone stelae decorated with bas-reliefs.

political and religious elite.

The most interesting discovery is the advanced form of agriculture practiced by the people of Tiwanaku. They dug deep channels in the fields about 50 feet from one another. Filled with water, the channels were used to hold fish and aquatic plants that were used respectively as food and fertilizer. Moreover, the water aided the formation of a warm blanket of humidity that protected the fields planted with potatoes from freezing, a frequent occurrence at an altitude of over 13,100 feet above sea level, as at Lake Titicaca.

Recently a farming project imitating the methods used at Tiwanaku has been launched among the Aymara living on the Bolivian shore of the lake, with surprising results. The potato crop has increased by 400 percent, and with the fish and geese raised in and around the channels, the diet of the population has improved substantially. Thus, thanks to the rediscovery of ancient knowledge, perhaps the Aymara too can overcome the pathologies linked to malnutrition, which today afflict a full half of the children of Bolivia.

The Serra da Capivara
BRAZIL

STATE OF PIAUÍ
REGISTRATION: 1991
CRITERIA: C (III)

The trip that, in the mid-1950s, took Brazilian archaeologist Niède Guidon to a virgin area in the wild southern region of the small northeastern state of Piauí was expected to be no more than a pleasurable excursion. Guidon was visiting the area to satisfy her curiosity about tales she had heard of the amazing vegetation and rock formations in the Serra da Capivara. The vegetation is part of the *caatinga*, a primary dry forest of which only a few oases remain in the immense arid stretch known as the *sertão*.

Though her expectations were already high, Guidon had no idea that this journey was about to change her life. Exploring the canyons of the Serra da Capivara, she came across extraordinary rock paintings. What made them so outstanding, as she intuited from the start, was not simply the skill with which they were drawn, nor the use of a vast range of mineral colors, but the mystery involving the remote period in which they were created by an equally mysterious people.

Over the next twenty years, Guidon and her colleagues scoured every inch of the zone, cataloguing 345 sites of archaeological interest, 240 of which contained a total of roughly 25,000 rock paintings. Unlike similar sites in the Americas and Europe, those in the Serra da Capivara contained mainly drawings of men rather than animals, and even when animals are present, they are part of hunting or fight scenes in which man is always the protagonist. Some of the most frequent scenes are those depicting dances and, in particular, a huge assortment of sexual practices, including those referred to as "of the round chamber," a sort of orgy involving numerous figures within a circle, probably holding some sort of ritual significance.

Nonetheless, the representations of animals, although less common, were what allowed Guidon to elaborate a revolutionary theory on the origin of man in the Americas. In addition to deer and big cats, the drawings show species

382 top A large cow was painted in a stylized manner. Though less frequent than human figures, the animals depicted are interesting because some of them are of species that have long been extinct.

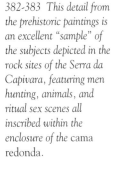

382-383 This detail from the prehistoric paintings is an excellent "sample" of the subjects depicted in the rock sites of the Serra da Capivara, featuring men hunting, animals, and ritual sex scenes all inscribed within the enclosure of the cama redonda.

the Bering Strait roughly 20,000 years ago would be brought down. At that time, the animals represented in the rock paintings in the Serra da Capivara had already become extinct due to the changes in climatic conditions that had transformed the sertão from a wet forest into a dry one. On the other hand, at the time of their disappearance, the last Ice Age was yet to come and the Arctic bridge had not yet been formed.

Carbon dating produced a definitive answer in the 1970s. The paintings date back to 48,000 years ago, and, in consequence, the Serra da Capivara earned itself the distinction of most interesting and astounding archaeological site on the continent.

A national park was set up in 1979 covering 48,000 square miles of land. Today visitors are only allowed to enter if accompanied by a guide. The interesting rock formations and caatinga zones can be visited along with thirty or so sites featuring rock paintings. These include the Toca da Boqueirão da Piedra Furada, a rock almost 200 feet high with a hole in its center about 50 feet in diameter that has become the park's "postcard" site.

At the entrance to the protected area, near the village of São Raimundo Nonato, stands the Museu do Homem Americano, featuring exhibits comparing evidence supporting the theory of migration across the Bering Strait to the results of Niéde Guidon's discoveries.

that have been extinct since remote prehistory: llamas, armadillos, bats, giant birds, and huge herbivores. Were they fantastic animals, born in the imagination of prehistoric man? Or, as the archaeologist believes, did the men who painted them actually live in the Americas at the same time as them? If the second case were true, then the universally accepted theory that man arrived on the American continent by crossing the land bridge from Siberia over

382 bottom The discovery of the rock paintings dating back to 48,000 years ago in this wild corner of Brazil has upset the theory in which man is said to have first arrived in the Americas across the Bering Strait 20,000 years ago.

383 top A wall of the Boqueirao de la Piedra Furada. It is the most dramatic site in the Serra da Capivara Park due to its paleo-ethnological interest and physical beauty.

383 bottom A representation of the hunt for a large animal. In the park, 345 sites of archaeological interest have been found, 240 of which contain roughly 25,000 rock paintings.

Rapa Nui National Park
CHILE

RAPA NUI

SANTIAGO

EASTER ISLAND
REGISTRATION: 1995
CRITERIA: C (II) (III) (V)

Convinced that Polynesia was populated by adventurous navigators from South America who were able to reach the far-away islands in the Pacific Ocean by traveling in primitive boats, in 1947 the Norwegian explorer and archaeologist Thor Heyerdahl organized an daring expedition. Aboard the Kon Tiki, a balsawood craft identical to the ones used by Polynesians, he set out to cover the 5,000 miles separating the Peruvian coast from the atoll of Raroia in the Tuamotu Archipelago.

Encouraged by the success of the expedition, eight years later he wanted to show that the same thing had happened with Easter Island, the solitary volcanic formation that lies 2,400 miles from the nearest human habitation. Heyerdahl and his team set out on an archaeological exploration of the island, discovering that it was once covered by forests, which had been completely cut down by the island's inhabitants. Carbon dating of some of the island's famous statues showed that it had

been populated since roughly A.D. 380, at least a thousand years before anyone had thought. The tradition of the inhabitants, however, claimed that their ancestors had arrived from the Far East. Over time, detailed analysis of the archaeology, physical anthropology, and genetics of the people confirmed that Heyerdahl had been wrong. The island was given its name by the sailor Jacob Roggeveen, because he had first seen it on Easter Day 1722. Only many years later, in 1863, it was called Rapa Nui by a group of Tahitian sailors who thought it looked like Rapa Iti, a small island in French Polynesia. To the local population, the island was Te Pito O Te Henua, meaning the Vessel of the World.

Polynesians were also the colonizers of Easter Island. In the fifth century, a complex and enigmatic culture began to develop there, producing Rongorongo, the only written language in Oceania. A number of rock inscriptions and the remains of houses, places of worship, wooden sculptures, clothes made from tree bark (tapa), and handicrafts have been found on the island. However, Rapa Nui is most famous for the Moai, the gigantic heads carved out of rock. At least 288 once stood upright on bases called ahu, which have counterparts in Polynesian culture. About 250 Moai encircle the edges of the island, while another 600, in different stages of production, are scattered around the coast and near Rano Raraku Volcano, where the quarries in which they were carved are located. Mostly executed between 1000 and 1650, they stand a maximum of 33 feet high with a weight of 80 or so tons. One of these, however, carved partially from its rock bed, is double the size and would have weighed, if completed, about

160 tons. The most accredited theory is that they had a religious value as they impersonated the mana, the spirits of the ancestors, in accordance with Polynesian tradition. To some experts, though, they are symbols of both religious and political authority. The society of Rapa Nui prospered for centuries, but with the growth of the population decline inexorably set in. At its peak, the island must have had around 10,000 inhabitants, but this number was too high for its 44 square miles of land. By the fifteenth century, the fragile eco-system was compromised to the point where there were no more trees to build canoes, as the last had been cut down to make space for crops. Rivalry broke out between clans that led to a breakdown in the social fabric, full-scale battles, and ultimately, cannibalism. The arrival of Europeans only worsened the situation. They brought disease, and many inhabitants of Rapa Nui were deported to be sold into slavery. In 1877, the population was reduced to 111 people (today it has once more grown to 2,000 inhabitants, many of whom are continental in origin). Though the worst was past, the violent and irreversible events in the island's history have led to Rapa Nui being considered a symbol of ecological catastrophe.

384 top The moai of Ahu To Ko Te Riku, with the characteristic block of lava (called a pukao) on the head.

384 center and bottom Groups of moai in the southeast part of the island. The statues vary in height from six to 33 feet and can weigh up to 80 tons each.

385 These moai stand in Anakena, the place where, according to tradition, the first ruler of Rapa Nui landed on the island.

The Cueva de las Manos in the Río Pinturas Valley

ARGENTINA

At the start of the nineteenth century, when the first European colonists arrived to populate Patagonia, the land at the southern tip of the world was inhabited by nomadic communities of Tehuelche aborigines. For them, the impact was fatal. Those who survived the massacres did not endure the enforced campaigns of "civilization." Those unaffected by European illnesses destroyed themselves with alcohol as they watched the land they had inhabited for more than 10,000 years be taken away from them.

Their ancestors were primitive *Homo sapiens* that had reached Tierra del Fuego and north Patagonia by crossing the Bering Strait from Asia when the land bridge was created during the last Ice Age at the end of the Pleistocene and start of the Holocene epochs. Divided into two groups, they had settled respectively on the islands and mainland where the former practiced fishing and the harvesting of mollusks, and the latter hunting. Thus it remained until the arrival of the Europeans.

Hunter-gatherers for millennia, the mainland Tehuelche "bequeathed" a vast, primordial land to the white man, which at first sight showed no signs of a human presence. Their ancestral spirits "lived" in the sacred grottoes hidden in almost inaccessible canyons that one could only find if driven by an insatiable curiosity. However, such a curious nature was found in Francisco Pascasio Moreno, a name that was to become famous after Patagonia's most outstanding natural feature was named the Perito Moreno

glacier in his honor. In 1877, he described the rock paintings he had discovered in the rocky ravines along the rivers and in the areas around Lago Argentina. The most extraordinary of these were found in the Cueva de las Manos, a cave in the canyon of Río Pinturas.

In this rather small space (the cave measures about 78 by 49 feet and is about 33 feet high, the same height as the entrance), there are about 890 rock paintings. As the name suggests, most of them are handprints, both of the hand itself or its outline, in various colors –

red, ocher, yellow, violet, white, black, and green – and generally of the left hand, though some of them include a part of the forearm. The hands belonged to both men and women, adults, adolescents, and even children. In addition to these, there are geometric shapes and scenes of groups hunting the guanaco (*Lama guanicoe*), the llama whose meat lay at the base of the diet of the Tehuelche and their ancestors.

Only around the mid-1900s was it possible to establish that the prints in the Cueva de las Manos dated back to prehistory. Argentine paleoethnologists carried out carbon-dating tests, identifying

387

stratigraphic sequences that allowed them to divide Patagonian prehistory into six distinct periods (or cultural levels) that occurred between 13,000 and 25,000 years ago. Diaphragmetric study of the different layers of pigments used in the paintings revealed how the colors had been prepared. The pigments were composed of chalk, sometimes mixed with clays of varying ferrous oxide content providing the various colorations, and sometimes with carbon or manganese powder. The color thus obtained was then calcined over a fire so that it would adhere to the rock.

Even if it is now known when and how the paintings of the Cueva de las Manos were made, the reason why the Tehuelche's prehistoric ancestors wanted to leave imprints of their hands on the rock walls is still uncertain. It may have been part of an initiation ceremony, but the most interesting theory is linked to the profound symbolism of the hand in the evolution of the human species. Because of the hand, man was able to forge tools and to consolidate his power over things and other creatures, thus being the means by which man "grasped" a conscious understanding of himself.

BUENOS AIRES

CUEVA DE LAS MANOS

386 Amphibians, guanacos, and human hands are among the most common subjects in the rock paintings at Cueva de las Manos. The earliest paintings date back to 13,000 years ago.

386-387 This is the rock wall with the greatest density of handprints. They are mostly of the left hand and were made by men, women, adolescents, and children.

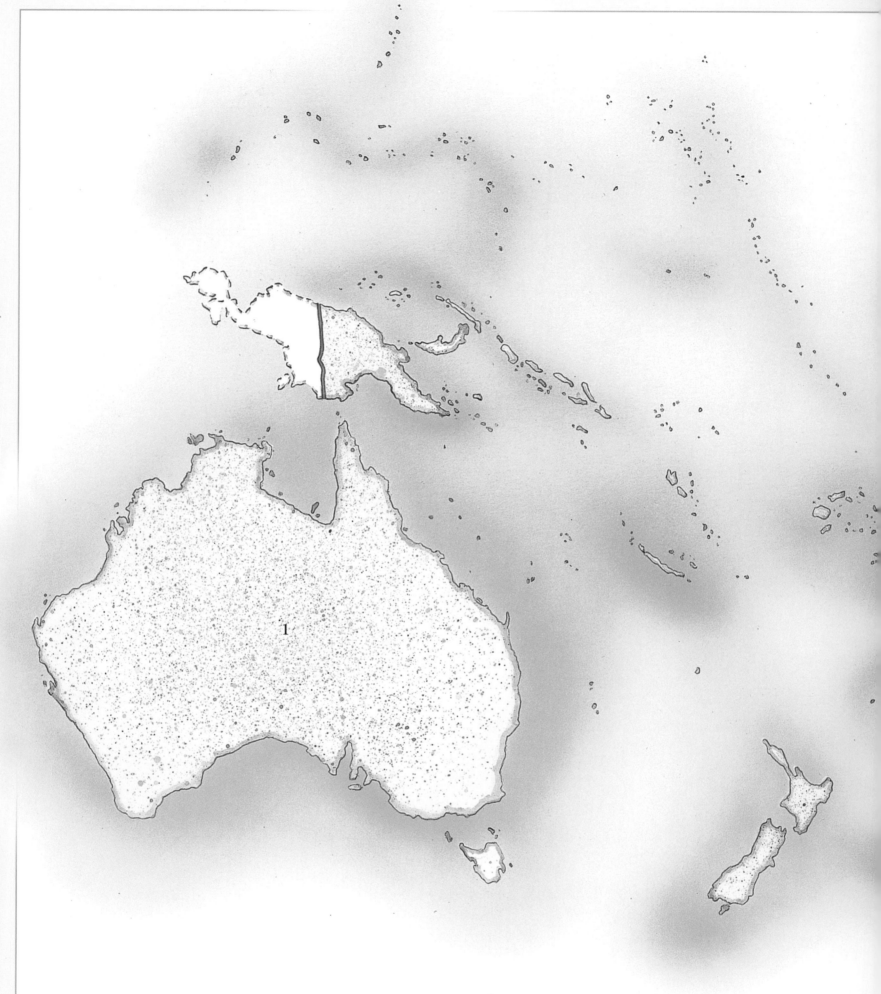

List of the Sites

Oceania

In the aboriginal culture of Australia, there is a rite called the Ceremony of the Dream of the Rain, performed to the sounds of the didgeridoo. This wind instrument is made from a long eucalyptus trunk that has been hollowed out by termites, stripped of its bark, cleaned up, and decorated with pictures from aboriginal mythology. Finally, beeswax is added to the mouthpiece.

The word didgeridoo is a western mispronunciation of one of the fifty or so names given it by the various aboriginal peoples. The instrument has been used for at least 15,000 years as documented by images engraved on rocks in Kakadu National Park in northern Australia, and, according to UNESCO, which has included aboriginal music in its collection of traditional music from around the world, the enigmatic and unique sound of the didgeridoo has remained unchanged for 40,000 years, or in other words, since the era immediately following the population of the continent of Australia.

During the Pleistocene Epoch, the sea level was several dozens of feet lower than it is today. Australia was probably joined to New Guinea by a low isthmus of land, in the same way that the islands of Southeast Asia were joined to the continent, forming a vast peninsula. The narrow stretch of sea that separated Asia from Australia – no wider than 40 or so miles – was easily crossed by the first inhabitants of the new land.

According to some archaeologists, the arrival of humans to Australia may have begun 70,000 or even 100,000 years ago, but the use of different dating criteria results in large variances on such distant epochs. However, no doubt exists that *Homo sapiens* had begun colonization of the continent more than 40,000 years ago, and any previous settlements would have been so dispersed and ephemeral that they left no traces of any archaeological note.

In any case, the aboriginal cultures never developed a civilization that constructed monuments of any kind or even structures able to survive the passing of the millennia, as has occurred on other continents. The customs of these peoples remained substantially unchanged until the arrival of Europeans in the eighteenth century. Nomads, organized in small communities of hunter-gathers, the aboriginals continued to live in temporary shelters or modest huts built from perishable materials. They never knew agriculture nor did they have a written language.

From an archaeological standpoint, all that remains of the Australian peoples, apart from the extraordinary cultural repertory passed down orally from generation to generation, is the history book represented by the rock paintings in Kakadu National Park, but it is unlikely that these will be of much help in lifting the veil of mystery that shrouds the history of man on this continent.

Kakadu National Park
AUSTRALIA

NORTHERN TERRITORY
REGISTRATION: 1981
EXTENSIONS 1987, 1992
CRITERIA: C (I) (VI); N (II) (III) (IV)

The first ancestors of Creation to paint pictures on the rocks were the Mimi, the spirits sent by Warramurrungundji, the "Mother of the Earth." Fundamental figures in the aboriginal cosmogony based on Dreamtime (the Creation), the Mimi taught the art of painting to some, while others learned by observation. At the end of their journey, some ancestors of the Creation painted their portraits on the rock walls, creating *djang* (Dream places) and *djang andjamun* (sacred and dangerous places of the Dream). Access to the latter is strictly limited to the Elders.

In general terms, this is the origin of the rock paintings for the Gagudju aboriginals in the Kakadu, the name of

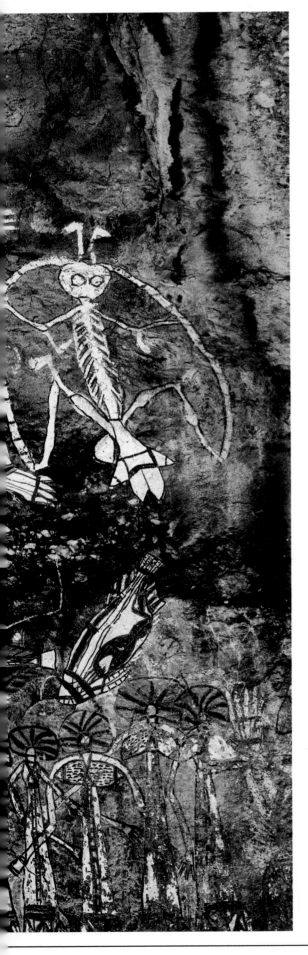

which is probably a mispronunciation of the name of the people. The paintings are spread across the territory, especially in the escarpment in Arnhem Land and the neighboring plateau and alluvial plain. For archaeologists, who have discovered around 5,000 sites in this remote region of northern Australia and who estimate there are another 10,000 waiting to be found, the 7,000 rock incisions identified in the Kakadu are a valuable tool in determining with precision when Australia was populated.

Until recently, carbon dating techniques made it possible to estimate that the zone was occupied about 25,000 years ago, but in 1990, using thermoluminescent methods, the Welsh archaeologist Rhys Jones discovered that tools found on the site of Nauwalabila, in particular fragments of ocher used in the painting, could be dated back to between 53,000 and 59,000 years ago.

One absolutely certain aspect of the rock art in the Kakadu is that the subjects painted aid in placing a limit on their age, as many of them depict animals that have been extinct on the continent, and therefore must have been painted at most a short while after their disappearance.

Like any other form of art, it is possible to notice developments in form and subjects in aboriginal painting. In the north, there are many naturalistic subjects, whereas in the south the prevalent themes are religious and linked to Creation. The pre-Estuarine style – in use between 50,000 and 8,000 years ago when the sea level was very low and the climate was drier – features "object prints," positive imprints of body parts, on the rock walls, as well as animals and human figures in action, such as the "dynamic" figures. During the Estuarine period, between 8,000 and 1,500 years ago, when the waters of the ocean began to rise and penetrate the valleys, depictions of sea fish begin to appear, and the use of beeswax was introduced to design simple patterns and human figures.

From 1,500 years ago on, the so-called "X-ray style" established itself, in which the forms of humans and animals are shown with their internal structures

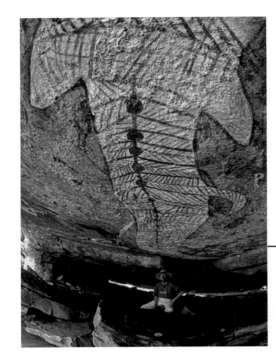

visible. Before the introduction of beeswax, the pigments used to give the most common colors were all mineral in origin, such as hematite, a rock rich in iron that provided a red pigment. Others used were limonite and goethite, which gave a yellow/orange color; ocher, for different hues of red, orange, and yellow; kaolin for white; and either manganese oxide or coal for black.

For Australian aborigines, rock painting has remained the most important form of art, even after contact with Europeans. One of the most important collections of paintings in the Kakadu exists in the Ubirr rock shelters. One painting shows a white man wearing trousers, a shirt, and boots with his hands in his pockets while another white man, with a pipe in his mouth and his hands on his hips "gives orders to us, the Aborigines, all around."

List of the Sites

Bibliography

UNESCO publications

On 18 April 1996, UNESCO began publication of the World Heritage Review, a quarterly, 80 page, color magazine that focuses on the *World Heritage sites*. The magazine is published simultaneously in English, French and Spanish.
The list of publications below includes those produced by UNESCO or in partnership with other publishing companies. All are available from the UNESCO offices in Paris. All enquiries should be sent to: The World Heritage Centre, UNESCO, 7 Place de Fontenoy, 75352 Paris, France.

Les villes du patrimoine mondial, CD-ROM, UNESCO Publishing/Cyberion, Paris.
The World Heritage Series for Children (recommended for children aged 8-15, available in English, French and Spanish), UNESCO Publishing/Childrens Press, Paris.
Patrimonio de la Humanidad (12 volume encyclopedia), Planeta/UNESCO Publishing, Madrid, 1995.
World Heritage Encyclopedia (in German), in 12 volumes, Verlagshaus Stuttgart/Plaza y Janes/UNESCO Publishing, Stuttgart, 1996/1997.
Schätze der Menschheit, Frederking & Thaler/UNESCO Publishing, Munich, 1996/1997.

The World Heritage Encyclopedia (in Japanese), in 12 volumes, Kodansha/UNESCO Publishing, Tokyo, 1996/1997.
Masterworks of Man and Nature, Harper-MacRae Publishing, Sydney, 1994.
Paradise on Earth, Harper-MacRae Publishing, Sydney, 1995.
World Heritage Twenty Years Later, by Jim Thorsell, IUCN, Switzerland and Great Britain, 1992.
World Cultural and Natural Property (available in Japanese), for children, Gakken, Tokyo, 1994.
Cultural Landscapes of Universal Value, by B. von Droste, H. Plachter, M. Rössler, Fischer Verlag, Jena, 1995.

Index

396

Photographic Credits

Page 292 left Cristiano Luparia/Archivio White Star
Page 292 right Livio Bourbon/Archivio White Star
Pages 292-293 Livio Bourbon/Archivio White Star
Page 293 top Livio Bourbon/Archivio White Star
Page 293 center AISA
Page 293 bottom Livio Bourbon/Archivio White Star
Page 294 top Livio Bourbon/Archivio White Star
Page 294 center left Livio Bourbon/Archivio White Star
Page 294 center right Livio Bourbon/Archivio White Star
Page 294 bottom left Livio Bourbon/Archivio White Star
Page 294 bottom right Livio Bourbon/Archivio White Star
Page 295 Livio Bourbon/Archivio White Star
Page 296 top Antonio Attini/Archivio White Star
Page 296 bottom Antonio Attini/Archivio White Star
Pages 296-297 Antonio Attini/Archivio White Star
Page 297 top left Antonio Attini/Archivio White Star
Page 297 top right Cristiano Luparia/Archivio White Star
Page 297 bottom left Antonio Attini/Archivio White Star
Page 297 bottom left Antonio Attini/Archivio White Star
Page 298 top Antonio Attini/Archivio White Star
Page 298 left Marcello Bertinetti/Archivio White Star
Pages 298-299 Antonio Attini/Archivio White Star
Page 299 top Antonio Attini/Archivio White Star
Page 299 center Antonio Attini/Archivio White Star
Page 299 bottom Antonio Attini/Archivio White Star

Sri Lanka
Page 300 top AISA
Page 300 center Jeremy Horner/Corbis/Contrasto
Page 300 bottom Bill Wassman/Lonely Planet Images
Pages 300-301 AISA
Page 301 top Cristiano Luparia/Archivio White Star
Page 301 bottom Christine Osborne/Corbis/Contrasto
Page 302 Getty Images/Laura Ronchi
Pages 302-303 AISA
Page 303 top left Cristiano Luparia/Archivio White Star
Page 303 top right AISA
Page 303 center AISA
Page 303 bottom AISA
Page 304 left Cristiano Luparia/Archivio White Star
Page 304 right Antony V Giblin/Lonely Planet Images
Pages 304-305 Gustavo Tomsich/Corbis/Contrasto
Page 305 top AISA
Page 305 center Jeremy Horner/Corbis/Contrasto
Page 305 bottom Jeremy Horner/Corbis/Contrasto
Page 306 left AISA
Page 306 right Lindsay Hebberd/Corbis/Contrasto
Pages 306-307 AISA
Page 307 top Andres Blomqvist/Lonely Planet Images
Page 307 bottom Michael Freeman/Corbis/Contrasto

Thailand
Page 308 top Cristiano Luparia/Archivio White Star
Page 308 center left Livio Bourbon/Archivio White Star
Page 308 center right Livio Bourbon/Archivio White Star
Page 308 bottom left Livio Bourbon/Archivio White Star
Page 308 bottom right Livio Bourbon/Archivio White Star
Page 309 Livio Bourbon/Archivio White Star
Page 310 Livio Bourbon/Archivio White Star
Page 311 top left Livio Bourbon/Archivio White Star
Page 311 top right Livio Bourbon/Archivio White Star
Page 311 bottom left Livio Bourbon/Archivio White Star
Page 311 bottom right Livio Bourbon/Archivio White Star

Cambodia
Page 312 top Livio Bourbon/Archivio White Star
Page 312 center Livio Bourbon/Archivio White Star
Page 312 bottom Livio Bourbon/Archivio White Star
Pages 312-313 Livio Bourbon/Archivio White Star
Page 313 Cristiano Luparia/Archivio White Star
Page 314 top Livio Bourbon/Archivio White Star
Page 314 left Livio Bourbon/Archivio White Star
Page 314 right Livio Bourbon/Archivio White Star
Pages 314-315 Livio Bourbon/Archivio White Star
Page 315 Livio Bourbon/Archivio White Star
Page 316 top Livio Bourbon/Archivio White Star
Page 316 center Livio Bourbon/Archivio White Star
Page 316 bottom Livio Bourbon/Archivio White Star
Pages 316-317 Livio Bourbon/Archivio White Star
Page 317 top Livio Bourbon/Archivio White Star
Page 317 right Livio Bourbon/Archivio White Star
Page 318 Livio Bourbon/Archivio White Star
Pages 318-319 Livio Bourbon/Archivio White Star
Page 319 top Livio Bourbon/Archivio White Star
Page 319 center Livio Bourbon/Archivio White Star
Page 319 bottom Livio Bourbon/Archivio White Star

Vietnam
Page 320 top Michael Freeman/Corbis/Contrasto
Page 320 left Michael Freeman/Corbis/Contrasto
Pages 320-321 Michael Freeman/Corbis/Contrasto
Page 321 left Michael Freeman/Corbis/Contrasto
Page 321 right Cristiano Luparia/Archivio White Star

Indonesia
Page 322 top Roger Ressmeyer/Corbis/Contrasto
Page 322 center Lindsay Hebberd/Corbis/Contrasto
Page 322 bottom Bernard Napthine/Lonely Planet Images
Pages 322-323 Bernard Napthine/Lonely Planet Images
Page 323 left Cristiano Luparia/Archivio White Star
Page 323 right Stephanie Colasanti/Corbis/Contrasto
Page 324 top Lindsay Hebberd/Corbis/Contrasto
Page 324 center Bernard Napthine/Lonely Planet Images
Page 324 bottom left AISA
Page 324 bottom right Lindsay Hebberd/Corbis/Contrasto
Pages 324-325 AISA
Page 326 left Marcello Bertinetti/Archivio White Star
Page 326 right Cristiano Luparia/Archivio White Star
Pages 326-327 Marcello Bertinetti/Archivio White Star
Page 327 top Angelo Tondini/Focus Team
Page 327 bottom Angelo Tondini/Focus Team
Page 328 left Marcello Bertinetti/Archivio White Star
Page 328 bottom Marcello Bertinetti/Archivio White Star
Pages 328-329 Marcello Bertinetti/Archivio White Star
Page 329 right Marcello Bertinetti/Archivio White Star
Page 329 bottom Marcello Bertinetti/Archivio White Star

THE AMERICAS
Page 330 Elisabetta Ferrero/Archivio White Star

United States
Page 332 top Richard A. Cooke/Corbis/Contrasto
Page 332 center Antonio Attini/Archivio White Star
Page 332 bottom David Muench/Corbis/Contrasto
Pages 332-333 Kraig Lieb/Lonely Planet Images
Page 333 Cristiano Luparia/Archivio White Star

Mexico
Page 334 left Antonio Attini/Archivio White Star
Page 334 right Cristiano Luparia/Archivio White Star
Pages 334-335 Yann Arthus-Bertrand/Corbis/Contrasto
Page 335 top left Antonio Attini/Archivio White Star
Page 335 top right Antonio Attini/Archivio White Star
Page 335 bottom Antonio Attini/Archivio White Star
Page 336 top Antonio Attini/Archivio White Star
Page 336 center top Antonio Attini/Archivio White Star
Page 336 center bottom Antonio Attini/Archivio White Star
Page 336 bottom Antonio Attini/Archivio White Star
Pages 336-337 Antonio Attini/Archivio White Star
Page 337 left Antonio Attini/Archivio White Star
Page 337 right Antonio Attini/Archivio White Star
Page 338 top Cristiano Luparia/Archivio White Star
Page 338 left Antonio Attini/Archivio White Star
Page 338 right Antonio Attini/Archivio White Star
Pages 338-339 Antonio Attini/Archivio White Star
Page 339 top Antonio Attini/Archivio White Star
Page 339 bottom left Antonio Attini/Archivio White Star
Page 339 bottom right Antonio Attini/Archivio White Star
Page 340 Massimo Borchi/Archivio White Star
Pages 340-341 Antonio Attini/Archivio White Star
Page 341 left Antonio Attini/Archivio White Star
Page 341 top right Antonio Attini/Archivio White Star
Page 341 bottom Archivio Scala
Page 342 left Massimo Borchi/Archivio White Star
Page 342 right Giovanni Dagli Orti
Pages 342-343 Massimo Borchi/Archivio White Star
Page 343 left Massimo Borchi/Archivio White Star
Page 343 right Cristiano Luparia/Archivio White Star
Page 344 top Massimo Borchi/Archivio White Star
Page 344 bottom Massimo Borchi/Archivio White Star
Pages 344-345 Massimo Borchi/Archivio White Star
Page 345 left Massimo Borchi/Archivio White Star
Page 345 right Massimo Borchi/Archivio White Star
Page 346 Massimo Borchi/Archivio White Star
Page 347 top Massimo Borchi/Archivio White Star
Page 347 center left Massimo Borchi/Archivio White Star
Page 347 center right Massimo Borchi/Archivio White Star
Page 347 bottom Cristiano Luparia/Archivio White Star
Page 348 top Massimo Borchi/Archivio White Star
Page 348 left Massimo Borchi/Archivio White Star
Page 348 right Massimo Borchi/Archivio White Star
Pages 348-349 Massimo Borchi/Archivio White Star
Page 349 Massimo Borchi/Archivio White Star
Page 350 Massimo Borchi/Archivio White Star
Pages 350-351 Massimo Borchi/Archivio White Star
Page 351 top left Massimo Borchi/Archivio White Star
Page 351 top right Cristiano Luparia/Archivio White Star
Page 351 center Massimo Borchi/Archivio White Star
Page 351 bottom Massimo Borchi/Archivio White Star
Page 352 Massimo Borchi/Archivio White Star
Pages 352-353 Massimo Borchi/Archivio White Star
Page 353 top left Massimo Borchi/Archivio White Star
Page 353 top right Massimo Borchi/Archivio White Star
Page 353 center Massimo Borchi/Archivio White Star
Page 353 bottom Massimo Borchi/Archivio White Star
Page 354 Massimo Borchi/Archivio White Star
Pages 354-355 Massimo Borchi/Archivio White Star
Page 355 top Massimo Borchi/Archivio White Star
Page 355 bottom Massimo Borchi/Archivio White Star

Guatemala
Page 356 top Giovanni Dagli Orti
Page 356 bottom Cristiano Luparia/Archivio White Star
Pages 356-357 Massimo Borchi/Archivio White Star
Page 357 top Massimo Borchi/Archivio White Star
Page 357 center Massimo Borchi/Archivio White Star
Page 357 bottom Massimo Borchi/Archivio White Star
Page 358 top Massimo Borchi/Archivio White Star
Page 358 center Massimo Borchi/Archivio White Star
Page 358 bottom left Massimo Borchi/Archivio White Star
Page 358 bottom right Massimo Borchi/Archivio White Star
Pages 358-359 Massimo Borchi/Archivio White Star
Page 359 top left Massimo Borchi/Archivio White Star
Page 359 top right Massimo Borchi/Archivio White Star
Page 360 top Massimo Borchi/Archivio White Star
Page 360 bottom Massimo Borchi/Archivio White Star
Page 361 left Massimo Borchi/Archivio White Star
Page 361 right Massimo Borchi/Archivio White Star
Page 361 bottom Cristiano Luparia/Archivio White Star

Honduras
Page 362 top Cristiano Luparia/Archivio White Star
Page 362 right Massimo Borchi/Archivio White Star
Page 362 center Massimo Borchi/Archivio White Star
Page 362 bottom left Massimo Borchi/Archivio White Star
Page 362 bottom right Massimo Borchi/Archivio White Star
Page 363 Massimo Borchi/Archivio White Star
Page 364 top left Massimo Borchi/Archivio White Star
Page 364 bottom left Massimo Borchi/Archivio White Star
Page 364 right Massimo Borchi/Archivio White Star
Page 365 top left Massimo Borchi/Archivio White Star
Page 365 top right Massimo Borchi/Archivio White Star
Page 365 bottom left Massimo Borchi/Archivio White Star
Page 365 bottom right Massimo Borchi/Archivio White Star

Perù
Page 366 top left Massimo Borchi/Archivio White Star
Page 366 top right Cristiano Luparia/Archivio White Star
Page 366 center Massimo Borchi/Archivio White Star
Page 366 bottom Massimo Borchi/Archivio White Star
Pages 366-367 Massimo Borchi/Archivio White Star
Page 367 top Massimo Borchi/Archivio White Star
Page 367 center Massimo Borchi/Archivio White Star
Page 367 bottom Massimo Borchi/Archivio White Star
Page 368 Cristiano Luparia/Archivio White Star
Pages 368-369 Charles et Josette Lenars/Corbis/Contrasto
Page 369 top Dave G. Houser/Corbis/Contrasto
Page 369 center Massimo Borchi/Archivio White Star
Page 369 bottom Massimo Borchi/Archivio White Star
Page 370 top Massimo Borchi/Archivio White Star
Page 370 bottom Massimo Borchi/Archivio White Star
Pages 370-371 Dave G. Houser/Corbis/Contrasto
Page 372 top Cristiano Luparia/Archivio White Star
Page 372 left Antonio Attini/Archivio White Star
Pages 372-373 Antonio Attini/Archivio White Star
Page 373 left Antonio Attini/Archivio White Star
Page 373 right Antonio Attini/Archivio White Star
Page 374 Antonio Attini/Archivio White Star
Pages 374-375 Antonio Attini/Archivio White Star
Page 375 Antonio Attini/Archivio White Star
Page 376 Antonio Attini/Archivio White Star
Pages 376-377 Antonio Attini/Archivio White Star
Page 377 top left Cristiano Luparia/Archivio White Star
Page 377 top right Antonio Attini/Archivio White Star
Page 377 center Antonio Attini/Archivio White Star
Page 377 bottom Antonio Attini/Archivio White Star
Page 378 top Cristiano Luparia/Archivio White Star
Page 378 bottom left Antonio Attini/Archivio White Star
Page 378 bottom right Antonio Attini/Archivio White Star
Pages 378-379 Antonio Attini/Archivio White Star
Page 379 left Antonio Attini/Archivio White Star
Page 379 right Antonio Attini/Archivio White Star

Bolivia
Page 380 top Antonio Attini/Archivio White Star
Page 380 center Antonio Attini/Archivio White Star
Page 380 bottom Antonio Attini/Archivio White Star
Pages 380-381 Antonio Attini/Archivio White Star
Page 381 Antonio Attini/Archivio White Star

Brazil
Page 382 top Ricardo Azoury/Pulsar Imagens
Page 382 bottom Ricardo Azoury/Pulsar Imagens
Pages 382-383 Ricardo Azoury/Corbis/Contrasto
Page 383 top Cristiano Luparia/Archivio White Star
Page 383 center Ricardo Azoury/Pulsar Imagens
Page 383 bottom Ricardo Azoury/Pulsar Imagens

Chile
Page 384 top left Wojtek Buss
Page 384 top right Cristiano Luparia/Archivio White Star
Page 384 center Kevin Schafer/Corbis/Contrasto
Page 384 bottom Gustavo Di Pace/Fotoscopio
Page 385 Wolfgang Kaehler/ Corbis/Contrasto

Argentina
Page 386 top Gustavo Di Pace/Fotoscopio
Page 386 bottom Hubert Stadler/Corbis/Contrasto
Pages 386-387 Hubert Stadler/Corbis/Contrasto
Page 387 Cristiano Luparia/Archivio White Star

OCEANIA
Page 388 Elisabetta Ferrero/Archivio White Star

Australia
Page 390 top Cristiano Luparia/Archivio White Star
Page 390 center Peter Ptschelinzew/Lonely Planet Images
Page 390 bottom Tom Boyden/Lonely Planet Images
Pages 390-391 AISA
Page 391 top John Van Hasselt/Corbis Sygma/Contrasto
Page 391 bottom Tom Boyden/Lonely Planet Images